FIRST COURSE
Sixth Edition

Keyboarding and Document Processing

Archie Drummond

Anne Coles-Mogford

McGRAW-HILL BOOK COMPANY

London · New York · St Louis · San Francisco · Auckland · Bogotá · Caracas
Hamburg · Lisbon · Madrid · Mexico · Milan · Montreal · New Delhi · Panama
Paris · San Juan · São Paulo · Singapore · Sydney · Tokyo · Toronto

Published by McGRAW-HILL Book Company Europe
Shoppenhangers Road, Maidenhead, Berkshire, SL6 2QL, England
Telephone 0628 23432 Fax 0628 770224

British Library Cataloguing in Publication Data

Drummond, A. M.
First Course: Keyboarding and
Document Processing. – 6Rev.ed
I. Title II. Coles-Mogford, Anne
652.3

ISBN 0-07-707605-2

Library of Congress Cataloging-in-Publication Data

Drummond Archie.
First course : keyboarding and document processing / Archie
Drummond, Anne Coles-Mogford. – 6th ed.
p. cm.
Rev. ed. of: Typing, first course. 5th ed. c1988
Includes index.
ISBN 0-07-707605-2
1. Word processing. 2. Typewriting. 3. Commercial
correspondence. I. Coles-Mogford, Anne. II. Drummond, Archie.
Typing, first course. III. Title.
Z52.4.D78 1993
652.3–dc20

1 2 3 4 5 97654 3
Typeset by Paston Press
and printed and bound in Great Britain at the University Press, Cambridge.

INDEX

wpm	Skill measurement no of mins	page
19	1	28
20	1	29
21	1	31
22	1	32
23	1	33
24	1	34
25	1	35
	1½	36
	2	37
	2½	38
	3	42
26	1	47
	1½	51
	2	55
27	1	62
	1½	69
	2	72
28	1	75
	2	78
29	1	88
	2	94
30	1	98
	1½	101
	2	113
	2½	117
	3	122
	3½	132
	4	137
	4½	141
	5	151
	5	155
	5	158

Record your progress

no of mins	no of words	page
1	28	30
1	30	31
1	35	32
1	35	33
1	38	34
1	38	34
1½	49	36
2	63	37
2½	75	38
3	90	42
1	41	47
1½	51	51
2	58	55
1	42	62
1½	52	69
2	63	72
1	44	75
2	68	78
1	46	88
2	70	94
1	47	98
1½	66	101
2	77	113
2½	96	117
3	124	122
3½	129	132
4	137	137
4½	169	141
5	188	151
5	195	155
5	189	158

PREFACE

Since its invention in the 1870s, the typewriter has been at the core of the processing of information and, today, the QWERTY keyboard is an integral part of many machines and the basic means for rapid communication of data: the family at home use the personal computer keyboard to play electronic games, to estimate their income tax liability, to find answers to problems; in business it is used to process an immense variety of documents, to input and retrieve information, to compute, to transmit and receive electronic communications locally, nationally and internationally; in schools and colleges it is used to teach the keyboard, to train typists, to calculate, to evaluate progress, and for examinations, etc.

First Course, Sixth Edition, offers a keyboarding course that has been tried, tested and used to train an inestimable number of typists. In addition, this text includes the best features from five prior editions. Eighty per cent of the production exercises are completely new and up to date.

The student who completes the course, and executes the directions as instructed will be:

(a) a competent copy typist;
(b) capable of passing an elementary typewriting examination;
(c) suitable for training as a word processor operator.

The purpose of *First Course, Sixth Edition*, is to help learners:

(a) acquire smooth and correct finger movement;
(b) operate all parts of the machine efficiently;
(c) raise the level and broaden the foundation of the skills and techniques practised in (a) and (b);
(d) apply the skills and techniques to practical work;
(e) acquire an insight into modern business terminology;
(f) apply basic language arts principles correctly.

Instructional design

UNITS 1–50 In all blocked exercises with open punctuation, consistency of style has been followed because we felt it was unfair to expect students, in the learning stage, to change from one style to another and thus become confused. The simplicity of presentation will help learners to eliminate errors because doubts about correct display have been removed and, therefore, the students can concentrate on accurate typing, speed and efficient manipulation of the equipment.

However, certain typewriting examiners will only accept documents set out in a particular style, and, to let students see some of the more traditional methods of display, we have included optional formats in the last section of *Handbook, Solutions, and Resource Material*. The requirements of the examining boards should be studied, and, if any of the displays in the *Handbook, Solutions, and Resource Material* are required in a particular examination, students should study and practise the appropriate exercises.

UNITS 51–56 These give continued emphasis on the points presented in the previous units, with exercises in open and full punctuation, blocked and centred styles.

Keyboard coverage

UNITS 1–22 Because it has proved very successful and popular, the keyboard approach used in previous editions has been retained with minor adjustments. To cover the needs of all learners, we have:

(a) introduced only two alphabet keys in each unit, and after the introduction of the home keys, only one new key is presented at a time;
(b) included only two lines of drills on each new key, followed by a further two lines of **Word family drills** on these keys;
(c) included three lines of **Review the keys you know** at the beginning of each keyboard unit and at the end of these units, three lines of **Apply the keys you know**;
(d) for students who prefer to spend a little more time on the alphabet keys, offered three **Improvement practice** units—8, 12 and 18—each with two pages of drills on the keys introduced prior to that particular unit;
(e) prepared special drills on:
    (i) homophones,
    (ii) words that are often misspelt, and
    (iii) agreement of subject and verb.

UNITS 23–28 Figures and symbols follow on immediately after the alphabet keys and because of the lack of standardization in the placement of symbols on keyboards used with electronic equipment, the figures have been presented as a group and the symbols introduced separately. In these six units there is a sequence of:

(a) **Alphabet reviews** that provide ample keyboard revision and practice.
(b) **Intensive drills** on figures/symbols.
(c) **Skill measurement** practice.
(d) **Record your progress** practice.

SKILL BUILDING AND PRODUCTION DEVELOPMENT From unit 29 onwards, **Skill measurement**, new work and production work are developed in a carefully balanced sequence of activities:

(a) **Skill building:**
    (i) **Keyboard techniques**;
    (ii) **Language arts drills** (spelling, apostrophe, subject and verb agreement);
    (iii) **Skill measurement**;
    (iv) **Record your progress**.

Important features

Features especially designed to develop and refine the important skills, knowledge, terminology and techniques that the changing office environment demands, have been built into the course.

SKILL MEASUREMENT As only the operator and/or the tutor will know whether, at any given time, the operator should be practising for speed or accuracy, we have called the speed/accuracy material **Skill measurement**, and a choice must be made as to whether the practice should aim at increasing speed or working for greater accuracy. There is a special **Skill measurement chart** in the *Handbook, Solutions, and Resource Material*.

PERSONALIZED AND REMEDIAL DRILLS These were a popular feature of the fifth edition and have been retained. Each drill gives intensive practice on a particular letter in combination with other letters. The **Personalized remedial drill sheet**, on which students can record drills practised, is in the *Handbook, Solutions, and Resource Material*.

RECORD YOUR PROGRESS Each **Record your progress** exercise contains every letter of the alphabet. The usual **Record your progress chart** is in the *Handbook, Solutions, and Resource Material*.

SYLLABIC INTENSITY This means the average number of syllables in the words of a passage and is used in the **Skill measurement** and **Record your progress** exercises. As in previous editions, we have used a controlled but random and unselected vocabulary.

BUSINESS VOCABULARY In the fourth edition, published 1982, we mentioned briefly word processing, computers and the electronic office. In the fifth edition, we brought in a much wider technical vocabulary, such as formatting, text editing, laser printing, word/data/text processing (today, more frequently referred to as information processing) etc. In this *First Course, Sixth Edition*, we have continued to widen the typist's knowledge of modern technology, which affects every aspect of office work, and we have also included a number of exercises embracing many facets of the Common Market.

DATA FILES In order to develop a student's initiative in the finding and utilizing of information, 20 exercises have details that need to be verified and/or require additional facts. The student is instructed to refer to the **Data files**, each of which is given a filename and presented in alphabetical order on pages 183–184. Other exercises may refer to data given on previous pages in the textbook, eg, names and addresses, dates, etc.

WORD PROCESSING PROCEDURES Although students may not have access to word processors, electronic typewriters and computers with word processing capabilities, they should take every opportunity to familiarize themselves with the terminology. We have included information processing terminology throughout the text, and wherever we considered it appropriate, we have mentioned word processing concepts and applications that would apply to the operations being practised. We hope that these points will enable students to prepare more fully for the electronic office. Further, we have suggested certain tasks that may be used as **input**, and **text-editing** changes are listed separately on pages 182–183.

INTEGRATED PRODUCTION TYPING PROJECTS These follow the same pattern as in the fifth edition. It is hoped that the thematic approach will develop the student's ability to follow through a project under simulated office conditions.

PROOFREADING Because proofreading is such an important part of the operator's training, we give it emphasis and offer a great variety of proofreading exercises on pages 178–180.

KEYBOARD AND PRODUCTION DEVELOPMENT SCHEDULE A copy of this schedule will be found in the *Handbook, Solutions, and Resource Material* and may be duplicated so that each operator will be able to record her/his progress.

Complementary aids

In addition to *First Course, Sixth Edition*, there are complementary aids that will be found helpful, such as:

Practical Typing Exercises—Book One

This contains further examples of exercises introduced in *First Course, Sixth Edition*. Many of these exercises give the exact layout of typed documents and, therefore, are very easy to follow.

Keyboarding software

The purpose of this disk is to train the individual to operate the keyboard by touch and use correct typing techniques in the shortest possible time. It is based on, and follows the same sequence and drills as, *First Course, Sixth Edition*, and quickly and easily develops basic speed and accuracy skills for the alphabet keys, punctuation, figures and symbols. By the end of this short course, the learner should be able to type at 25 words a minute for three minutes, making not more than three errors. The following demonstration disks are available on 14 days' free inspection: 40 Track, 80 Track, IBM Version.

Handbook, Solutions, and Resource Material

Part I contains:

(a) A brief explanation of how *First Course, Sixth Edition*, was planned so that it incorporates a complete and systematic skill-building plan.
(b) A brief but concise review of the basic principles of how typing skill is acquired and developed.
(c) Syllabuses and schemes of work.
(d) Ideas on the presentation of a lesson.
(e) Recommendations for classroom management.
(f) Points on profiling.
(g) The office environment, ergonomics, Repetitive Strain Injury (RSI).

Part II contains a review of each unit of *First Course, Sixth Edition*, and all exercises not displayed in this edition are set out as they should look when typed. The many charts and letterheads may be copied and duplicated.

At the end of each unit, in Part II, we have included a page of supplementary exercises based on the new work in that unit. Tutors will find these additional exercises beneficial for the student who works more quickly and needs extra material, and for the operator who has typed before and requires a revision course. There is also a new section **Variations in display**.

Acknowledgements

The contents of this book reflects the comments, suggestions and recommendations made to us by tutors who have used previous editions, and we attach a great deal of value to their contributions which, over the years, have helped enormously in the effectiveness and popularity of our typing publications.

We also wish to thank our colleagues for their helpful advice and assistance given in copying the manuscript exercises.

We sincerely hope that students and tutors enjoy working through the Sixth Edition and the supplementary books and aids, and that they will also find pleasure and reward from using the second series, details of which are given on the back cover of this text.

The IBM Personal Computer and printer have been reproduced by kind permission of IBM UK Ltd; the Apple Macintosh Computer by kind permission of Apple Computer U.K. Limited.

Archie Drummond
Anne Coles-Mogford

NOTE References in this book to the *Handbook, Solutions, and Resource Material* are to the sixth edition.

CONTENTS

GREEN

The items should read:

47 kilos of plastics
32 kilos of metal
45 kilos of food
74 kilos of glass

HOST

Mr and Mrs D Gowering
11 The Bridleway
SHIPTON-UNDER-WYCHWOOD
Oxon OX7 6BP

HOUR

Flight LH1661 departs at 1900 hours.

ISLE

The population of Northern Ireland is 1.5 million.

KING

Olav was succeeded by son Harald V on 17 January 1991.

LEC

Monday 25 October at 1930 hours

MENU

The following words require accents: Château ragoût Café

PET

The programme began in 1989.

P/T

The hours will be as follows:

Mondays and Fridays	0900–1230 hours
Tuesdays	0900–1100 hours
Wednesdays	0900–1130 hours
Thursdays	1000–1230 hours

SEC

Dates for the German refresher courses:

GR1/1	Thursday 16 September
GR1/2	Thursday 23 September
GR1/3	Thursday 30 September

SPAIN

All the times are correct.

TEC

(iii)[2] Providing free quality training and work experience leading to national vocational qualifications.

(iv)[3] Providing vital financial help for those wanting to set up their own business.

VDU

Workstations already in use have until 1996 to be adapted.

WORK

The residence permit is obtainable from the local police.

YDS

* It would seem preferable to add an **s** for the plural of yd and qr (yds and qrs). This style is recommended by the *Oxford Dictionary for Writers and Editors*; however, the British Standards Institution gives both examples without the **s**. Follow the author's copy and/or housestyle.

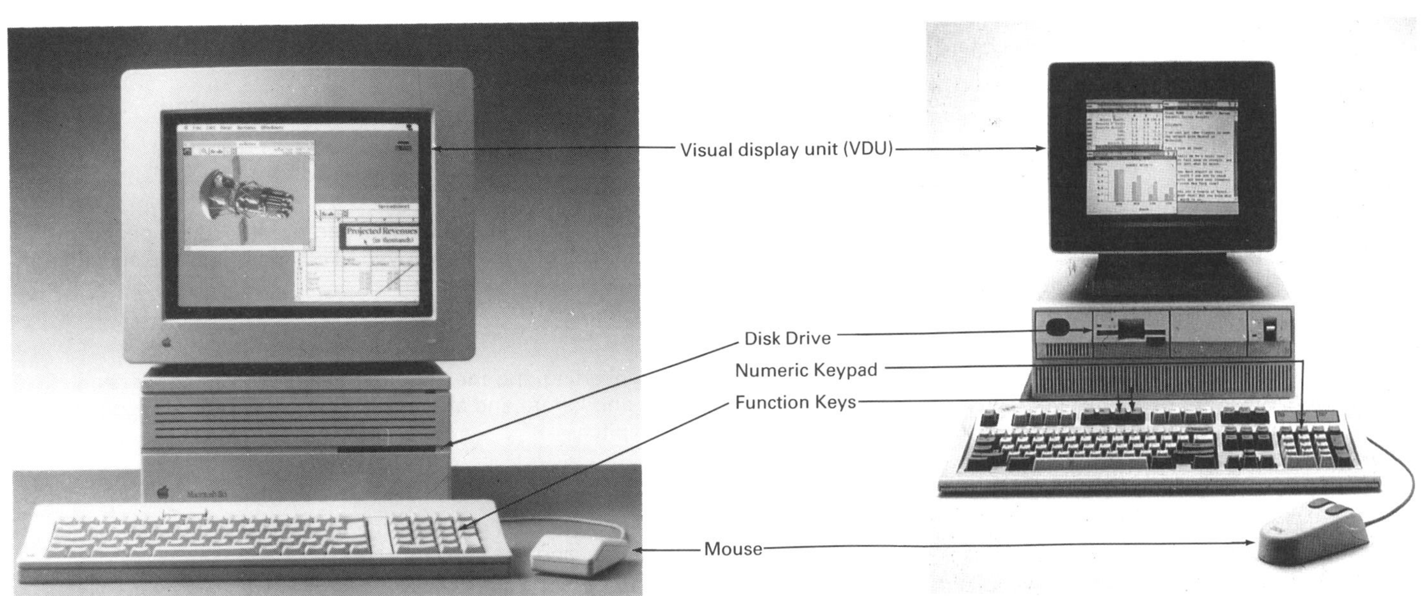

Apple Macintosh Computer

IBM Personal Computer

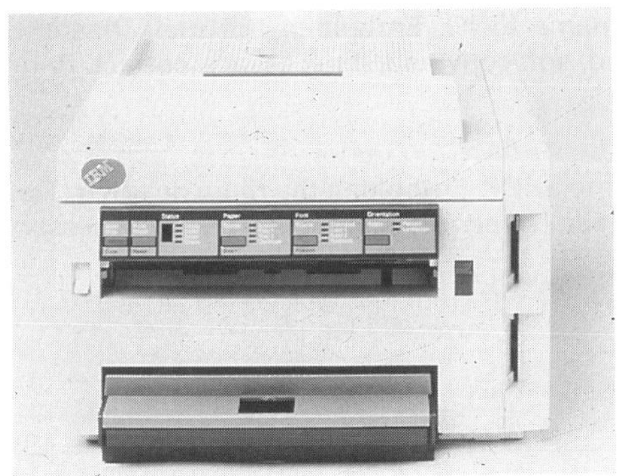

Printer

Disk drive—a diskette is inserted into the disk drive where it is rotated and a read/write head reads from or writes on to the diskette.

Function keys—special keys on the keyboard that command the machine to perform certain functions such as centring a line, emphasizing in bold type, etc.

Keyboard—the alphabetic and numeric keys are the same as any typewriter keyboard—known as the QWERTY keyboard.

Mouse—an electronic, hand-operated input device. When moving the mouse on a flat surface, the cursor on the screen also moves.

Numeric keypad—a bank of keys on the keyboard containing the figures 1–9 and 0 and arranged in a pattern similar to that of a calculator. It is usually operated by the right-hand fingers only.

Printer—the machine that produces characters on paper (hard copy). There are a variety of printers available: daisywheel, dot matrix, laser, etc.

Visual display unit (VDU)—a screen, similar to a television screen, on which the text is displayed (soft copy).

Page 154

Recall the document stored under filename MENU. Embolden the words Dinner Menu. Insert the following two single lines after '(Wild strawberry sorbet)': 'Fromages'
'(Cheese board)'

Leave three single lines after typing the above. Proofread (screenread) soft copy and, if necessary, correct. Print out original only in 12 pitch.

Page 156

Recall the document stored under filename EDU. Add the following sentence at the end of the first paragraph. 'Young people in the European Community account for 20% of the potential workforce, but 40% of the unemployed.' Transpose items (i) and (iii). Proofread (screenread) soft copy and, if necessary, correct. Print out original only in 12 pitch.

Page 157

Recall the document stored under filename ISLE. Embolden the main heading and the shoulder headings. Change to single spacing, but leave double where necessary, ie, after the main heading and before and after each shoulder heading. Proofread (screenread) soft copy and, if necessary, correct. Print out original in 10 pitch.

Page 160

Recall the document stored under filename RSI. Emphasize the main heading and reformat the letter to fully-blocked style. Proofread (screenread) soft copy and, if necessary, correct. Print out original and one copy in 10 pitch.

Page 163

Recall the document stored under filename BUB. Change the final sentence to read as follows: 'Please send me full details, and prices, of your range of bubble jet printers, as well as details of any laser printers you supply.' Proofread (screenread) soft copy and, if necessary, correct. Print out original in 12 pitch.

Page 166

Recall the document stored under filename KING. Embolden the main heading. Re-arrange so that the countries are in alphabetical order. Proofread (screenread) soft copy and, if necessary, correct. Print out original in 10 pitch.

Page 167

Recall the document stored under filename SHOP. Embolden the main heading. Transpose the last two columns in the table, so that London comes before Berlin. Proofread (screenread) soft copy and, if necessary, correct. Print out original in 10 pitch.

DATA FILES

The following office files contain information that you will need when typing certain documents.

AIR

(D) *Finally*, seal the bag using the Airstream label.

CORK

Subject	*Possible hours*	*Actual hours*
Communication	33	30
Shorthand	110	106
Typewriting	80	78
Secretarial Services	33	30
Business Administration	33	31
Information Processing	33	30
Accounts	33	32

EDU

Students have the opportunity of 6 months' training, not 9.

FAX

The address of DUBOIS & CIE is 2 Avenue de la Republique
37100 TOULOUSE France

GNP

The GNP per capita is 6 208 Lira.

This is the symbol that we will use to draw your attention to information and instructions about word processing concepts and applications. In business today, it is important that you understand how modern machines with the QWERTY keyboard may be employed to format more easily a great variety of documents.

If you are typing on an electronic typewriter, a word processor, or a computer with word processing software, study the manufacturer's handbook that accompanies your machine, and practise the functions, movements and settings. You will probably find that there are a number of automatic operations. As it is essential for you to know the types of errors you make and how to overcome errors, **do not** employ the correction key during the keyboard-learning stage or when typing exercises from **Skill measurement**, **Record your progress** or **Skill building** pages.

Cursor

When a VDU (visual display unit) is used in conjunction with an electronic machine, the typing appears on the VDU screen. On the screen there is a movable dot (hyphen) that indicates the typing point at which the next typed character will appear. This movable dot/hyphen is called the cursor. At the end of the typing line the cursor will return to the left margin automatically or when the return key is pressed.

Margins

To save the operator's time, many electronic typewriters and word processors have pre-stored margin settings, tab settings, page length, etc, which may be changed to suit the layout required for a particular document. When any of these pre-stored settings are not appropriate for a particular exercise in this textbook, we suggest that you may wish to change the setting(s) by following the instructions given in the manufacturer's handbook.

Pitch

When only manual typewriters were marketed, the two typefaces available were 10 pitch (pica) or 12 pitch (elite). Then the golf ball electric typewriter brought dual pitch and a choice of 10 or 12 on any one typewriter. Most electronic typewriters and word processors now offer 10, 12 and 15 pitch; however, on the more sophisticated machines there is a wider selection including proportional spacing (PS). The instructions and exercises in this edition are based on 10 or 12 pitch, and we use the word pitch when referring to margin settings.

Single-element typewriters

Nearly all electric and electronic typewriters have single-element heads. These typewriters have no movable carriage, and there are no type bars. Instead, they have a printing head attached to a carrier that moves across the page from left to right, stroke by stroke. When you wish to return the carrier to the left margin, you press the return key as you would with the electric typewriter. On most electronic keyboards, the automatic carrier return is employed.

The printing element is usually a daisywheel which is a rapidly spinning disk with flexible arms. On the tip of each arm there is a typeface character. The required character stops at the printing point and is struck by a small hammer which imprints the image on the paper.

Word processor operators—Text-editing instructions

Page 99

Recall the document stored under filename AIR. Add the following sentence to the end of the first paragraph. 'The Post Office will supply bags and labels.' Proofread (screenread) soft copy and, if necessary, correct. Print out original only in 12 pitch.

Page 100

Recall the document stored under filename MARK. Embolden the letters CE each time they occur; inset the numbered items three character spaces, not five as previously asked for. Proofread (screenread) soft copy and, if necessary, correct. Print out original only in 15 pitch.

Page 106

Recall the document stored under filename BOOK. Embolden the subject heading. Add a third book to the list as follows: 'European Management by F T Chance—£32.00' and change the first paragraph to read '. . . the following 3 books.' Proofread (screenread) soft copy and, if necessary, correct. Print out original and one copy in 12 pitch.

Page 119

Recall the document stored under filename FOOD. Change the final full stop to a comma and add the following: ', with the exception of charity home-bakers who make cakes, etc, for their fund-raising coffee mornings!' Proofread (screenread) soft copy and, if necessary, correct. Print out original only in 12 pitch.

Page 120

Recall the document stored under filename PET. Embolden the main heading. Start a new paragraph with the words 'The Commission believes . . .', and NOT with the words 'The British Government . . .'. Proofread (screenread) soft copy and, if necessary, correct. Print out original only in 10 pitch.

Page 121

Recall the document stored under filename VDU. Embolden all headings in capitals; transpose the paragraphs WORKSTATIONS and REQUIREMENTS. Proofread (screenread) soft copy and, if necessary, correct. Print out original and one copy in 12 pitch.

Page 126

Recall the document stored under filename TRAV. Emphasize the shoulder heading. Transpose items (a) and (c) and add a further item (d) as follows: 'Do not attract ants by leaving crumbs lying around. Keep food under lock and key.' Proofread (screenread) soft copy and, if necessary, correct. Print out original and one copy in 10 pitch.

Page 134

Recall the document stored under filename LEG. Embolden the main heading. Insert the following paragraph after the subheading and before the table and column headings. 'If you are not aware of the provisions of any of the measures listed below, and you require further information, you should contact your single market adviser.' Proofread (screenread) soft copy and, if necessary, correct. Print out original and one copy in 15 pitch.

Page 138

Recall the document stored under filename WORK. Embolden the main and side headings. Change to single spacing. Proofread (screenread) soft copy and, if necessary, correct. Print out original only in 10 pitch.

Page 139

Recall the document stored under filename GAUL. Start a new paragraph at the point 'On 7th April 1921 . . .' and add the following sentence to that paragraph. 'Charles had 3 brothers and a sister all of whom were tall, but Charles, who was 6′ 5″, was the tallest.' Leave 12 single lines clear for the photograph, not 10 as originally instructed. Proofread (screenread) soft copy and, if necessary, correct. Print out original only in 12 pitch.

Page 140

Recall the document stored under filename EFTA. Embolden the main heading, the side headings and the abbreviation EFTA each time it appears. Add the following as a new paragraph, typing it before the final paragraph in the original exercise. 'Agreements establishing industrial free trade between most of the other EFTA member states and the enlarged EC came into force on 1 January 1973. The free trade agreement, therefore, now applies to trade between the 6 countries remaining in EFTA and Portugal.' Proofread (screenread) soft copy and, if necessary, correct. Print out original only in 15 pitch.

Page 153

Recall the document stored under filename METRIC. Alter the footnote so that it appears after the last sentence in the second paragraph. Delete the asterisk signs. Justify the right margin. Proofread (screenread) soft copy and, if necessary, correct. Print out original only in 10 pitch.

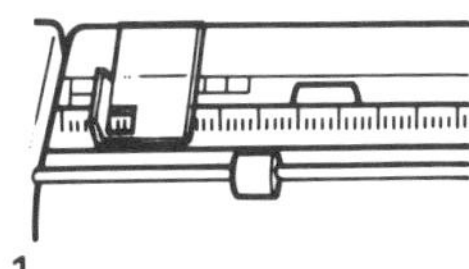

1

1 Paper guide

One of the marks on the paper rest shows where to set the paper guide so that the left edge of the paper will be at '0' on the paper guide scale. Check that the paper guide is set at that mark.

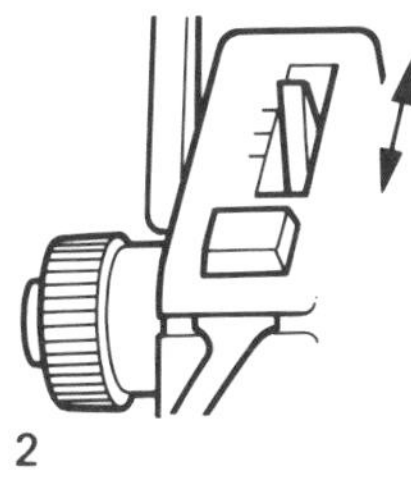

2

2 Linespace selector

The linespace selector has a 1, a 2 and in some cases a 3 printed on or beside it. In addition, many machines are now fitted with half-line spacing to give $1\frac{1}{2}$ and $2\frac{1}{2}$ linespaces. Use the manufacturer's handbook and make sure you know how to set the selector. Always adjust the selector so that it is at the required position.

3 Margins

See previous page and manufacturer's handbook.

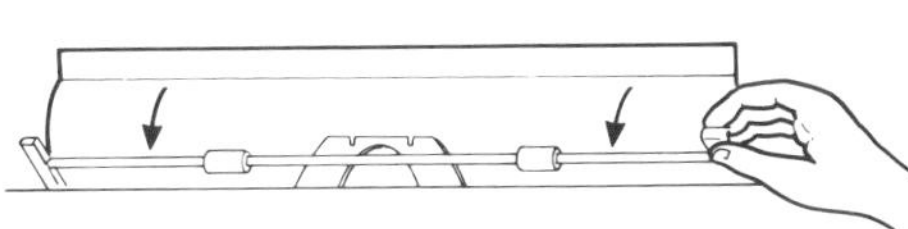

4 Paper bail

Before inserting the paper into the typewriter or printer, pull the paper bail forward, away from the cylinder, so that you may insert the paper without it bumping into the paper bail.

5 Inserting paper—typewriters and printers

To prevent damage to the cylinder of the typewriter, use a piece of stout paper as a backing sheet.

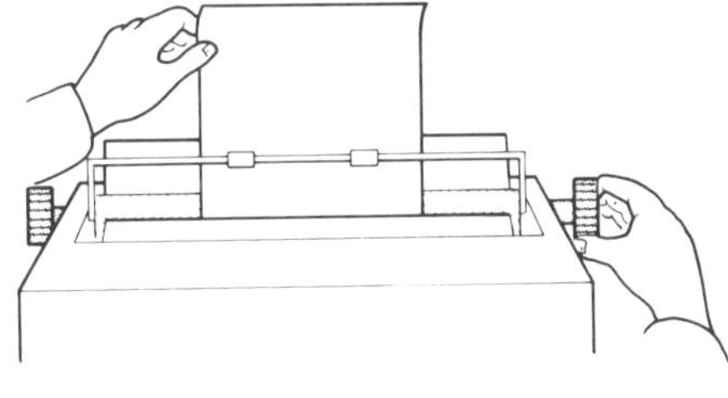

5.1 Hold the sheet in your left hand. Place the paper behind the cylinder, against the raised edge of the paper guide. Turn the right cylinder knob to draw the paper into the machine. Many machines now have a special paper insertion key that should always be used when inserting the paper.

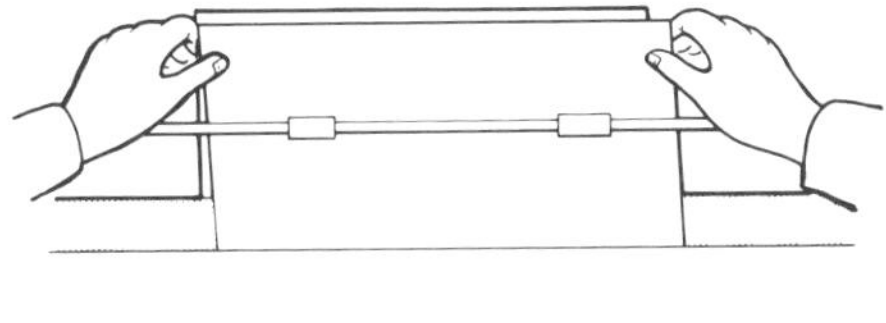

5.2 **Check that the paper is straight**
Push the top of the paper back. If the left side of the paper, at top and bottom, fits evenly against the paper guide, your paper is straight. If it is not straight, loosen the paper (use the paper release), straighten it, and return the paper release to its normal position.

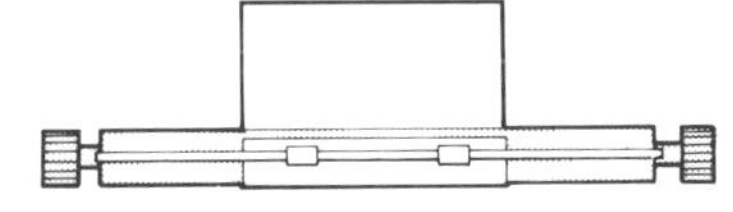

5.3 **Place the paper bail against the paper**
Slide the rubber rollers on the bail to the right or left to divide the paper into thirds. Then, position the bail back against the paper.

5.4 **Top margin**
For most exercises, it is usual to leave 25 mm (1 inch) clear at the top of the page. Many machines now have a pre-stored top margin setting; if necessary, change this so as to leave 25 mm (1 inch) clear. Where an automatic paper insertion key is not provided, turn up seven single spaces which will leave 25 mm (1 inch) clear.

Proofreading

Page 178 (a): line 1—program; line 2—visual; line 3—100; line 4—a daisy-wheel printer; line 5—stock; line 6—Spreadsheet.
Page 178 (b): line 1—your; line 2—top and bottom; line 3—interrupt; line 4—dictation.; line 5—omit the word 'the'; line 6—omit comma after 'pencil'.
Page 178 (c): line 1—GARDENING; line 2—month; line 3—or; line 4—lettuces; line 5—spring-flowering; line 6—line not at left margin; line 7—omit the word 'ANY'.
Page 179 (d): line 1—definite; line 2—two spaces after full stop; line 3—handling; line 4—index cards; line 5—loose-leaf; line 6—omit 'they may'.
Page 179 (e): line 1—retrieval; line 2—accessed; line 3—insert 'an' before annual; line 4—varied,; line 5—retrieve; line 6—a telephone line; line 7—adapted; line 8—insert full stop after 'use'.
Page 180 (f): line 1—disks; microcomputers; line 2—disk,; line 3—two spaces after full stop; 800; line 4—$3\frac{1}{2}$"; line 6—disks,; line 7—Winchester; line 8—computer,; line 9—large; space before and after dash; megabytes.
Page 180 (g): line 1—two spaces after 'advantages'; line 3—roll; 3,000; to; line 4—10 m; 10.5 cm; line 5—500; cheap; line 6—made,; line 7—handle; line 8—35 mm; line 9—insert 'not' before deteriorate.

Spelling skills—words misspelt

Page 42—until, separate, accommodation
Page 51—necessary, truly, stationery
Page 62—privileges, committees, advertisement
Page 72—sheriffs, guaranteed, committees
Page 78—admissible, withhold, cheque
Page 94—knowledge, inaccessible, incompetent
Page 101—arguments, possesses, underrate
Page 47—believe, cancel, temporary
Page 55—cursor, develop, liaison
Page 69—benefited, Wednesday, manufacturer's
Page 75—inconvenience, unnecessarily, believe
Page 88—parallel, miscellaneous, discretion
Page 98—occasion, guardian, familiar
Page 113—ensuing, eighths, arrogance

Language arts—apostrophe

Page 117—lines 6 and 8	Singular (one only) nouns not ending in **s**, add an apostrophe **s**
lines 7 and 9	Plural nouns ending in **s**, add an apostrophe
Page 122—lines 10 and 12	Singular nouns not ending in **s**, add an apostrophe **s**
lines 11 and 13	Plural nouns not ending in **s**, add apostrophe **s**
Page 132—line 10	Singular noun (Mary) not ending in **s**, add an apostrophe **s** Plural noun (weeks) ending in **s**, add an apostrophe
line 11	The contraction **it's** needs the apostrophe before the **s** to show the omission of the letter **i**. The pronoun **its** (The dog chased its tail.) does not require an apostrophe.
line 12	To avoid confusion, the apostrophe is used for the plural of single letters and numbers (2 **c's** and 2 **m's**).
line 13	Single quotes (apostrophe) is sometimes used in place of the quotation marks to indicate the exact words of a speaker or writer.

Language arts—agreement of subject and verb

Page 137—line 6	**Keyboarding** (singular noun) requires singular verb **is**.
line 7	**keys** (plural noun) requires plural verb **are**.
line 8	A plural verb is always necessary after **you**.
line 9	Although **s** or **es** added to a noun indicates the plural, **s** or **es** added to a verb indicates the third person singular.
Page 141—line 2	The subject is **box** (singular); therefore, the singular verb **is** should be used.
line 3	Singular subjects (**report** and **letter**) joined by **and** require a plural verb (**are**).
line 4 line 5	Two subjects (**name** and **address**) preceded by, or joined by, **every** (**each**, **neither**, **one**, **another**) require a singular verb.
Page 151—line 2	When singular subjects are joined by **nor** the verb should be singular; however, if one of the subjects is plural **(students)** the verb should agree with the subject immediately preceding it (**students are**).
line 3	Parenthetic expressions such as, **including**, **together with**, **as well as**, do not affect the number of the verb and should be ignored.
line 4	**None** means **not one**; therefore, singular verb **is** should be used.
line 5	Use singular verb after a phrase beginning **one of**, or **one of the**.
Page 155—line 2	Words like, **works**, **news**, **means**, etc, take singular verbs.
line 3	You would say: My shoes are missing; but you require a singular verb after **pair**. Plural words such as **wages**, **valuables**, **headquarters**, etc, take a singular verb when they are singular in meaning.
line 4	Collective nouns (**committee**) take a singular verb when the nouns apply to a group or unit, and a plural verb when the members of the group are thought of as acting separately.
Page 158—line 2	**Set** is singular and, therefore, requires a singular verb (**has**).
line 3	Subject consists of two singular nouns (**friend** and **neighbour**) joined by **and**, but both nouns denote the same person, therefore, the verb is singular.
line 4	**Neither** always takes a singular verb.

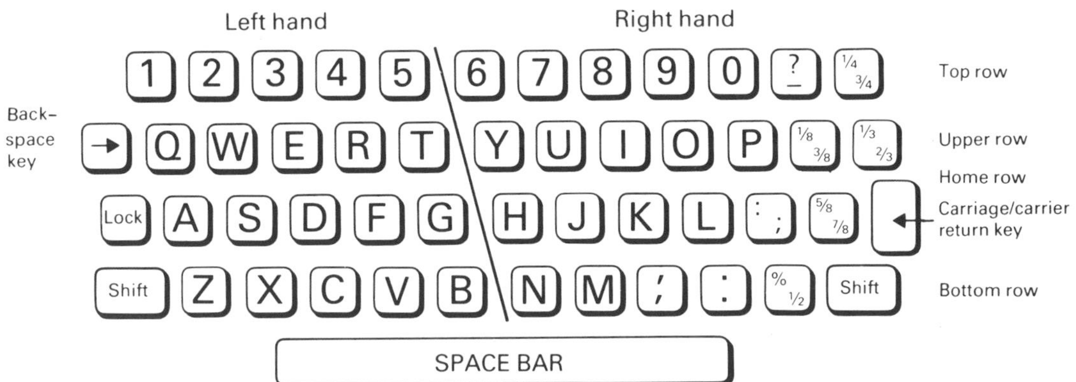

Preliminary practice

1 Place your book on the right-hand side of your machine, or as indicated by your tutor. Whenever possible use a copy holder.
2 Place your finger tips above the home keys. Left finger tips above **A S D F** and right finger tips above **J K L ;** check that you place them correctly.
3 Keep your left thumb close to your left first finger.
4 Extend your right thumb so that it is slightly above the centre of the space bar.
5 Now check your **posture**.
Your head—hold it erect, facing the book.
Your shoulders—hold them back and relaxed.
Your body—centre yourself opposite the J key a hand-span away from the machine.
Your back—straight, with your body sloping slightly forward from the hips.
Arms and elbows—let them hang loosely by your sides.
Wrists—keep them low, barely clearing the machine.
Hands—close together, low, flat across the backs.
Fingers—slightly curved.
Waist—sit back in the chair.
Feet—on the floor, one foot slightly in front of the other. If necessary, a foot rest should be used.
6 **VDU screen**
Wherever possible:
6.1 Position the body so that you are looking straight ahead at the VDU—avoid looking at the screen sideways.
6.2 Eyes should be level with the top of the screen and between 406 mm (16 inches) and 762 mm (30 inches) from the screen.
6.3 Use adequate lighting and see that there is no glare on the screen from daylight or artificial light.
NOTE RSI (Repetitive Strain Injury) may be caused by repetitive use of fingers when sitting incorrectly.

Finger movement drill

1 Without typing, practise the finger movement for the exercise you are about to type. During this preliminary practice, you may look at your fingers. You will find it helpful to say the letters to yourself. Continue the preliminary practice until your fingers 'know' where to move from the home key. Always return finger to its home key.
2 When you are confident that your fingers have acquired the correct movement, repeat this practice **without looking at your fingers**. Keep your eyes on the copy in your book and do not strike the keys. If you hesitate in making the finger movement, go back and repeat step 1.
3 Practise the finger movement for each new key until your finger moves confidently to that key and back to the home key.

The following two exercises contain 12 errors each. Read each passage carefully, and compare with the correct copy typed below. When you have found and noted the errors, type the corrected passage using margins of 12 pitch 22–82, 10 pitch 12–72. Use blocked paragraphs. Do not type the figures down the left side.

Line number

(f) Exercise to be corrected

There are 3 main types of discs used for micro computers. The most common is the 5¼" floppy disk which is permanently protected by a plastic sleeve. This disk holds between 100 and 8000 kilobytes. Then there is the 3¼" disk which is built into a rigid plastic box with a cover which slides back when you put the disk into the machine. These disks have a similar capacity to the 5¼" disk, ie, between 100 and 800 kilobytes. The winchester disk is a hard disk which is permanently built into the Computer, and has a very big capacity-several megabites.

Correct copy

There are 3 main types of disks used for microcomputers. The most common is the 5¼" floppy disk, which is permanently protected by a plastic sleeve. This disk holds between 100 and 800 kilobytes. Then there is the 3½" disk which is built into a rigid plastic box with a cover which slides back when you put the disk into the machine. These disks have a similar capacity to the 5¼" disks, ie, between 100 and 800 kilobytes. The Winchester disk is a hard disk which is permanently built into the computer, and has a very large capacity - several megabytes.

(g) Exercise to be corrected

There are various advantages of using a microfilm system of filing. Obviously expensive filing space is saved, viz, a microfilm jacket holds up to 70 documents, role film holds from 3 000 - 20,000 documents per 10 mm, and microfiche 15 cm x 10.6 cm holds from 98 to 5000 images. The film is cheep to send through the post, duplicates can be easily made storage costs are less and the system is easy to handel and control. Documents are filmed on 16 mm or 35 cm roll film, which means that originals are not constantly handled and do deteriorate or become torn.

Correct copy

There are various advantages of using a microfilm system of filing. Obviously expensive filing space is saved, viz, a microfilm jacket holds up to 70 documents, roll film holds from 3,000 to 20,000 documents per 10 m, and microfiche 15 cm x 10.5 cm holds from 98 to 500 images. The film is cheap to send through the post, duplicates can be easily made, storage costs are less and the system is easy to handle and control. Documents are filmed on 16 mm or 35 mm roll film, which means that originals are not constantly handled and do not deteriorate or become torn.

Practise carriage/carrier/cursor return

1 MANUAL MACHINES

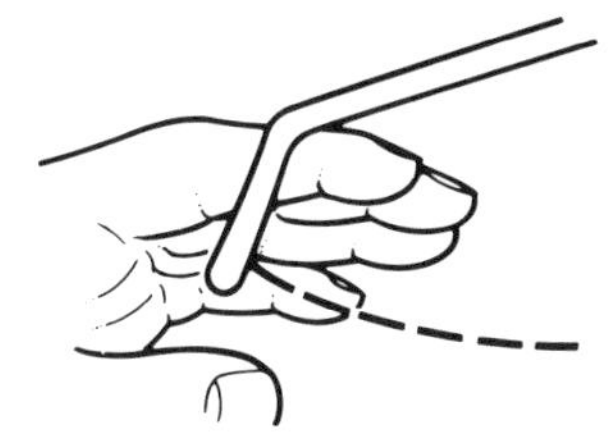

1.1 Preliminary practice *without returning the carriage*. Look at the carriage return lever and raise your *left hand* and put the first finger, supported by the other fingers, against the lever. Practise the movement from the HOME KEYS to carriage return lever and back to HOME KEYS.

1.2 Right-hand fingers always remain on JKL;

1.3 With eyes on textbook:

- 1.3.1 raise left hand and return carriage,
- 1.3.2 return left hand to ASDF immediately.

2 ELECTRIC MACHINES

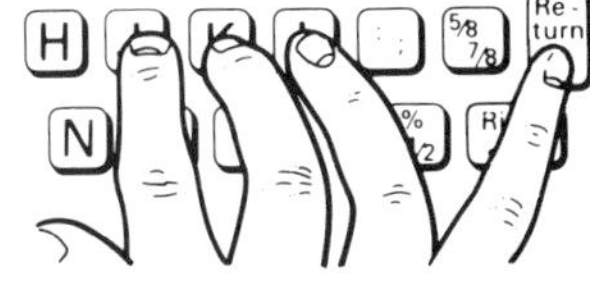

2.1 Preliminary practice *without returning the carriage/carrier*. Look at the carriage/carrier return key (on the right-hand side of the keyboard) and make the reach with your right-hand little finger from its HOME KEY to the return key and back to the HOME KEY.

2.2 All fingers remain just slightly above their HOME KEY except the right-hand little finger.

2.3 With eyes on textbook:

- 2.3.1 raise the little finger of the right hand and lightly press the return key,
- 2.3.2 return the little finger to the HOME key immediately.

3 ELECTRONIC MACHINES

With electronic keyboards you can, by depressing a function key, use automatic carrier/cursor return. You will notice that the carrier/cursor returns automatically at the set right margin when the line is full. This is often referred to as word wraparound. Follow the instructions given in the machine handbook or ask your tutor for advice.

Striking the keys

Manual machines—strike keys firmly and sharply.
Electric/electronic machines—stroke keys lightly and quickly.

Prepare to type

In order to prepare yourself and your machine for typing, take the following action:

1. Electric/electronic machines—insert plug in socket, switch on socket, and switch on machine.
2. Place book on right-hand side of machine or as instructed by your tutor.
3. Place blank typing paper on left-hand side of machine or as instructed by your tutor.
4. Set left margin at 12 pitch 30 (64 mm—$2\frac{1}{2}$ inches) 10 pitch 20 (51 mm—2 inches).*
5. Set linespace selector on '1'.
6. Set paper guide on '0'.
7. Move paper bail out of the way.
8. Insert sheet of A4 paper.
9. If necessary, straighten paper.
10. Return paper bail to normal position.
11. If necessary, turn the paper back, using right cylinder knob, until only a small portion of paper shows above paper bail.
12. Place front of keyboard level with edge of desk so that the J key is opposite the centre of your body.
13. If necessary, adjust chair height so that your forearms are on the same slope as the keyboard.
14. Place chair so that you are about a hand-span away from edge of desk.
15. Feet apart and flat on floor or, if necessary, on a foot rest.
16. See that carriage/carrier/cursor is at left margin.

NOTE Until you are instructed otherwise, all exercises should be typed line for line as in the text—use return key.

* You may use a pre-stored margin setting if you wish.

Computers, word processors and electronic typewriters may be programmed to provide whatever top, bottom and side margins you consistently require.

Proofreading target: 4 minutes } for each
Typing target: 5 minutes } exercise

Read each passage carefully and compare with the correct copy typed below. Each line in the incorrect copy contains an error that may be spelling, spacing, hyphenation, omission of apostrophe, etc. When you have found and noted the errors, type the corrected passage using margins of 12 pitch 22–82, 10 pitch 12–72. Use blocked paragraphs. Do not type the figures down the left side.

Line number

(d) Exercise to be corrected

Visible indexing systems have the definate advantages of easy access and clear labelling or indexing. The information can be seen at once with very little or no handeling. Also cards can be inserted or removed without disturbing others in the container. Visible card indexes may be held flat in trays, in loose leaf binders, or they may hang from walls, or they may be free-standing on table tops or desks.

Correct copy

Visible indexing systems have the definite advantages of easy access and clear labelling or indexing. The information can be seen at once with very little or no handling. Also cards can be inserted or removed without disturbing others in the container. Visible index cards may be held flat in trays, in loose-leaf binders, or they may hang from walls, or be free-standing on table tops or desks.

(e) Exercise to be corrected

Prestel is a public database Retrieval service operated by British Telecom. The data is stored on computers and accesed via telephone lines. Various agencies subscribe to input information for annual fee. The information is very varied: eg, household hints, sports results. In order to retreive information a Prestel user can call the computer centre on telephone lines, using a keypad. The information will be shown on his television screen, which can be adopted for Prestel use

Correct copy

Prestel is a public database retrieval service operated by British Telecom. The data is stored on computers and accessed via telephone lines. Various agencies subscribe to input information for an annual fee. The information is very varied, eg, household hints, sports results. In order to retrieve information a Prestel user can call the computer centre on a telephone line, using a keypad. The information will be shown on his television screen, which can be adapted for Prestel use.

Introduction to home keys

Type the following drills.

Exercise 1

1.1 Curve fingers slightly.
1.2 Look at keyboard and place fingertips over HOME KEYS—left hand **A S D F**, right hand **J K L ;**
1.3 Type the two lines exactly as they are—**do not look at the keyboard**.

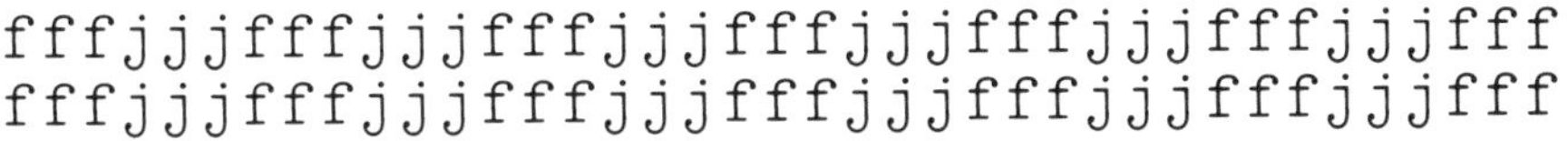

```
fffjjjfffjjjfffjjjfffjjjfffjjjfffjjjfff   Return carriage/carrier/cursor
fffjjjfffjjjfffjjjfffjjjfffjjjfffjjjfff   Return carriage/carrier/cursor twice
```

1.4 Sit back, relax and look at what you have typed.

Exercise 2—operating the space bar

A clear space is left between each group of letters and between words. This is done by tapping the space bar with the right thumb. Keep your other fingers over the HOME KEYS as you operate the space bar. Practise operating the space bar and returning carriage/carrier/cursor.

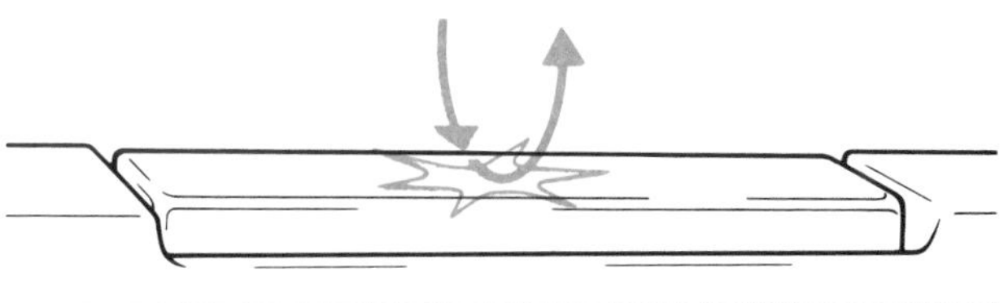

See that carriage/carrier/cursor is at left margin.

Exercise 3

3.1 Curve fingers slightly.
3.2 Look at the keyboard and place your left-hand fingertips over **A S D F** and right-hand fingertips over **J K L ;**
3.3 Type the three lines exactly as they are—**do not look at the keyboard**.

```
fff jjj fff jjj fjf jfj fff jjj fff fjfj   Return carriage/carrier/cursor
fff jjj fff jjj fjf jfj fff jjj fff fjfj   Return carriage/carrier/cursor
fff jjj fff jjj fjf jfj fff jjj fff fjfj   Return carriage/carrier/cursor twice
```

3.4 Sit back, relax and look at what you have typed.

Exercise 4

Repeat exercises 1, 2 and 3.

Proofreading target for each exercise: 2 minutes
Typing target for each exercise: 3 minutes

In the exercises below, the sentences in COLUMN ONE have been repeated in COLUMN TWO. Those in column one are correct, but in each sentence in column two there is a typing error. Compare the sentences and see how quickly you can spot the errors. Then type the sentences correctly.

(a) Column one

1 A program for a computer is recorded on a disk.
2 The visual display unit looks like a TV screen.
3 A disk can hold 100 kilobytes or more.
4 A matrix printer is faster than a daisy-wheel printer.
5 Bar codes may be used in stock control.
6 Spreadsheet programs may be used for management accounting.

Column two

1 A programme for a computer is recorded on a disk.
2 The vizual display unit looks like a TV screen.
3 A disk can hold 101 kilobytes or more.
4 A matrix printer is faster than daisy-wheel printer.
5 Bar codes may be used in Stock control.
6 Spread sheet programs may be used for management accounting.

(b) Column one

1 Keep your shorthand notebook handy.
2 Date each page at top and bottom.
3 Do not interrupt the dictator.
4 Raise any queries at the end of dictation.
5 Rule a left margin for reminders.
6 Keep a pen or pencil by your notebook.

Column two

1 Keep you shorthand notebook handy.
2 Date each page at bottom and top.
3 Do not interupt the dictator.
4 Raise any queries at the end of dictation
5 Rule a left margin for the reminders.
6 Keep a pen or pencil, by your notebook.

(c) Column one

G A R D E N I N G - October

Tasks for the month

Plant fruit trees or soft fruit canes

Transplant cabbages, and lettuces

Plant hardy, spring-flowering plants

Mark out boundaries of new borders

SWEEP UP DEAD LEAVES

Column two

G A R D N I N G - October

Tasks for the Month

Plant fruit trees of soft fruit canes

Transplant cabbages, and lettuce

Plant hardy, spring flowering plants

 Mark out boundaries of new borders

SWEEP UP ANY DEAD LEAVES

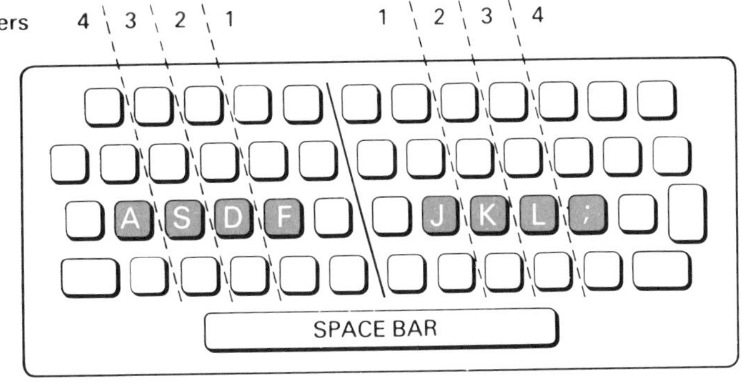

Follow the routine suggested on page 6 under the heading **Prepare to type**, then type each line or sentence three times, saying the letters to yourself. If time permits, complete your practice by typing each group of lines as it appears. Keep your eyes on the copy while you type and also when returning the carriage/carrier/cursor. The carriage/carrier/cursor must be returned **immediately** after the last character in the line has been typed. Set left margin stop at 12 pitch 30 (64 mm—2½ inches) 10 pitch 20 (51 mm—2 inches) and use single spacing with double between exercises. Pre-stored margin settings may be used.

A Practise F and J keys—First fingers

Keep fingers curved over home keys

1 fff jjj fjf jfj fjf jfj fff jjj fff fjfj

Always turn up twice between exercises

B Practise D and K keys—Second fingers

Keep fingers curved over home keys

2 ddd kkk dkd kdk dkd kdk ddd kkk dkd dkdk

3 fff jjj ddd kkk fkf kfk jdj djd fjk fdjk

Use an even stroke for space bar

C Practise S and L keys—Third fingers

Keep fingers curved over home keys

4 sss lll sls lsl sls lsl sss lll sls slsl

5 fff jjj ddd kkk sss lll fds jkl fds jklj

Both feet flat on floor/foot rest

D Practise A and ; keys—Little fingers

Keep fingers curved over home keys

6 aaa ;;; a;a ;a; a;a ;a; aaa ;;; ;a; a;a;

7 f;f jaj d;d kak a;s lal aaa ;;; a;a a;a;

E Word-building

8 aaa lll all lll aaa ddd lad ddd aaa dad;

9 fff aaa ddd fad sss aaa ddd sad fad lad;

F Apply the keys you know

10 dad fad sad lad ask all dad fad sad lad;

11 lass fall lads fads lass fall dads fads;

12 all sad lads; a sad lass; a lad asks dad

13 all sad lads ask a dad; a sad lass falls

14 as a lass falls dad falls; all lads fall

One space after semi-colon

G At the end of typing period

Remove paper by using paper release.
If electric, turn off machine, switch off at socket, and remove plug from socket.
Cover machine.
Remove used and unused paper.
Leave desk tidy.

W wages weary which widow write Wyatt drawl awoke
dwell ewers Gwent kiwis Elwin owner swing twist
byway Wales fewer Irwin swims dwarf crews awful

Berwyn Dewhurst lived in Cwmbran, Gwent, Wales, and never wearied in winding his way through the byways and highways of that wonderful land. I always find that waterway awkward but worthwhile for our visit.

X axiom excel oxide exact mixed pyxie exert exits
expel extra exude Xiang Xebec Xenon X-ray oxbow
proxy maxim toxin Xerox Oxfam annex affix mixer

We will examine the text of the excellent tax guide which Maxine bought. Sixty days ago Max Wilcox saw the quixotic and exquisite film EXULTANT XYLOPHONE. Rex offered no excuse for losing the toxic mixture.

Y yacht yearn yield Ypres yucca Ayers bylaw cynic
Dyfed eyrie gypsy hymns lynch myths nymph pygmy
Ryder synod tyres vying crazy wryly unify syrup

Sydney sent sympathy to Sally who cycled home after they lost a typing test. You were ruled by tyranny and an arbitrary bully. In the dusty, shady area I saw a gypsy help a very tiny, bonny baby to safety.

Z Zaire zebra zippy azure czars ozone zonal zooms
adzes maize Franz graze pizza dizzy aztec oozes
waltz Czech gauze dozes zeros zloty zones Zulus

Puzzled but zealous Zelda won both my quizzes about zebras living in zoos in New Zealand. The owner of the dozen sheep grazing in the field won an amazing prize of a gazelle. This sizzling sun is a hazard.

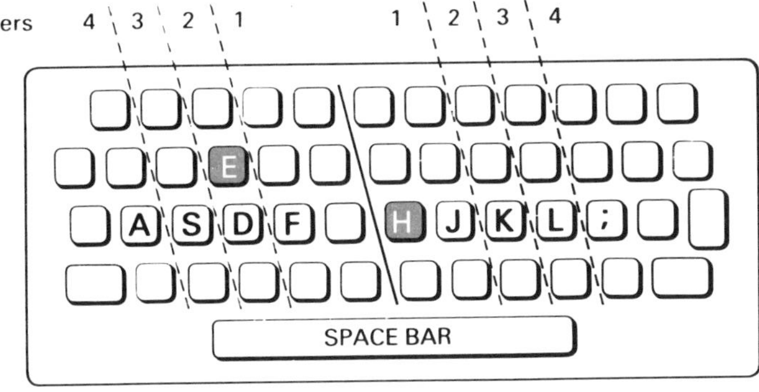

Follow the routine suggested on page 6 under the heading **Prepare to type**, then type each line or sentence three times, saying the letters to yourself. If time permits, complete your practice by typing each group of lines as it appears. Keep your eyes on the copy while you type and also when returning the carriage/carrier/cursor. The carriage/carrier/cursor must be returned **immediately** after the last character in the line has been typed. Set left margin stop at 12 pitch 30 (64 mm—2½ inches) 10 pitch 20 (51 mm—2 inches) and use single spacing with double between exercises. Pre-stored margin settings may be used.

A Review the keys you know

1 aaa ;;; sss lll ddd kkk fff jjj asd jkl;
2 ask a lad; ask all lads; ask a sad lass;
3 all lads fall; dad falls; dad asks a lad

Return carriage/carrier/cursor without looking up

Turn up twice between exercises

B Practise E key—D finger

Practise D to E back to D. Keep other fingers curved over home keys

4 ddd eee ded ded see ded lee ded fee ded;
5 ded sea ded lea ded led ded fed ded eke;

C Practise H key—J finger

Practise J to H back to J. Keep other fingers curved over home keys

6 jjj hhh jhj jhj has jhj had jhj she jhj;
7 jhj has jhj had jhj she jhj ash jhj dash

Do not rest your hands on the frame of the machine

D Practise word-building

8 hhh eee lll ddd held jjj aaa fff jaffas;
9 sss hhh aaa lll shall fff eee ddd feeds;

E Apply the keys you know

10 see lee fee sea lea led fed eke see lee;
11 ash dash fash sash hash lash; heel shed;
12 a lass has had a salad; dad sees a lake;
13 a jaffa salad; she held a sale; he shall
14 she feeds a lad; dad has a hall; a shed;

Use right thumb and even stroke for space bar

NOTE To help you complete your keyboarding more quickly and efficiently, why not use our keyboarding software? It covers the QWERTY keyboard and ACCURACY/SPEED up to 25 words a minute. For details see Preface.

Q quote quail quart queen query quest quiet quite
quail quote quick queue equal equip pique quack
squad quake quilt quits quirk query quart quick

I questioned the value of the unique aquarium which Quinton Asquith had acquired. A subsequent enquiry queried an odd bequest of quartz glass to the quisling. I had an adequate quantity of new equipment.

R rapid reach rhyme round rules arise brand cream
drive error fruit group irate kraft order print
trade urges write yards birch scarf shrub arson

That thrill of securing rare turquoise curtains and carpet was truly appreciated. The corvette carried one tier of crude guns which were fired when on the practice trials. Carmel saw the lark near a barge.

S saves scale serve short sight skirt sleep small
snowy solid squad asset stuck suits sweet sylph
aside goods issue essay calls osmic users bombs

Sally Tompson stayed on for a course in Spanish for summer visitors. I disbelieve that the mischievous lad tried to bring disgrace to a distressed family. The shrewd businessman should buy that system soon.

T talks tease those tired today trend rests myths
tulip tweed typed atlas ether width doubt rifts
night items kilts boots optic start utter extol

She substituted battle tactics to settle the territorial dispute. The partition of Vietnam started a quarrel that had devastating results. The title of Tom's textbook is certainly ecstatic and traumatic.

U ulcer umbra union upper upset urban usage utile
uvula Uzbek audit build cured ducks funny guide
hurry jumbo lungs muddy nurse pulse quick rural

On a sunny day the ubiquitous uncle wore a tunic of unusual blue when he queued for his supper. Truthfully, the manufacturer pursued an unequalled and a unique course to further our aims for extra output.

V valid verbs vigil vocal avoid event civil elves
envoy overt ivory delve vivid verve every solve
valve vogue haves ovens overs saves vocal Olive

Vivian provided a vivid picture of Valery Vowles on a visit to prevail upon her sister. He was invited to play the provocative villain. Very soon Vanessa will involve Vi in a vicious and vituperative book.

Follow **Prepare to type** on page 6 and instructions given at top of page 9.

Margins: 12 pitch 30 (64 mm—2½ inches) 10 pitch 20 (51 mm—2 inches) and use single spacing with double between exercises. Pre-stored margin settings may be used.

A Review the keys you know

1 asd ;lk ded jhj def khj fed has lee had;
2 add salads; a sea lake; lads feed seals;
3 add leeks; she had leeks; he has a hall;

Wrists and arms straight

Turn up twice between exercises

B Practise G key—F finger

Practise F to G back to F. Keep other fingers curved over home keys

4 fff ggg fgf fgf fag fgf lag fgf sag fgf;
5 fgf jag fgf gag fgf hag fgf keg fgf leg;

C Practise U key—J finger

Practise J to U back to J. Keep other fingers curved over home keys

6 jjj uuu juj juj due juj sue juj hue juj;
7 juj sug juj jug juj dug juj hug juj lug;

D Practise word-building

8 uuu sss eee ddd use uses used useful us;
9 jjj uuu ddd ggg eee judge judges judged;

E Apply the keys you know

10 fag sag lag jag gag hag keg leg egg keg;
11 dues hues jugs hugs lugs suds eggs legs;
12 he had a dull glass; a judge has a flag;
13 see she has a full jug; she used jaffas;
14 dad had a full keg; he shall guess; use;

Feet firmly on floor

F At end of typing period

Remove paper by using paper release.
If electric, turn off machine, switch off at socket, and remove plug from socket.
Cover machine.
Remove used and unused paper.
Leave desk tidy.

K Katie kebab kicks knock Korea krona eking bulky
lurks flack works seeks black kilns picks skews
Akron khaki knelt quake Kevin fluke locks junky

Karen and Jack had bulky packages which they bought in the market from a gawky crook. The lucky worker lunched with a well-known cricketer who spoke in an unkind, husky voice. Take the bricks to the truck.

L label legal Lloyd lodge lunch alike bluff claim
elegy flour glove Klein older place slang ultra
Allen idled ankle madly pylon altar allow ankle

Lily Lyles delivered an excellent table to my uncle living at Blind Alley Bay. Walters was not able to collect the lion and alligator from Lulworth. Call on Liz Bolton when you are in Ballinluig next July.

M makes merge Miami mount mufti myrrh amuse emend
imply omega small combs dogma tramp calms McNee
Amman charm pigmy films dummy remit admit human

Mrs Mimms was empowered to promote Marjory McMaster to Games Mistress. Mary may have committed herself to take command of the mission to Mexico. In a moment a memorandum will be mailed to my new Manager.

N names needs night nouns nudge ankle enjoy index
onion under meant thing spend prawn tongs tense
scent lynch thank penny fungi ankle fence sneak

Nancy announced that she cannot attend the national plant exhibition until next Monday when another man from Tanner and Company's Personnel Department will be absent. The ninety-ninth meeting was mentioned.

O oasis obese ocean odour offer Ogden olive Omagh
onion opera orbit Oscar other ought ovens owner
oxide ozone borne count doves forms goats homes

This forenoon another of our followers will hope to visit the zoological forest. Young Jon Morley rode south through many towns in my well-worn Zodiac car and Nora Porters located a hotel in Colwyn for him.

P paper Peter photo piano plans ports press pulls
Pyrex apart empty input opens space upper warps
expel gipsy helps optic alpha apply pupil quips

Philip put his computer on display so as to explain the preparation of proper programmes. Please put a copy of the opposition's campaign pictures in Peter Philpott's post before he opens the people's parks.

Follow **Prepare to type** on page 6 and instructions given at top of page 9.

Margins: 12 pitch 30 (64 mm—2½ inches) 10 pitch 20 (51 mm—2 inches) and use single spacing with double between exercises. Pre-stored margin settings may be used.

A Review the keys you know

1 fds jkl ded juj fgf jhj hag jug dug leg;
2 a lass uses a flask; all lads had a jug;
3 sell us a full keg; see she has a glass;

Eyes on copy always

B Practise R key—F finger

Practise F to R back to F. Keep other fingers curved over home keys

4 fff rrr frf frf jar frf far frf rag frf;
5 frf are frf ark frf red frf fur frf rug;

C Practise I key—K finger

Practise K to I back to K. Keep other fingers curved over home keys

6 kkk iii kik kik kid kik lid kik did kik;
7 kik dig kik fig kik rig kik jig kik gig;

D Practise word families

8 fill hill rill drill grill skill frills;
9 ark lark dark hark; air fair hair lairs;

E Apply the keys you know

10 fill his flask; he is here; he had a rug
11 her red dress is here; she has fair hair
12 she likes a fair judge; he has dark hair
13 his lad fills a jug; she has rare skills
14 she is sure; ask her here; he likes figs

Keep your elbows in close, hanging loosely by your sides

F Size of type faces

10 pitch 10 characters take up 25 mm or 2.5 cm (1 inch) of space.
12 pitch 12 characters take up 25 mm or 2.5 cm (1 inch) of space.
15 pitch 15 characters take up 25 mm or 2.5 cm (1 inch) of space.

NOTE To help you complete your keyboarding more quickly and efficiently, why not use our keyboarding software? It covers the QWERTY keyboard and ACCURACY/SPEED up to 25 words a minute. For details see Preface.

E eaten edges eerie Egypt eject elder embed entry
epics equal erase estop evade duvet cells Derby
feign heavy keeps merge peeks weary years blaze

The messengers had to proceed to the exit gates and collect the receipts from the referees. It will be expedient not to reject the guarantee given for the new temperature gauges you received only yesterday.

F fatal fewer fifty flame focus frank fully cliff
turfs often after refer lifts cleft elfin offer
infer wharf staff affix edify forms tufts feign

After Frank referred to Faith's offer of a fabulous car as a gift to the fighting fund, they found that an unfriendly thief had faked the accounts. Father fought to safeguard the foolish and fretful fellow.

G gains germs cough given glare gnome going grand
guard Gwent gypsy again Egypt aggro igloo Ogden
argue sugar Edgar bulge muggy edged guard Gregg

Gideon, who played the guitar, gained good marks at college for giving regular concerts. The great and gracious Grace giggled as she guided the genial guy through the aged and lengthy thoroughfares to town.

H hands heard hired hoard human ahead chase photo
shout there rough south night harsh laugh thugs
honey ghost teach phone aloha ghoul rhino abhor

Their teacher showed them how to centre headings in a horizontal fashion. We went ahead throughout the harsh, dark night and reached the hallowed halls at a late hour. Hugh and Homer hailed Hal and Hellen.

I Ibiza icing ideal igloo image index ionic irate
issue items ivory aisle birth cigar diary first
girls hired kinds light miles ninth piece right

Visibility was very poor and we did not participate in the official visit to that island. It is surely not permissible for pensioners to give publicity to their objective. The privilege had been withdrawn.

J Japan jetty joker judge jolly joins enjoy major
Bejam fjord banjo jazzy jaded jaunt jewel jerky
Fijis juror jinks jumps jolly jeans jeers jelly

Judith and John listened to Junior's disjointed and jumbled speech. My prejudices were justified and I rejected the joyful joker whose jacket is jade. He jumped and jeered at the jockeys injured yesterday.

Follow **Prepare to type** on page 6 and instructions given at top of page 9.

Margins: 12 pitch 30 (64 mm—$2\frac{1}{2}$ inches) 10 pitch 20 (51 mm—2 inches) and use single spacing with double between exercises. Pre-stored margin settings may be used.

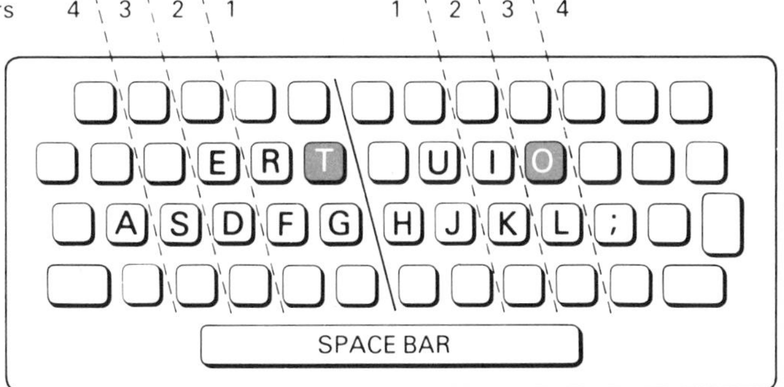

A Review the keys you know

1 fgf jhj frf juj ded kik aid did her rug;
2 his full fees; she likes a dark red rug;
3 his girl is here; he is glad she is sure

B Practise T key—F finger

Practise F to T back to F. Keep other fingers curved over home keys

4 fff ttt ftf ftf fit ftf kit ftf lit ftf; Check your posture
5 ftf sit ftf hit ftf sat ftf hat ftf fat;

C Practise O key—L finger

Practise L to O back to L. Keep other fingers curved over home keys

6 lll ooo lol lol lot lol got lol hot lol;
7 lol rot lol dot lol jot lol tot lol sot;

D Practise word families

8 old hold sold gold; look rook hook took;
9 let set jet get ret; rate late hate date

Homophones

These are words that are similar in sound but spelt differently and have different meanings. It is often difficult to decide which of a pair is the correct one to use in particular circumstances; therefore, use your dictionary to check the meaning of any word you are not sure about. **Always** check on the meaning and spelling if you are in doubt.

E Homophones Use your dictionary to check the meaning

10 sea see; here hear; tide tied; aid aide;
11 ail ale; right rite; tare tear; fir fur;

F Apply the keys you know

12 get her a set; he took a full jar to her Back straight
13 he had sold the gold; at this late date;
14 that old dress looks just right for her;

Individual letter drills

As each individual has different weaknesses when using the keyboard, you will require individual remedial practice based on your needs; therefore, we have prepared the following drills for corrective practice on keyboarding errors made during **Record your progress** practice. Of course, there is no reason why you should not use the drills for remedial practice on any alphabetic keystroking errors.

When you examine the drills that follow, you will see that each letter drill gives practice in typing a particular letter in combination with other letters. For example, in drill **A** below, the first word begins with Aa, the second word with ba, the third word with ca and so on to the last word which begins with Za. It is not necessary for the purpose of the drill that the letters within any one drill are presented in any particular order.

Type each line of words at least twice, and each paragraph at least once. Use a left margin of 12 pitch 30, 10 pitch 25.

If you type the first exercise once, you will have typed the letter **A** 65 times (in 45 different combinations); the letter **E** 34 times; the letters **R** and **T** 20 times; and the letter **S** 15 times.

```
A    Aaron baled cares dazed eager gains major ahead
     trial kayak aorta axles naked oasis paced Qatar
     radio saved table aquae vague aware exact Zaire

I am rather glad that these facts were available at
the hearing last May.  Aunt May was not afraid when
I travelled on Arabian Airways, and she appreciated
the caviar, bread and tomato sandwiches, and cakes.

B    badly begin bible black board brick build byway
     about ebony Ibsen obese ember unbar blurb rugby
     cubic oxbow Bobby elbow maybe doubt abhor abide

Her absence seemed abnormal but she was subdued and
bright when Barbara Babbacombe bought a brown ball.
Betty Gibson sat by Bobby Dobson at the back of the
bright blue mobile bus bound for beautiful Babylon.

C    cable check cedar claim McGee civil cover cocoa
     black crack cupid cycle Czech acted icing birch
     uncut ulcer eclat incur octet occur scion excel

The committee met in Cwmbran in October.  The cool,
practical mechanic accepted the challenges and com-
pleted the service on the bicycle.  That clock they
acquired is scratched, and they are much concerned.

D    daily defer dhobi dials dodge draft dunce dwell
     dying hands admit edict ideas odour oddly badge
     older order fudge Floyd fluid idiom crowd outdo

They decided to double the dividend and to readjust
and adapt the oddments.  Edwin sold the cuddly bear
and my rowdy admirers said he was a dutiful dodger.
David had daffodils in his garden beyond the dykes.
```

Follow **Prepare to type** on page 6 and instructions given at top of page 9.

Margins: 12 pitch 30 (64 mm—2½ inches) 10 pitch 20 (51 mm—2 inches) and use single spacing with double between exercises. Pre-stored margin settings may be used.

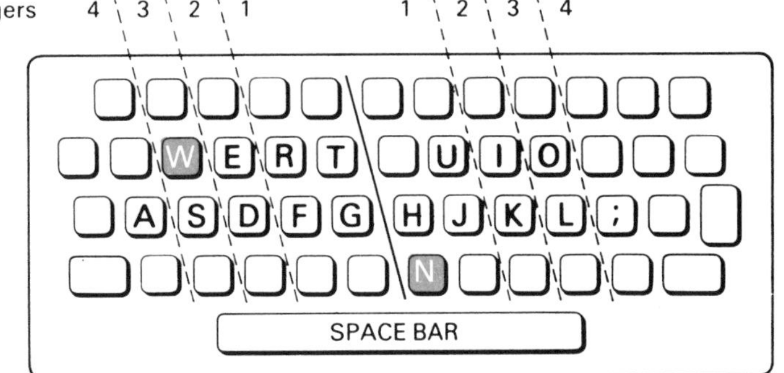

A Review the keys you know

1 ftf lol frf juj ded kik tot out rot dot;
2 this is a red jet; the lad took the gold
3 he asked a just fee; the old folk agree;

Return carriage/carrier/cursor without looking up

B Practise W key—S finger

Practise S to W back to S. Keep other fingers curved over home keys

4 sss www sws sws low sws sow sws row sws;
5 sws hew sws few sws dew sws sew sws tew;

C Practise N key—J finger

Practise J to N back to J. Keep other fingers curved over home keys

6 jjj nnn jnj jnj fan jnj ran jnj tan jnj;
7 jnj sin jnj kin jnj din jnj lin jnj tin;

D Practise word families

8 end send lend tend fend rend wend trend;
9 low sow how row tow saw law daw jaw raw;

E Homophones *Use your dictionary to check the meaning*

10 sew sow; weak week; wear ware, fair fare
11 oar ore; new knew; knead need; not knot;

F Apply the keys you know

12 we saw her look at the new gate; we knew
13 he sent us a gift of red jeans last week
14 we had left a jade silk gown and the rug

Wrist and arms straight, fingers curved

NOTE To help you complete your keyboarding more quickly and efficiently why not use our keyboarding software? It covers the QWERTY keyboard and ACCURACY/SPEED up to 25 words a minute. For details see Preface.

PARKER, MORRELL & CO

Telephone: 0926 078331
Fax: 0926 754092

46 Augustus Road
KENILWORTH
Warwickshire
CV8 2QP

TO:

G Knight + Co
1 Chestnut Square
LEAMINGTON SPA
Warwickshire CV32 9HJ

Purchase Order No PO/JRM/180

Date Today's

Deliver to address above

Please supply

36 Fold-back clips @ £1.20 ea (Ref X 29) → Price £ 43-20

2 Rotary paper trimmers @ £30 ea (Ref A457) 60-00

2 Heavy-duty staplers @ £40.50 ea (Ref HS 900) 81-00

Typist – use special purchase order form (Parker, Morrell + Co) from Handbook, Solutions, and Resource Material

TOTAL £ 184.20

JOHN R MORELAND
PURCHASING DEPARTMENT

Improvement practice

Margins: 12 pitch 30 (64 mm—$2\frac{1}{2}$ inches) 10 pitch 20 (51 mm—2 inches) and use single spacing with double between exercises. Pre-stored margin settings may be used.

A Improve control of carriage/carrier/cursor return

1 Type the following lines exactly as shown. Repeat the exercise twice.

```
as a lass
as a lass falls
as a lass falls dad falls
```

Return carriage/carrier/cursor without looking up

In the following exercises type each line three times, saying the letters to yourself.

B Improve control of T and H keys

```
2  the then than that this thus these there
3  she thus feels that this is rather good;
4  these lads are there for the third week;
```

C Improve control of space bar

```
5  a s d f j k l ; g h w e r t u i o a s d;
6  at it we he go to as are not for did ask
7  we are sure he did not ask us for these;
```

Use right thumb and even stroke

D Improve control of R and O keys

```
8  our for road work word offer order other
9  she works near our road; the other word;
10 he wrote the order; sort out our offers;
```

E Improve control of paper insertion

Practise inserting and straightening the paper ready for printout/typing. Repeat the drill several times a day so that the operation can be completed in a few seconds. Unless there are instructions to the contrary, it is usual to leave 25 mm—1 inch (typing on the seventh line) clear at top of the page.

NOTE RSI—In order to avoid Repetitive Strain Injury, it is essential that you follow our instructions about **posture** on page 5, items 5 and 6.

Task 4

(TYPIST – Please type an envelope for this memo)

From Emma Cohetwynd　　　　Ref EC/(Yr initials)
To Frederick Gilby　　　　　Date (Tomorrow's)

Travelling on the Continent of Europe ← (CAPS)

As you wl be travelling to Belgium & Germany by car within the next month for the Co, it is important th you are aware of the following differences in the law ~~relating~~ affecting driving.

Belgium

The speed limit on motorways is 120 Km per hour; on other roads it is 90 Km per hr, while in built-up areas it is 60 Km per hr. It is compulsory to ~~carry~~ stet/ a red warning triangle in case of breakdown.

Germany

The speed limit on motorways is 130 Km per hour; on other roads it is 120 Km ph, while in built-up areas it is 50 Km ph. You wl note th there is a slight difference. Again it is compulsory to carry a red warning triangle.

(K shd be in lc in the abbreviations Km)

Task 5

(A5 headed paper. Take a carbon copy & insert tomorrow's date)

Our Ref TD/ Yr initials
Mr Norman Kendle
(Insert address here – as in T1)

Dear Mr K——　　　(SOCIAL CHARTER)

I am so sorry to hear from my sec th you wl be on business on the Continent during the next few weeks, & will not be able to hv a discussion as I had hoped. [Could you delegate someone to come in yr place? I feel th the issue is of such importance th we shd try to gain as much info as we can. [I look forward to hearing from you, or yr rep, as soon as poss.

Yrs sinc

TRISTAN DEACON

F Improve control of E *and* N *keys*

11 en end tend new keen then when need near;
12 then she went; he knew the news was sent
13 we need the new jugs; near here; the end

Feet flat on floor

G Improve control of W *and* I *keys*

14 win wish wife with will wait writ while;
15 his wife will wait with us; the wise lad
16 we will wish to write while we are there

H Improve control of U *key*

17 our hour sour dull lull full hull gulls;
18 all our dull hours; he ruled for a week;
19 use our usual rules; let us rush out now

Elbows in close to sides

I Improve control of G *key*

20 go got good goods sigh sight light right
21 urge her to get a rug; the girl is right
22 go on the green light; the night is long

J Improve control of suffix ING

23 ing going taking selling dealing heating
24 he is going; we are selling; owing to us
25 ask if she is dealing with that heating;

K Apply the keys you know

26 now that joke is not good; our old safe;
27 for fun ask if the jars she got were old
28 do join us; walk to that green fir tree;

Shoulders back and relaxed

L Typing errors

If you make a mistake, ignore it until the end of the exercise, then look at the keyboard and study the reach(es) for accurate finger movement. Do not type while you look at the keyboard. *Never* overtype, ie, type one character on top of another.

TYPIST – Use A4 paper. Leave one clear line at the point marked (X), and 2 clear lines at (XX). Insert leader dots as indicated.

COMPARISON OF CLOTHING MEASUREMENTS[1]

(X)

~~European~~ Continental and British systems

(XX)

	British	Continental
Shoes[2]	4	37
	5	38
	7	41
	6	39
(XX)		
Ladies' dresses	10	38
	12	40
	14	~~2~~4
	16	44
	18	46
	20	48
(XX)		
Men's shirts	14	35/36
	14½	37
	15½	39/40
	16	41
	16½	42
	17	43
	17½	44

(15 38) (to be inserted after 14½)

(XX)

1 Approx equivalents

(X)

2 Half sizes are not always indicated on the continent, eg, (ucl)

4½ = 38; 5½ = 39; ~~6½~~ 6½ = 40

(XX)

TD/yr initials

Tomorrow's date

Follow **Prepare to type** on page 6 and instructions given at top of page 9.

Margins: 12 pitch 30 (64 mm—2½ inches) 10 pitch 20 (51 mm—2 inches) and use single spacing with double between exercises. Pre-stored margin settings may be used.

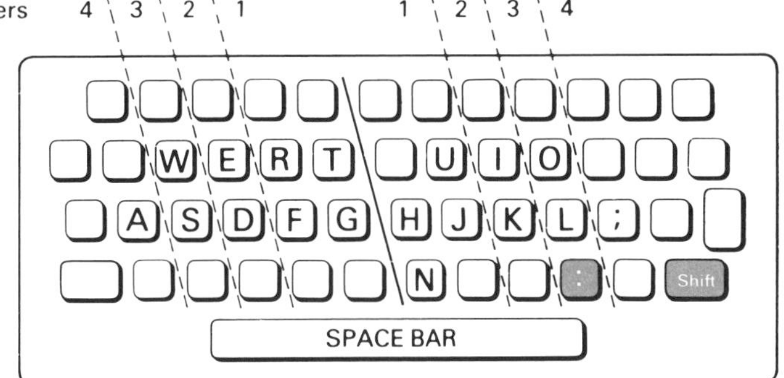

A Review the keys you know

1 sws jnj ftf lol frf jhj won win new now; Eyes on copy
2 we do not like those jars she got for us
3 the red dogs will go for a walk just now

B Practise right shift key

To make capitals for letters typed by the left hand:
(a) With right-hand little finger depress and hold right shift key well down.
(b) Strike left-hand capital letter.
(c) Remove finger from shift key and return all fingers to home keys.

4 fF; dD; sS; aA; Ada; Sad; Dad; Fad; Wade
5 Gee; Reg; Ted; Sue; Flo; Ede; Dora; West

C Practise full stop key [:] —L finger

Practise L to . back to L. Keep other fingers curved over home keys

6 lll ... l.l f.l j.l Good. Dear. Ellis.

Leave 2 spaces after full stop at end of sentence

7 Ask her. Ted is sad. Do go. She will.

NOTE In this book, we always leave two spaces after a full stop at the end of a sentence. However, one space is acceptable, provided you remember always to leave the same number every time. Some electronic equipment, with the automatic return function at the line end, may carry the second space to the beginning of the next line.

D Practise word families

8 Wee; Weed; Feed; Reed; Seed; Deed; Greed
9 And; Sand; Wand; Rand; Send; Tend; Fend;

E Homophones *Use your dictionary to check the meaning*

10 altar alter; guessed guest; aught ought.
11 dear deer; aloud allowed; threw through.

F Apply the keys you know

12 Ask Ed Reid if we should join the Swede. Check your posture
13 She was right. Dirk was jealous. Fine.
14 Flora would like to go; just state when.

SEAT BELTS

Belt-up in the Back

Wearing a seat belt in the front seat of a car has been the law since 1983. This has saved at least 200 deaths and 7000 serious injurys each year. In 1989 It became law for children under the age of 14 years to be restrained in the rear seats of cars ~~in 1989~~ 1988. From 1 July 1991 it became law for adults also to wear seat belts when riding in the back seats of cars, provided that they were already fitted.

Other points to note are -

Single spacing with double between each item

i for children between 1 and 4 years of age, an appropriate child seat, or a cushion booster with the adult seat belt, must be used;

ii children under one must be in an approved infant carrier, designed for the babys size and weight, or a carrycot restrained by straps;*

iii For medical reasons you may be exempt from wearing the seat belt. Contact your doctor if you think you should not wear a seat belt on medical grounds.

It is not only your life which is at risk if you do not wear an available seat belt. You are also risking the lives of the driver and other passengers.

If you do not wear an available seat belt, you is liable to a fixed penalty, or a fine if the case goes to court.

---

* Approved child restraints must carry the BS "Kitemark", or the United Nations "E" mark.

Follow **Prepare to type** on page 6 and instructions given at top of page 9.

Margins: 12 pitch 30 (64 mm—$2\frac{1}{2}$ inches) 10 pitch 20 (51 mm—2 inches) and use single spacing with double between exercises. Pre-stored margin settings may be used.

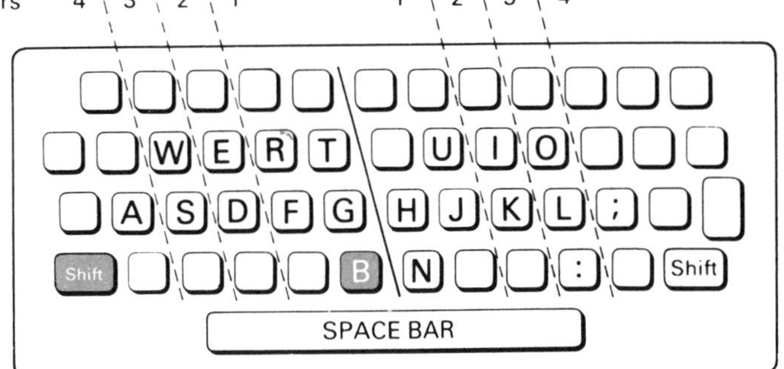

A *Review the keys you know*

1 aA; sS; dD; fF; wW; eE; rR; Red; Gee; As
2 Ask Flo. See Roger. Tell Fred. Go in.
3 Ede had gone. Write to us. A fake jug.

Leave 2 spaces after full stop at end of sentence

B *Practise left shift key*

To make capitals for letters typed by the right hand:
(a) With left-hand little finger depress and hold left shift key well down.
(b) Strike right-hand capital letter.
(c) Remove finger from shift key and return all fingers to home keys.

4 jJa kKa lLa jUj kIk Judd Kidd Lode Hoad;
5 Ida Ken Len Jude Owen Hilda Oakes Usual;

Eyes on copy

C *Practise* B *key—F finger*

Practise F to B back to F. Keep other fingers curved over home keys

6 fff bbb fbf fbf bud fbf bus fbf but fbf;
7 fbf rob fbf sob fbf fob fbf hob fbf job;

D *Practise word families*

8 Nib Jib Lib Job Lob Hob Hail Jail Nails;
9 Jill Hill Kill Lill Tall Ball Fall Wall;

E *Homophones* *Use your dictionary to check the meaning*

10 break brake; bare bear; blue blew; suite
11 sweet; whether weather; road rode rowed;

F *Apply the keys you know*

12 She will be taking those salads to Jane.
13 Jill knows. Kit had to bluff Bob Green.
14 Fred will ask us to do those jobs again.

NOTE RSI—In order to avoid Repetitive Strain Injury, it is essential that you follow our instructions about **posture** on page 5, items 5 and 6.

Monday 6 December 1993 **Time allowed—2 hours**

Notes

Your centre number is 7566/R23.
Calculators and English dictionaries may be used in this examination.
Type your name and centre number at the top of each page that you type.
Use headed paper where appropriate.
Put your completed work in task number order.
Put a pencil mark through any work which you do not wish the examiner to mark.

Task 1

Our Ref TP/(Yr initials)
(Today's date)

Mr Norman Kendle
Kendle Engineering Works
Carrington Industrial Estate
Avenue 4
Warwick CV35 8NA

Please use letterhead paper – Parker, Morrell & Co – and type an envelope of a suitable size

Dear Mr K——

SOCIAL CHARTER
I understand th you will attend the Conference, wh I am to chair, to discuss the Social Charter, planned by the EC, & how it wd affect small businesses, such as ours, wh employ a large no of prt-time & casual staff. // I believe th some of the proposals are –
(a) That rights enjoyed by full-time ~~workers~~ staff be extended to part-timers.
(b) Restrictions on night & shift work.
(c) Certain stipulations on overtime & annual holidays.
(d) A right to maternity leave with full pay for part-time employees, as well as rights to education & vocational trg enjoyed, at the moment, by full-time staff.
The idea of this Charter is, I know, to improve employee protection but as a small business employing a large no of p/t female staff, it is going to cost us a great deal of money. As I am sure you are in a similar situation, I shd be glad of a discussion with you before the conference. // Perhaps you wd contact my sec to arrange a suitable date & time.
Yrs sinc

TRISTAN DEACON

Follow **Prepare to type** on page 6 and instructions given at top of page 9.

NOTE Margin settings have changed.

Margins: 12 pitch 24 (51 mm—2 inches) 10 pitch 15 (38 mm—1½ inches). Pre-stored margin settings may be used. Spacing: single, with double between exercises.

A Review the keys you know

1 fbf sws jnj ftf lol frf jhj Len Ken Hen Ian Win Go
2 Dan and Rob left. He will go just now. Ask Nell.
3 Lois and Earl will see June. Go with Fred Bolton.

Leave 2 spaces after full stop at end of sentence

B Practise M Key—J finger

4 jjj mmm jmj jmj jam jmj ham jmj dam jmj ram jmjmj;
5 jmj rum jmj hum jmj sum jmj mum jmj gum jmj strum;

Practise J to M back to J. Keep other fingers curved over home keys

C Practise left and right shift keys

6 Ada Ben Dan East Fred Green Hilda Irwin James King
7 Lil Mark Nell Owen Rene Sara Todd Usher Wills Watt

Little fingers for shift keys

D Practise word families

8 arm farm harm warm alarm art hart tart darts mart;
9 game name dame fame same lame home dome some foam;

E Homophones *Use your dictionary to check the meaning*

10 there their; moan mown; air heir; eminent imminent
11 missed mist; mail male; aid aide; morning mourning

F Apply the keys you know

12 Most of the fame goes to John who had been working
hard for his father but he has now left the works.
I think he is now at home.

Centred ruled tabulation with leader dots

The method used for typing leader dots in ruled tables is the same as that given on page 134 when typing unruled tables. Refer to the points given on page 134 before typing exercise 8.

8 Type the following table on A4 paper. (a) Centre the table vertically and horizontally on the paper. (b) Use centred style. (c) Double spacing. (d) Leave three spaces between the columns. (e) Rule horizontal lines by underscore and vertical lines in ink. (f) Insert leader dots.

THE COST OF SHOPPING IN THE COMMUNITY*

August 1991

Goods	Brussels	Paris	Berlin	London
	£	£	£	£
Plain white flour	0.26	0.23	0.24	0.32
White sugar	0.68	0.60	0.61	0.66
lc / Frozen Chips	0.64	0.59	0.75	0.70
Margarine	1.58	1.84	0.68	1.21
Rump steak	7.90	8.50	6.13	8.75
Carrots	0.64	0.59	0.47	0.64
Full-fat milk ...	0.31	0.51	0.34	0.51
trs / Pure orange juice	1.96	0.71	0.30	1.52

* Price per kilo/litre

Create a new document (filename SHOP) and key in document 8 for 10-pitch printout. When you have completed this task, proofread (screenread) carefully and correct if necessary. Print out original and store on disk under filename SHOP. Follow the instructions for text editing on page 183.

Improvement practice

Follow **Prepare to type** on page 6 and instructions given at top of page 9.

Margins: 12 pitch 24 (51 mm—2 inches) 10 pitch 15 (38 mm—1½ inches). Pre-stored margin settings may be used. Spacing: single, with double between exercises.

A Improve control of home row keys

1 add had jag gas ask ash sash dash glad flags flash
2 Dad has a flag. Sal had a sash. A lass asks dad.
3 A lass had had a jag. A glad lad. Ask a sad lad.

Leave 2 spaces after full stop at the end of sentence

B Improve control of O and U keys

4 to go now out our hour tour sour would house shout
5 Ask Ruth if she would like to go to our house now.
6 Tell Flo we will start out on our tour in an hour.

C Improve control of carriage/carrier/cursor return

7 I will go
I will go soon
I will go as soon as
I will go as soon as I get there.

Do not look up

D Improve control of  *keys*

8 we wet were west tree tell test where threw refers
9 We were all in here. I saw those trees last week.
10 She referred to the tests. Tell her to rest here.

E Improve control of shift keys

11 He Ask Jon Sara Kite Dale Lord Ford Hall Iris Tait
12 Ask Miss Ford if she will see Mrs Tait in an hour.
13 Owen Dale and Gerald Reid are going to Harrow now.

No full stop after Mrs

NOTE To help you complete your keyboarding more quickly and efficiently, why not use our keyboarding software? It covers the QWERTY keyboard and ACCURACY/SPEED up to 25 words a minute. For details see Preface.

Centred tabulation—Horizontal and vertical ruling

When ruling centred tabulation, the same procedure is adopted as for blocked tabulation. Refer to page 136 and revise the points given before attempting the following exercises.

6 Type the following table on A5 portrait paper. (a) Centre the table vertically and horizontally on the paper. (b) Use centred style. (c) Double spacing. (d) Leave three spaces between columns. (e) Rule horizontal lines by underscore and vertical lines in ink.

MONTHS OF THE YEAR

English/Spanish/French

English	Spanish	French
January	Enero	Janvier
February	Febrero	Février
March	Marzo	Mars
April	Abril	Avril
May	Mayo	Mai

7 Type the following table on A5 landscape paper. (a) Centre the table vertically and horizontally on the paper. (b) Use centred style. (c) Double spacing. (d) Leave three spaces between columns. (e) Rule horizontal lines by underscore and vertical lines in ink.

TYPIST – King Olav of Norway died in 1991. You wl find the name of the present monarch, + the date of his accession, in the Data Files (filename KING) on page 184.

EUROPEAN MONARCHS

Dates of Accession

Country	Sovereign	Date
Norway	Olav V	21 September 1957
Sweden	Carl Gustaf XVI	15 September 1973
Denmark	Margrethe II	14 January 1972
Great Britain	Elizabeth II	6 February 1952
The Netherlands	Beatrix	30 April 1980
Belgium	Baudouin	17 July 1951
Spain	Juan Carlos I	22 November 1975

Create a new document (filename KING) and key in document 7 for 10-pitch printout. When you have completed this task, proofread (screenread) carefully and correct if necessary. Print out original and store on disk under filename KING. Follow the instructions for text editing on page 183.

F Improve control of I and N keys

14 an is in into line infer night noise injure inside
15 Irene infers Nina was injured one night this week.
16 The noise is inside the inn. Neither one will go.

G Improve control when typing phrases

17 to go to us to see to ask to take to fill to write
18 I wish to see Wales. Ask her to fill in the date.
19 Leslie would like to take Jill to the new theatre.

Maintain an even pace

H Improve control of B key

20 bid but bad best both able book begin about better
21 Both of us will be better off when he begins work.
22 Bob has been able to book a table for Bill and me.

I Improve control of M key

23 am me man seem make main must item them from might
24 I am making out a form for the main items we lost.
25 I must tell him that the amount seems to be right.

J Improve control of space bar

26 a w s e d r f t g b h j n u m k i o l f b j n m l.
27 is it if in as an at am on or of to go he me we be
28 He did go to tea. It is now time for us to go on.

Use right thumb and even strokes

K At end of typing period

Remove paper by using paper release.
If electric, turn off machine, switch off at socket, and remove plug from socket.
Cover machine.
Remove used and unused paper.
Leave desk tidy.

3 Type the following exercise on A5 portrait paper. (a) Use centred style of display. (b) Centre the table vertically and horizontally. (c) Double spacing. (d) Leave three spaces between columns.

N U M B E R S

Spanish/French

Numbers	Spanish	French
1	uno	un
2	dos	deux
3	tres	trois
4	cuatro	quatre

Double spacing

Typing column headings—Centred style

If the column heading is shorter than the longest item in the column (as in exercise 4 below), the column heading is centred over the longest item:

(a) Set left margin and tab stops as usual.

(b) Find the centre point of the column by tapping space bar once for every two characters and spaces in the longest column item, beginning from the point set for the start of the column. This will bring the printing point to the centre of the column.

(c) From the point reached in (b), backspace once for every two characters and spaces in the column heading. Type the column heading at the point reached.

(d) The column items will start at the tab stop already set for each column.

4 Type the following exercise on A5 landscape paper. (a) Use centred style of display. (b) Centre the table vertically and horizontally. (c) Centre headings over longest item in each column. (d) Double spacing. (e) Leave three spaces between columns.

MEMBERS OF THE EUROPEAN PARLIAMENT

MEP	Country	Committee
Bianco, Maria	Italy	Institutional Affairs
Maire, Michele	France	Political Affairs
Bayer, Thomas	Germany	Budgets
Hajos, Florus	The Netherlands	Transport and Tourism

5 Type the following exercise on A5 portrait paper. (a) Use centred style of display. (b) Centre the table vertically and horizontally. (c) Single spacing. (d) Leave three spaces between columns.

EUROPEAN INVESTMENT BANK

Loans - 1990

Country	ECU (millions)
Belgium	153
Denmark	81
Irish Republic	334
UK	688
Italy	1 153
Germany	14
France	279

See Practical Typing Exercises, Book One, page 63, for further exercises on

Check your work after each exercise

After returning the carriage/carrier/cursor at the end of an exercise, check your typing carefully and circle, and note, any errors. **Always** check *before* removing the paper from the machine, or printing out a hard copy.

	They have to leave early.
1 Each incorrect character is one error.	1 Theu have to leave early.
2 Each incorrect punctuation is one error.	2 They have to leave early?
3 An extra space is one error.	3 They have to leave early.
4 Omitting a space is one error.	4 They haveto leave early.
5 When using a manual machine, a raised/lowered capital is one error.	5 They have to leave early.
6 When using a manual machine, an uneven left margin is one error.	6 They have to leave early.
7 Omitting a word is one error.	7 They have leave early.
8 Inserting an extra word is one error.	8 They have to to leave early.
9 Inserting an extra letter is one error.	9 They have to leaves early.
10 Omitting a letter is one error.	10 They have to lave early.

Half- or one-minute goals

1 Type the exercise. If any word causes you to hesitate, type that word three times.
2 Take a half- or one-minute timing.
3 If you reach the goal or beyond, take another timing and see if you can type the same number of words but with fewer mistakes.
4 If you do not reach the goal after three tries, you need a little more practice on the key drills. Choose the previous exercise(s) that gives intensive practice on the keys that caused difficulty.

NOTES
(a) There is little to be gained by typing any one drill more than three times consecutively. When you have typed it three times, go on to another drill; then, if necessary, go back to the original drill.
(b) At present, techniques (keeping an even pace, good posture, eyes on copy) are very important and you should concentrate on good techniques. If your techniques are right, then accuracy will follow. However, if you have more than two errors for each minute typed, it could mean that you have not practised the new keys sufficiently and that you should go back and do further intensive practice on certain key drills.

Measure your speed

Five strokes count as one 'standard' word. In a typing line of 50 spaces, there are ten 'standard' words. The figures to the right of each exercise indicate the number of 'standard' words in the complete line, and the scale below indicates the number across the page. If in the exercise below you reach the word 'we' in one minute, your speed is 10 + 6 = 16 words per minute. You will now be able to measure your speed.

Type the following exercise as instructed under points 1–4 of 'Half- or one-minute goals'.

Margins: 12 pitch 24 (51 mm—2 inches) 10 pitch 15 (38 mm—$1\frac{1}{2}$ inches). Pre-stored margin settings may be used.
Spacing: double.

Goal—8 words in half a minute 16 words in one minute

```
We will take her to see our new house on(8) the north    10

side of the new estates and we(16) shall ask George to   20

join us at that time.  (SI 1.04)                          24

 1 | 2 | 3 | 4 | 5 | 6 | 7 | 8 | 9 | 10 |
```

NOTE RSI—In order to avoid Repetitive Strain Injury, it is essential that you follow our instructions about **posture** on page 5, items 5 and 6.

Fully-centred tabulation

In previous exercises on tabulation all the tables were blocked. You should also become proficient in centring column work. The following points should be noted:

(a) Refer back to pages 80 and 81 for horizontal and vertical centring.

(b) The main heading and subheading (if there is one) are centred on the paper, ie, backspace once for every two characters and spaces from the centre of the paper.

(c) As in previous exercises on tabulation, backspace once for every two characters and spaces in the longest line in each column, plus half the number of spaces to be left between columns. Set your left margin at the point reached.

(d) Tap forward from left margin and set tab stops.

NOTE Any one piece of tabulation must be blocked or centred—a combination of the two is unacceptable.

1 Type the following exercise on A5 landscape paper. (a) Centre the exercise vertically and horizontally. (b) The main heading should be centred on the paper. (c) Double spacing. (d) Leave three spaces between columns. (e) Before you type the exercise, make sure you know in which city you would find the buildings listed.

FAMOUS BUILDINGS IN EUROPE

Eiffel Tower	Brandenburg Gate	St Peter's
Arc de Triomphe	Rialto Bridge	St Paul's Cathedral
Leaning Tower of Pisa	Acropolis	Houses of Parliament
Colosseum	Tower Bridge	Notre-Dame

Typing column headings—Centred style

If the column heading is the longest item in the column (as in exercise 2 below), the column items are centred under the headings as follows:

(a) Type the column headings at the left margin and at the tab stops set.

(b) Find the centre of the heading by tapping the space bar once for every two characters and spaces in the heading, starting from the left margin or the tab stop set for the heading. This will bring the carriage/carrier/cursor to the centre point of the heading.

(c) From the point reached in (b), backspace once for every two characters and spaces in the longest line under the heading. This gives you the starting point for EACH ITEM in the column. Make a note of the point reached, and set a tab stop here. Then cancel the tab stop for the start of the headings.

2 Type the following exercise on A5 landscape paper. (a) Centre the exercise vertically and horizontally. (b) Centre the column items under the column headings. (c) Double spacing. (d) Leave three spaces between columns.

MEMBER COUNTRIES

<u>Dates of joining the Community</u>

Name of country	Date joined	Name of country	Date joined
UK	1974	Spain	1986
Portugal	1986	Netherlands	1957
Luxembourg	1957	Italy	1957
Greece	1981	France	1957

See Practical Typing Exercises, Book One, page 63, for further exercises on

Follow **Prepare to type** on page 6 and instructions given at top of page 9.

Margins: 12 pitch 24 (51 mm—2 inches) 10 pitch 15 (38 mm—1½ inches). Pre-stored margin settings may be used. Spacing: single, with double between exercises.

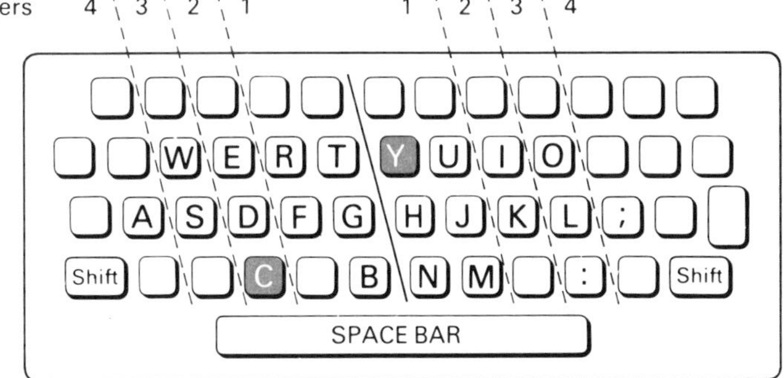

A Review the keys you know

1 jmj fmj kmk fmf lml am; Mat Tom Ham Sam Lamb Farm;
2 Mrs Lamb would like to take on the job we offered.
3 None of them would go with Job down the long road.

Eyes on copy

B Practise C *key—D finger*

4 ddd ccc dcd dcd cod dcd cot dcd cob dcd cog dcdcd;
5 dcd cut dcd cub dcd cur dcd cud dcd cab dcd cat cd

Practise D to C back to D. Keep other fingers curved over home keys

C Practise Y *key—J finger*

6 jjj yyy jyj jyj jay jyj hay jyj lay jyj bay jyjyj;
7 jyj say jyj day jyj ray jyj may jyj gay jyj way jj

Practise J to Y back to J. Keep other fingers curved over home keys

D Practise word families

8 sty try fry dry cry wry dice rice mice nice trice;
9 shy sky sly try sty slay stay fray gray dray stray

Even strokes

E Homophones *Use your dictionary to check the meaning*

10 sealing ceiling; council counsel; cent sent scent;
11 stationery stationary; creak creek; cereal serial;

F Apply the keys you know

Goal—8 words in half a minute 16 words in one minute Use double spacing

12 He is not able to find a nice jacket which he says 10

he lost on the way to your farm. He will send you 20

his bill in a week or so. **(SI 1.08)** 25

1 | 2 | 3 | 4 | 5 | 6 | 7 | 8 | 9 | 10 |

Semi-blocked personal letter with home address blocked at right margin

When your home address is not printed on your stationery, you may wish to block it at the right margin. This is done in the same way as you backspaced for the date when typing it in exercise 1, on page 159; from the right margin backspace once for each character and each space in a line and, from the point reached, start typing that line. Before starting the first line of your address, turn up four single spaces and turn up two single spaces before typing the date.

6 Type the following letter on a sheet of plain A5 portrait paper. (a) Block the home address at the right margin. (b) Use margins of 12 pitch 13–63, 10 pitch 6–56. (c) Use open punctuation and semi-blocked style.

```
                                      17 High Street
                                               RUGBY
                                        Warwickshire
                                            CV22 5QE

                                   27th October 1993

The Managing Director
Kenkott Scotia PLC
Byrnes Terrace
Langside
GLASGOW      G41 3DI

Dear Sir

     I wish to purchase a new printer for my port-
able laptop computer.

     I understand that, next to lasers, bubble jet
printers give quality, speed and flexibility as
well as being cost effective.  I require a quiet,
portable printer that gives a clean, crisp finish
to the printed copy.

     Please send me full details of your range.

                        Yours faithfully





                        Amy Robertson (Miss)
```

Create a new document (filename BUB) and key in document 6 for 12-pitch printout. When you have completed this task, proofread (screenread) carefully and correct if necessary. Print the document and store on disk under filename BUB. Follow the instructions for text editing on page 183.

Centring the home address on the page

Another way of typing your home address on plain paper is to centre each line on the page in the same way that you displayed the notice on page 154 when you backspaced one for every two letters and spaces from the centre point of the paper. This style is acceptable for blocked or semi-blocked letters.

7 Type the above letter again, but this time centre the home address on the page. As usual, turn up four single spaces before the first line and two single spaces before typing the date at the right margin.

See Practical Typing Exercises, Book One, page 62, for further exercises on

Follow **Prepare to type** on page 6 and instructions given at top of page 9.

Margins: 12 pitch 24 (51 mm—2 inches) 10 pitch 15 (38 mm—1½ inches). Pre-stored margin settings may be used. Spacing: single, with double between exercises.

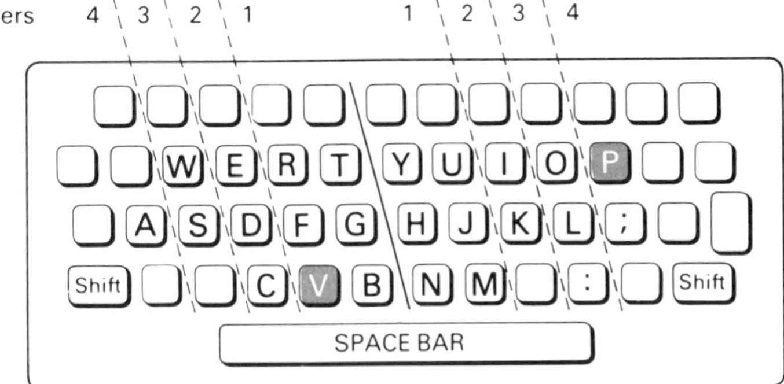

A Review the keys you know

1 dcd jyj dcd fbf jhj fgf lol yet coy yes call come.
2 Her mother had brought a new kind of jersey cloth.
3 He sent us a ticket for the jumble sale on Monday.

Eyes on copy

B Practise P *key—; finger*

4 ;;; ppp ;p; ;p; cap ;p; lap ;p; rap ;p; jap p;p;p;
5 ;p; pip ;p; dip ;p; sip ;p; hip ;p; lip ;p; nip p;

Practise ; to P back to ;. Keep other fingers curved over home keys

C Practise V *key—F finger*

6 fff vvv fvf fvf vow fvf van fvf vat fvf vet fvfvf;
7 fvf eve fvf vie fvf via fvf very fvf give fvf live

Practise F to V back to F. Keep other fingers curved over home keys

D Practise word families

8 tup cup pup sup lop pop fop hop cop top tops mops;
9 live jive hive dive give rave pave save wave gave;

E Homophones *Use your dictionary to check the meaning*

10 canvas canvass; reviews revues; patients patience;
11 principle principal; presents presence; site sight

F Apply the keys you know

Goal—9 words in half a minute 17 words in one minute Use double spacing

12 She moved a pink jug away from the very back [9] shelf 10

where it had been hidden from sight.[17] It now shows 20

up better on that top shelf. **(SI 1.15)** 26

1 | 2 | 3 | 4 | 5 | 6 | 7 | 8 | 9 | 10 |

Revise the points given on page 76 about the typing of memos. The layout of the printed forms used for memos varies considerably, but the same rules for typing them apply. It is preferable to leave two clear character spaces after the words in the printed headings before typing the insertions, and to use the variable linespacer to ensure their alignment. Never type a full stop after the last word of an insertion, unless it is abbreviated and full punctuation is being used. A memo form with printed heading is given in the *Handbook, Solutions, and Resource Material*, and copies may be duplicated.

4 Type the following memo on a printed A4 memo form. (a) Use margins of 12 pitch 13–90, 10 pitch 11–75. (b) Take a carbon copy and address an envelope. (c) Use full punctuation and semi-blocked style.

PERSONAL MEMORANDUM

From Frederick Gilby, Management Officer Ref. FG/tel/12/PW

To Jack Barclay, Head of Resources Date 14 December 1993

TELEPHONE DIALLING CODES

You are no doubt aware that as from 3 April 1994 every telephone dialling code is to be changed to cope with the boom in faxes and portable handsets.

STD CODES

Every number will have the digit 1 inserted into it's current STD code. For example, the code for inner London will change from 0171 to 071; Bristol will change from 0272 to 01272, and Edinburgh's 031 prefix will become 0131.

LOCAL CALLS

These will not be affected.

International Code ← CAPS

At the same time

l.c. / International codes will change from the currant 010 to 00, a step designed to bring Britain into line with other countries.

We sh need to circulate staff in plenty of time as well as change all headed notepaper. Wd you please see to this? Thank you.

5 Type the following memo on a printed memo form. Use suitable margins and semi-blocked style.

To Frederick Gilby, Management Officer Ref. JB/(Yr initials)

From Jack Barclay, Head of Resources Date 16 December 1993

Thank you for yr memo dated 14 Dec. I hv noted the contents & wl make sure th headed notepaper is ordered ready for use on 3 April 1994, as well as circulating all staff in plenty of time before the changeover.

Insert heading – TELEPHONE DIALLING CODES

Follow **Prepare to type** on page 6 and instructions given at top of page 9.

Margins: 12 pitch 24 (51 mm—2 inches) 10 pitch 15 (38 mm—1½ inches). Pre-stored margin settings may be used. Spacing: single, with double between exercises.

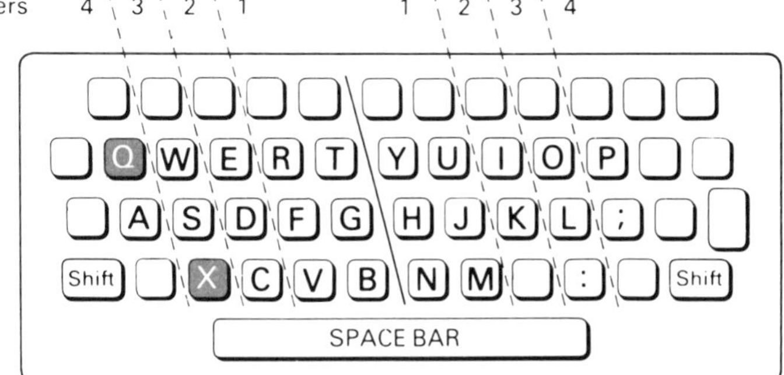

A Review the keys you know

1 ;p; fvf ftf jhj dpf apf kpf pot van cop map eve p;
2 Jack was glad my family all moved to North Avenue.
3 Daniel may have to give back a few paper journals.

Fingers curved

B Practise X key—S finger

4 sss xxx sxs sxs tax sxs lax sxs pax sxs wax sxsxs;
5 sxs sex sxs hex sxs vex sxs rex sxs cox sxs vox sx

Practise S to X back to S. Keep other fingers curved over home keys

C Practise Q key—A finger

6 aaa qqq aqa aqa quad aqa aqua aqa equal aqa quick;
7 aqa quin aqa quit aqa quite aqa equal aqa query qa

Practise A to Q back to A. Keep other fingers curved over home keys

D Practise word families

8 qua quad squad quit quip quins quill quint quilts;
9 fox cox mix fix nix axe lax pax wax tax taxi taxed

E Homophones *Use your dictionary to check the meaning*

10 accede exceed; accept except; access excess; stake
11 steak; checks cheques; choir quire; coarse course;

F Apply the keys you know

Goal—9 words in half a minute 17 words in one minute Use double spacing

12 Joe quickly moved the gross of new boxes for [9] which 10

you had paid and then took an extra [17] box of the red 20

quilts and sheets you wanted. **(SI 1.15)** 26

1 | 2 | 3 | 4 | 5 | 6 | 7 | 8 | 9 | 10 |

Displayed matter in semi-blocked letters

The usual method for displaying matter in semi-blocked letters is to arrange for the longest line of the matter to be centred in the typing line. To do this:

(a) Find the centre point of the body of the letter by adding together the points at which the left and right margins are set and divide by two.

(b) Bring printing point to this scale point and backspace once for every two characters and spaces in the longest line of the displayed matter. This is the starting point for all items.

(c) ALWAYS leave one clear space above and below displayed matter.

With computers, word processors and electronic typewriters you could use the automatic centring device and/or the temporary second margins.

3 Type the following letter from Eastways Developments (UK) Ltd on A4 letterhead paper. (a) Use semi-blocked style with full punctuation. (b) Take a carbon copy and centre the subject heading and displayed portion. (c) Margins: 12 pitch 22–82, 10 pitch 12–72.

Our Ref. LAB/PAC.398

Your Ref. CCS/ma

9 September 1993

T. Ryland p.l.c.,
65 Durham Road,
Central Estate,
HARTLEPOOL,
Cleveland. TS24 7RQ

Dear Sirs,

"TRANSLATOR"

Thank you for your enquiry about our "Translator". It weighs only 285 g and is easily portable. It has a qwerty keyboard and, by pressing only one button, instruction messages pop up in one of 10 languages on an LCD screen. The language cards are in French, German, Italian, Spanish, Dutch, Swedish, Norwegian, Finnish, Danish and English.

The cost is as follows:

6126	"Translator" with LCD screen	£180.00
6127-16	Language card	£45.00

Another useful feature for travel abroad is the calculator which can convert tax and currency in 5 different exchange rates.

Yours faithfully,

Backing sheets

These can be used for the following purposes:

(a) To prevent damage to the cylinder of the typewriter.

(b) To hold the paper in place when typing near the bottom of a page, and prevent the bottom lines from 'running off' the sheet.

(c) To help you find the horizontal and vertical centre of the page by drawing a vertical line down the centre and a horizontal line across the centre.

(d) To remind you to leave an inch clear at the top of a page by drawing a heavy horizontal line one inch from the top.

See Practical Typing Exercises, Book One, pages 59–60, for further exercises on

Follow **Prepare to type** on page 6 and instructions given at top of page 9.

Margins: 12 pitch 24 (51 mm—2 inches) 10 pitch 15 (38 mm—1½ inches). Pre-stored margin settings may be used. Spacing: single, with double between exercises.

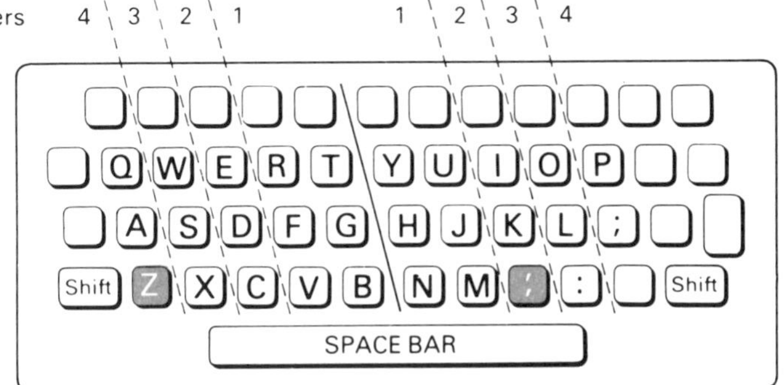

A Review the keys you know

1 axs aqa fxf fcf axs xaj sex vex tax quit aqua quad
2 Just have one box of new grey mats packed quickly.
3 With extra help Clive found many quite black jugs.

B Practise Z key—A finger

4 aaa zzz aza aza zoo aza zinc aza zeal aza azure za
5 aza zip aza zero aza size aza gaze aza jazz aza za

Practise A to Z back to A. Keep other fingers curved over home keys

C Practise , key—K finger

6 kkk ,,, k,k k,k l,k a,k s,k j,k d,k f,k hj,k g,f,k

One space after comma

7 at, it, is, or, if, one, can, yes, may, for, cross

Practise K to , back to K. Keep other fingers curved over home keys

D Practise word families

8 daze haze gaze laze maze, lazy hazy crazy, puzzle.
9 zeal zero zest zone, size prize, buzz fuzz, azure.

E Homophones *Use your dictionary to check the meaning*

10 affect effect; style stile; deference difference;
11 born borne; complement compliment; miners minors;

F Apply the keys you know

Goal—9 words in half a minute 18 words in one minute Use double spacing

12 We do hope the right size is in stock; yes, it[9] is; 10

we have just a few boxes, but the colour[18], although 20

quite pretty, is not the same. **(SI 1.15)** 26

1 | 2 | 3 | 4 | 5 | 6 | 7 | 8 | 9 | 10 |

Feet apart, flat on floor

Semi-blocked letters with attention line, enclosure and subject heading

The **attention line** and **enclosure** are typed in the same style and position as in fully-blocked letters (see pages 59–60).

Turn up two single spaces after the salutation and centre the subject heading over the body of the letter. To do this:

(a) Add together the points at which the left and right margins are set and divide by two.

(b) Bring the printing point to the scale point found when you divided by two and backspace once for every two characters and spaces in the subject heading.

(c) Type the heading.

(d) Turn up two single spaces before starting the body of the letter.

2 Type the following letter from Eastways Developments (UK) Ltd on A4 letterhead paper. (a) Use semi-blocked style and take a carbon copy. (b) Full punctuation. (c) Margins: 12 pitch 22–82, 10 pitch 12–72.

Our Ref. PJG/riv 9th September, 1993

NOTE A comma may be inserted after the month

Your Ref. LAB/PAC

FOR THE ATTENTION OF MS J. R. DEACON

O. E. Allinson & Co. Ltd.,
38 St. Mary's Road,
SOUTH SHIELDS,
Tyne and Wear.
NE33 1AA

Dear Sirs,

REPETITIVE STRAIN INJURIES

I enclose a leaflet which gives details of a special new chair that can help to eliminate RSI pains after only a week or 2 of use. It has elbow rests to support the upper arms, so that the neck and shoulders are not strained while working at the keyboard.

Since the number of RSI sufferers is said to have more than doubled since 1980, it could be worth investing in one or more of these chairs, even if your employees suffer only the occasional twinge.

Prevention is better than cure. If you place your order before 1st October, 1993, you will be eligible for a 10% discount.

NOTE To be consistent insert comma after month

Yours faithfully,

PETE J. GILBY

Enc.

Create a new document (filename RSI) and key in document 2 for 10-pitch printout. When you have completed this task, proofread (screenread) carefully and correct if necessary. Print out original and one copy and store on disk under filename RSI. Follow the instructions for text editing on page 183.

See Practical Typing Exercises, Book One, page 58, for further exercises on

Improvement practice

Follow **Prepare to type** on page 6 and instructions given at top of page 9.

Margins: 12 pitch 24 (51 mm—2 inches) 10 pitch 15 (38 mm—1½ inches). Pre-stored margin settings may be used. Spacing: single, with double between exercises.

A Improve control of carriage/carrier/cursor return

1 Type the following lines exactly as shown.
Repeat the exercise and see if you can type it in one minute

```
It was good
It was good to see
It was good to see you
It was good to see you today
```

Return carriage/carrier/cursor without looking up

B Improve control of  *keys*

```
2  mob bump brim Mabel blame bloom climb bombs became
3  Blame Mabel.  The mob climbed in through a window.
4  My rose bloom became well known.  I bumped my car.
```

Leave 2 spaces after . at end of sentence

C Improve control of punctuation

```
5  I shall tell Wilfred.  No, he may be rather angry.
6  We are pleased to hear from you; but we cannot go.
7  John, Mary and Elsie are going.  You may come too.
```

One space after ; and ,

D Improve control of C and Y keys

```
8  cry city clay copy cozy carry yacht comply certify
9  We certify that this is a correct copy made today.
10 Cathy must comply with the order.  The yacht left.
```

E Improve control of space bar

```
11 at it up on to we an be go of so am by do as no he
12 Go to her.  It is up to us.  I am here.  Tell him.
13 If you go to the shop now, he will still be there.
```

Use right thumb and even strokes

F Typing from manuscript

You may have to type business documents from handwritten drafts. Take particular care to produce a correct copy. **Before typing**, read the manuscript through to see that you understand it. Some words or letters, not very clear in one part, may be repeated in another part more clearly.

Semi-blocked letters

The following points should be noted when typing semi-blocked letters.

(a) *Date*: This ends flush with the right margin. To find the starting point, backspace from right margin once for each character and space in the date.

(b) *Reference*: Type at left margin on same line as the date.

(c) *Body of letter*: The first word of each paragraph is indented five spaces from the left margin. Tap in and set tab stop for paragraph indent.

(d) *Complimentary close*: Start this approximately at the centre of the typing line.

(e) *Signature*: As in fully-blocked letters, turn up a minimum of five single spaces to leave room for signature. Type name of person signing, starting at the same scale point as the complimentary close.

(f) *Designation*: Begin to type official designation (if any) at the same scale point as complimentary close, ie, immediately below the name of person signing.

(g) *Punctuation*: Semi-blocked letters may be typed with open or full punctuation.

1 Type the following semi-blocked letter from Eastways Developments (UK) Ltd on headed A5 portrait paper. (a) Margins: 12 pitch 13–63, 10 pitch 6–66. (b) Use open punctuation.

```
Our ref  AK/HS                                 6 September 1993

Paul T Emerson Esq
R J Components (UK) Ltd
19 Trafalgar Street
TRURO
Cornwall
TR1 2DN

Dear Mr Emerson

     You are no doubt aware that EC legislation states that
employers should provide a means of reducing glare and reflec-
tion from VDU screens, as well as providing some means of
holding documents required for copy typing.

     We have a good range of copyholders as well as an anti-
glare filter which reduces on-screen glare whilst improving
the contrast of text.

     Enclosed is an illustrated leaflet showing the range of
our office equipment.

                               Yours sincerely




                               Amir Khan
                               Sales Executive

Enc
```

Set tab stop for paragraph indents at 18(11)

↑ Start approximately at the centre of the typing line

See Practical Typing Exercises, Book One, page 57, for further exercises on

G Improve control of P and V keys

14 pave prove vapour provide private prevent provoked
15 I will provide a private plane. We will prove it.
16 Prevent Peter from provoking Val and Victor Payne.

H Improve control of shift keys

17 Sal Joe Fay Ida Roy Lee Don Gay Bob Your Mary Hall
18 Tell Joe, Fay, Lee and Marie to call on Roy Young.
19 Edna Kelly and Nan Peters will visit Olive Walker.

Hold shift key well down with little finger

I Improve control of Q and X keys

20 mix tax vex exit next taxi; quay quiz quite quiet;
21 A taxi will be at the quay exit; expect him there.
22 Keep quite quiet in that queue for this next quiz.

J Improve control of phrases

23 to go, to ask, to see, to pay, to hear, to let him
24 I am pleased to hear that you are going to see me.
25 Remember to go and to ask her to pay for the flat.

K Improve control of Z and , keys

26 zip, size, lazy, zeal, zone, prize, dozen, amazed,
27 I was amazed, quite amazed, to see a dozen prizes.
28 We gazed at the zebra, also a gazelle, in the zoo.

L Apply the keys you know

Goal—9 words in half a minute 18 words in one minute Use double spacing

29 The whizzing of a jet plane across the sky had[9] now 10
become such a normal event that it won but[18] a quick 20
glance from the young boys in the crowd. **(SI 1.14)** 28

1 | 2 | 3 | 4 | 5 | 6 | 7 | 8 | 9 | 10 |

Follow instructions given at the top of page 42. Margins: 12 pitch 22–82, 10 pitch 12–72.

A Review alphabet keys

1 We saw the five models at the waxworks, which were just
amazing, as the exact resemblances to folks in the past were
quite remarkable.

B Language arts—agreement of subject and verb *(See explanation on page 181)*

2 A new set of wheels and axles has been fitted to my old van.
3 My friend and neighbour has moved to 4 High Street, Falkirk.
4 Neither of the golfers was prepared to play in the new year.

Skill measurement *30 wpm 5 minutes Not more than 5 errors*

SM40 Have you ever 'met' a person for the first time over 10
the telephone? How did you know what kind of person she/he 22
was? By the voice, of course! Was it gruff or pleasant, 34
calm or excited? How do you appear over the telephone? You 46
cannot be seen, only heard, and your voice will convey your 57
personality. 59

You should speak clearly and distinctly, and be tactful 70
and logical in expressing your thoughts. The good telephon- 82
ist will handle all telephone calls courteously and intelli- 94
gently by speaking in a well-modulated voice, enunciating 105
distinctly, choosing words that convey her thoughts clearly, 117
and expressing through her tone sincere interest in the per- 129
son calling. How well you represent your employer on the 140
telephone will depend on your telephone technique. **(SI 1.45)** 150

1 | 2 | 3 | 4 | 5 | 6 | 7 | 8 | 9 | 10 | 11 | 12 |

Record your progress *5 minutes*

R31 A low, well-controlled voice carries better and is more 11
pleasant to listen to than one pitched high. Your voice 22
should not be raised above normal; if anything, talk in a 34
lower tone than you are accustomed to use in speaking. 45

One of the great advantages of using the telephone is 55
the saving of time. This advantage is lost unless your con- 67
versation is to the point and concise. Avoid sounding curt, 79
and avoid using jargon or slang expressions such as 'O.K.', 91
'Yeah', etc. If you are cut-off during a call initiated by 103
you, it is your place to ring again. This accepted proced- 115
ure ensures that both parties are not simultaneously ringing 127
each other and finding the lines engaged. 134

To save time, list frequently used numbers in an alpha- 145
betic index which should be kept up to date. When a client 157
notifies you of a change of address and/or telephone number 169
amend your records immediately. Also, to save time, use a 181
standardized form for taking messages. **(SI 1.40)** 189

1 | 2 | 3 | 4 | 5 | 6 | 7 | 8 | 9 | 10 | 11 | 12 |

Open punctuation

Many businesses and most examining bodies prefer this style for business documents. It means that the full stop is omitted from an abbreviated word (except at the end of a sentence) and is replaced by a space. Example: Mr (space) J (space) Smith, of W M Smith & Co Ltd, will discuss the terms of payment, etc, with Mrs U E St John-Browne.

Where an abbreviation consists of two or more letters with a full stop after each letter, the full stops are omitted and no space is left between the letters, but one space (or comma) after each group of letters. Example: Mrs G L Hunt, 21 South Road, will call at 7 pm today. She requires past examination papers from several bodies, eg, LCCI, RSA and PEI.

Grammatical punctuation must still be used.

The major part of this book is written in open punctuation, ie, no full stops are given in or after abbreviations.

Improve your typing technique

If a technique is faulty, check with the following list and carry out the remedial drill.

Faulty technique		*Remedy*
Manual machines		
Raised capitals caused by releasing shift key too soon.	I may go.	Drills 4–9 page 16; drills 4–9, page 17.
Uneven left margin, caused by faulty carriage return.	I may go.	Return carriage without looking up. Any **Apply the keys you know**.
Heavy strokes, caused by not releasing keys quickly.	I mmay go.	Practise finger movement drills. Any **Apply the keys you know**.
Light strokes, caused by not striking the keys hard enough.	I may go.	Practise finger movement drills. Any **Apply the keys you know**.
Manual, electric, and electronic machines		
Omitting or inserting words (looked up from the copy).	may I go	Eyes on copy always. Page 25—lines 1, 2 and 3 backwards.
Extra spaces, caused by your leaning on the space bar.	I may go.	Right thumb slightly above space bar. Drills 5–7, page 14.
Omitting spaces, caused by poor wrist position.	I maygo.	Say 'space' to yourself each time you tap space bar. Drills 5, 6 and 7, page 14. Drills 26, 27 and 28, page 20.
Fingers out of position.	I ,au go.	Return fingers to home keys. Any **Apply the keys you know**.
Turning letters around—eyes get ahead of fingers.	I may og.	Eyes on copy always. Say each letter and space to yourself as you type. Any preceding drills.
Extra or wrong characters caused by accidentally depressing keys.	KKK may go.	Keep all fingers slightly above home keys—especially with electronics.

Skill measurement

Practice routine for all **Skill measurement** exercises:

1. Type a copy of the exercise in double spacing, although these exercises are not always shown in double spacing.
2. Check and circle any errors.
3. Compare your errors with those shown above.
4. Practise the **Remedial drills**.
5. Type as much of the exercise as you can in the time suggested.
6. Check and circle any errors.
7. On your **Skill measurement table** (see *Handbook, Solutions, and Resource Material*) record actual number of words typed in a minute and number of errors, if any.
8. If you made more than the stipulated number of errors, continue with the timed practice and aim for accuracy.
9. If your errors were below the tolerance given, type the exercise again (timed) and endeavour to type a little faster.
10. Margins: 12 pitch 24 (51 mm—2 inches) 10 pitch 15 (38 mm—1½ inches). Pre-stored margin settings may be used. Spacing: double.

Skill measurement *19 wpm* *One minute* *Not more than one error*

SM1 As those shoes are too small, you should take them 10

back and have them changed for the right size. **(SI 1.00)** 19

1 | 2 | 3 | 4 | 5 | 6 | 7 | 8 | 9 | 10 |

Indented paragraph headings

See guide given on page 49 for paragraph headings. The paragraphs may be indented and the headings typed in either of the forms given on page 49. A full stop may be typed after the paragraph headings, two spaces should be left after the full stop.

2 Type the following on A5 landscape paper. (a) Double spacing. (b) Indented paragraphs. (c) Underline the paragraph headings and type a full stop after each, as shown. (d) Margins: 12 pitch 13–90, 10 pitch 11–77. (e) Make your own line-endings. (f) Centre the main heading.

I R E L A N D

Indent → Area. Ireland is 84 402 km^2 in area. The Republic of Ireland takes up 70 282 km^2, and Northern Ireland 14 120 km^2.

Population. About 3.5 million people live in the Republic and ↰ in Northern Ireland. (TYPIST – Insert the no of people who live in N. Ireland here. You wl find the figure in the Data Files (filename ISLE) on page 184.)

Currency. The unit of currency in the Republic is the Irish pound or punt, which is divided into 100 pence.

Shoulder headings

See guide on page 50 for shoulder headings. Paragraphs that follow shoulder headings may be indented.

3 Type the following exercise on A4 paper. (a) Double spacing. (b) Indented paragraphs. (c) Suitable margins. (d) Centre the main heading. (e) Type the shoulder headings at the left margin in capitals.

(Typist – Correct the 4 circled errors.)

THE EMERALD ISLE

SCENERY

Ireland is famous for its beautiful scenery. The land is fairly flat in the central plain, but in the west (their) are steep, rugged ranges + cliffs 200 metres high. ↑

WEATHER

Rainfall is not usually heavy, but it is frequent. This is the main reason for the rich grass + fertile land + why it is called 'The Emerald Isle'.

Rivers

Irish rivers run usually slowly + sometimes flow thro' lakes (loughs) + marshes wh makes (there) progress even more (liesurely). The River Shannon is 384 kilometres long, longer than any other river in Ireland or Britain.

LOUGHS

South-west of Dublin is a (mountaneous) region, including the Wicklow mountains, with deep valleys cut by glaciers long ago.

Create a new document (filename ISLE) and key in document 3 for 10-pitch printout. When you have completed this task, proofread (screenread) carefully and correct if necessary. Print out original and store on disk under filename ISLE. Follow the instructions for text editing on page 183.

See Practical Typing Exercises, Book One, pages 55–56, for further exercises on

Each line or sentence in the lettered exercises should be typed three times and, if time permits, type each complete exercise once. Single spacing, with double between exercises. For **Skill measurement** follow instructions on page 28. Left margin: 12 pitch 24, 10 pitch 15.

A Review alphabet keys

1 Five excellent school prizes were awarded and Jamy qualified for the best work in his group.

Placement of certain characters

The location of the hyphen, question mark, underscore, etc may vary with the make of machine. This also applies to a few of the signs, symbols and marks keys such as the oblique and quotation marks. When practising these keys, make sure you know whether or not you have to use the shift key, decide on the correct finger, and then practise the reach from the home key; then type the drills given.

B Practise [-] (hyphen) key—; finger

```
2 ;-; ;-; p-; p-;-; blue-grey, one-fifth, part-time,
3 Over one-third are part-time day-release students.
4 Her father-in-law asked for all-wool yellow socks.
```

No space before or after hyphen

C Practise [?] key—; finger

```
5 Now? When? Where? May she? Must we? Will you?
6 Who said so? What is the time? Is it late? Why?
```

Spacing after question mark at end of sentence

Leave the same spacing as you leave after the full stop at the end of a sentence. If you leave two spaces after a full stop, then leave two spaces after the question mark; one after a full stop, then leave one after the question mark at the end of a sentence.

D Practise [:] (colon) key—; finger

```
7 ;;; ::: ;;; a:; l:; s:; k:; d:; j:; f:; hj:; gf:;a
8 Delivery Period: One month.  Prices: Net ex Works.
```

Depress left shift key :
One space after colon

E Homophones *Use your dictionary to check the meaning*

```
9  board bored; sight cite; chute shoot; birth berth;
10 recover re-cover; hair hare; key quay; peace piece
```

Skill measurement *20 wpm* *One minute* *Not more than one error*

```
SM2 If you are good at figures, and are keen to have a   10
    job in our firm, we should like you to call on us.   20
                                              (SI 1.05)
SM3 I wish that you could have been with us on Tuesday   10
    to see the new office machines which were on view.   20
                                              (SI 1.15)
```

1 | 2 | 3 | 4 | 5 | 6 | 7 | 8 | 9 | 10 |

Headings centred in the typing line

To centre headings in the typing line, find the centre point of the line by adding the two margins together and dividing by two.* Then backspace from this point, one space for every two characters and spaces in the heading.

Examples: Margins set at 12 pitch 22–82 22 + 82 = 104 ÷ 2 = 52 (centre point)
10 pitch 12–72 12 + 72 = 84 ÷ 2 = 42 (centre point)
12 pitch 13–63 13 + 63 = 76 ÷ 2 = 38 (centre point)

* When dividing by two, ignore any fractions.

Main headings centred

See guide given on page 48 for main headings. Centred headings may be used with indented or blocked paragraphs. The heading is centred in the typing line.

Subheadings centred

See guide given on page 48 for subheadings. If the main heading is centred, it is usual to centre the subheading in the typing line.

Enumerated items—Roman numerals blocked to the right

See information given on pages 99 and 124 about enumerated items. As well as being blocked to the left, roman numerals may be blocked to the right, with or without full stops. Full stops are never used with brackets. There are two spaces after the full stop, bracket and after the figure without a full stop. With open punctuation, there is no full stop after an enumeration. As indented paragraphs are used in the exercise below, the roman numeral with the most characters (in this case iii) starts at the indent, which means, that from the indent there are two spaces before the i, one space before the ii.

1 Type the following exercise on A4 paper in double spacing. (a) Margins: 12 pitch 18–88, 10 pitch 15–75. (b) Indented paragraphs (turn up one double line only between paragraphs). (c) Centre the main heading and subheading in the typing line.

OBJECTIVES FOR EDUCATION

<u>Within the European Community</u>

Since 1983, member States are pledged to grant a 'social guarantee' to young people who leave school without qualifications, that they will have the opportunity of 9 months' training. lc/

TYPIST – Please check in the Data Files, page 183, (filename EDU) that the training given is for 9 months.

Commission objectives include -

(i) more exchanges of information;

(ii) emphasis on the teaching of foreign languages;

(iii) education in European current affairs.

Two types of grant are available for helping in the exchange of information and experience. The first is for short study visits, the second helps with joint study programmes.

Create a new document (filename EDU) and key in document 1 for 12-pitch printout. When you have completed this task, proofread (screenread) carefully and correct if necessary. Print out original and store on disk under filename EDU. Follow the instructions for text editing on page 183.

See Practical Typing Exercises, Book One, page 54, for further exercises on

These drills have been specially prepared for corrective practice on keystroking errors made when typing the **Record your progress** exercises. For further information about the drills, read the information below and the introduction to **Personalized remedial drills** on page 173.

Record your progress exercises

Each **Record your progress** exercise contains *all the letters* of the alphabet.

Instructions for all **Record your progress** exercises:

(a) Use double spacing, although the exercises are not always shown in double spacing.
(b) Type the exercise *once* as practice.
(c) Check and circle any error.
(d) Record the individual letter errors on your **Personalized remedial drill sheet**—see *Handbook, Solutions, and Resource Material* for a copy.
(e) Turn to the **Individual letter drills** on pages 173–177 and type (at least once) the appropriate words and sentences for each letter on which you made a mistake.

NOTE If you made no errors, turn to the **Individual letter drills** and type the words and sentences for any letters that cause you difficulty.

(f) Return to the **Record your progress** exercise and type as much of the passage as you can in the time allotted.
(g) Record the number of words typed and the number of errors (if any) in the second typing, on your **Record your progress chart**—see *Handbook, Solutions, and Resource Material* for a copy.

NOTE Over a period of time you will see from the **Personalized remedial drill sheet** which finger reaches initially caused difficulties and have now been mastered, and which reaches still require concentrated practice.

Record your progress *One minute*

R1 I know you will be pleased to hear that Zola Coles 10
joined this firm on a part-time basis. Chris said 20
I must give her a quick test next week. **(SI 1.08)** 28

1 | 2 | 3 | 4 | 5 | 6 | 7 | 8 | 9 | 10 |

Follow instructions given at top of page 42. Margins: 12 pitch 22–82, 10 pitch 12–72.

A Review alphabet keys *(Indent first line)*

1 The quiz was ranked as being very difficult requiring a great deal of thought and adjustment on the part of the contestants, who were of mixed ability.

B Language arts—agreement of subject and verb *(See explanation on page 181)*

2 The works is to be closed from 1800 hours on 23 August 1994.
3 A pair of shoes is missing from the stockroom in the office.
4 The committee is to prepare its final report by 14 December.

Skill measurement *30 wpm 5 minutes Not more than 5 errors*

(Use indented paragraphs for Skill measurement and Record your progress)

SM39 Input is the data prepared by the author and entered 10
into the system by means of the keyboard. The input may be 21
in the form of typed or handwritten drafts, or shorthand/ 33
audio dictation. Whatever kind of input you work from, pre- 45
paring correspondence and reports will be your task. You 56
must use: the correct paper for the printout - letterhead, 68
memo, plain bond, and, of course, bank paper for the carbon 80
copies; the preferred house style; accurate spelling, gram- 92
mar, and punctuation. You must proofread thoroughly, making 103
any corrections on the soft copy before printout. 113

You should follow instructions precisely, use your time 124
wisely, apply common sense and initiative, and type mailable 136
copy, within a given time, ready for approval, signing and/ 148
or comment. **(SI 1.48)** 150

1 | 2 | 3 | 4 | 5 | 6 | 7 | 8 | 9 | 10 | 11 | 12 |

Record your progress *5 minutes*

R30 Any document which is not 'mailable' is not acceptable. 11
By mailable copy we mean: the contents must make sense; no 23
omissions; no uncorrected errors (misspellings, incorrect 34
punctuation, typing errors, etc); no careless corrections 46
(if part of the wrong letter(s) is showing, the correction 57
is not acceptable); no smudges; no creases. 65

With your VDU screen it is fairly easy to text edit a 76
document that has been amended by the author. The data is 88
retrieved from the file and displayed on the screen. The 99
backspace-strikeover method is normally used to correct typ- 111
ing errors and, with the use of the function keys, text- 123
editing techniques are used to change information in the 134
text. If the text on the VDU looks hazy, you should clean 146
the screen or adjust the luminous intensity. 155

While corrections and amendments are easily made on 165
the VDU screen, these changes may take up a lot of time 176
which could better be spent on other work. Try to produce a 188
correct copy on the first printout. **(SI 1.43)** 195

1 | 2 | 3 | 4 | 5 | 6 | 7 | 8 | 9 | 10 | 11 | 12 |

Each line or sentence in the lettered exercises should be typed three times and, if time permits, type each complete exercise once. Single spacing, with double between exercises. For **Skill measurement** follow instructions on page 28 and for **Record your progress** follow instructions on page 30. Left margin: 12 pitch 24, 10 pitch 15.

A Review alphabet keys

1 The taxi ranks were busy because of a sizeable jam
which caused very long queues of cars up the hill.

Shift-lock key

When you need to type several capital letters one after the other, the shift lock must be used. When it is depressed, the shift key remains engaged until the lock is released, and you will be able to type capitals without using the shift key. The following steps should be practised:

(a) Depress shift lock, using 'A' finger of left hand.
(b) Type capital letters.
(c) Depress left-hand shift key to release shift lock.

B Practise shift-lock key

2 BEFORE lunch please ring me in LUDLOW next MONDAY.
3 MEETINGS held in LONDON, LIVERPOOL and MANCHESTER.
4 Both LAURA and KATHLEEN were present at the party.

Skill measurement 21 wpm One minute Not more than one error

SM4 We trust that the hints we gave for the removal of 10
stains will be found to be of great help to all of 20
you. **(SI 1.09)** 21

1 | 2 | 3 | 4 | 5 | 6 | 7 | 8 | 9 | 10 |

Record your progress One minute

R2 At what time does the Zurich bus arrive? You must 10
equip yourself with: extra shoes, raincoats, brown 20
socks, a warm jumper, a large torch, and the maps. 30
(SI 1.23)

1 | 2 | 3 | 4 | 5 | 6 | 7 | 8 | 9 | 10 |

Horizontal centring—All lines centred

Follow the points given for horizontal centring on page 44, but do not set a left margin, and centre each line, not just the longest one. For this purpose set a tab stop at the horizontal centre point of the paper and backspace one space for every two characters and spaces as before. (See last section of *Handbook, Solutions, and Resource Material*, for the arithmetical method of horizontal centring.)

Vertical centring

To centre the matter vertically on a sheet of paper, follow the points (a) to (f) as given on page 45.

6 Type the following notice on A5 landscape paper. Set a tab stop at the horizontal centre point of the page, ie, 12 pitch 50, 10 pitch 41, and centre each line horizontally and the whole notice vertically.

THE IMPACT OF THE SINGLE MARKET

↓ 2 clear spaces

Easier travel - the channel tunnel

Frontier controls all but abolished

Mutually recognized qualifications

- TOWARDS EUROPEAN UNITY -

↓ 2 clear spaces

More opportunities - greater efficiency

7 Type the following menu on A5 portrait paper. Set a tab stop at the horizontal centre point, ie, 12 pitch 35, 10 pitch 29, and centre each line horizontally and the whole notice vertically.

D I N N E R   M E N U

12 August 1993

2 clear spaces ↓

TYPIST – Please check in the Data Files (filename MENU) on page 184, to see if accents are req'd. If so, insert them either in ink or using yr machine.

Soupe de poisson
(Fish soup)

Tournedos
(Fillet of beef in a red wine sauce)

Ratatouille et Pommes de Terre Chateau
(Mixed vegetable ragout and braised potatoes)

Sorbet aux fraises de bois
(Wild strawberry sorbet)

Cafe et petits fours

Create a new document (filename MENU) and key in document 7 for 12-pitch printout. When you have completed this task, proofread (screenread) carefully and correct if necessary. Print out original and store on disk under filename MENU. Follow the instructions for text editing on page 183.

Each line or sentence in the lettered exercises should be typed three times and, if time permits, type each complete exercise once. Single spacing, with double between exercises. For **Skill measurement** follow instructions on page 28, and for **Record your progress** follow instructions on page 30. Left margin: 12 pitch 24, 10 pitch 15.

A Review alphabet keys

1 You will of course realize it is very important to acquire excellent skills; you may well be rejected for a post yet again.

B Practise [-] *(dash key)—; finger*

Practise ; to — back to ;. Keep first finger over home key

One space *before* and *after* dash

2 ; - ; ; - ; Call today - no, tomorrow - after tea.
3 The book - it was his first - was a great success.
4 It is their choice - we are sure it will be yours.

Upper and lower case characters

Characters requiring use of shift key are called UPPER CASE characters. Characters not requiring use of shift key are called LOWER CASE characters.

C Homophones *Use your dictionary to check the meaning*

5 ascent assent; carat caret carrot; incite insight;

6 dependent dependant; incidence incident; rap wrap;

Skill measurement *22 wpm One minute Not more than one error*

SM5 We want a first-class employee: one who has a good 10
knowledge of accounts. She must be able to manage 20
a section. **(SI 1.32)** 22

1 | 2 | 3 | 4 | 5 | 6 | 7 | 8 | 9 | 10 |

Record your progress *One minute*

R3 No charge will be made for any extra copies of the 10
GAZETTE: but their account must be paid at the end 20
of the quarter. Will this suit Kate? James would 30
like to have your reply. **(SI 1.20)** 35

1 | 2 | 3 | 4 | 5 | 6 | 7 | 8 | 9 | 10 |

4 Type the following exercise on A4 paper. (a) Margins: 12 pitch 22–82, 10 pitch 12–72. (b) Although the exercise is set out in single spacing, please type it in double spacing. (c) Make your own line-endings. (d) Open punctuation. (e) Indented paragraphs. (f) Note the use of abbreviations.

TYPING MEASUREMENTS

When typing measurements, always use the small 'x' for the multiply sign, and leave one space either side of the 'x', eg, 20½ (space) ft (space) x (space) 10¼ (space) ft = 20½ ft x 10¼ ft. The same spacing is necessary when using metric measurements, eg, 1 m = 100 cm; 1 m = 1000 mm; 1 m x 1000 = 1 km.

Note the use of apostrophe for feet and double quotation marks for inches

You can also use the sign for feet and inches, eg, 9 ft 10 5/16 in x 15 ft 9 7/12 in = 9' 10 5/16" x 15' 9 7/12". You will see that, when using the signs, there is no space between the figure and the sign, but there is one space after the sign.

Do not add 's' to the plural of ft, in, lb, m, kg, etc.* In imperial measurements a full stop is used after an abbreviation when using full punctuation, but in metric measurements full stops are never used after symbols even with full punctuation, except at the end of a sentence, eg, 210 mm x 197 mm.

TYPIST – You wl find the footnote in the Data Files on page 184. (filename Y05). Please type it here in single spacing.

5 Type the following exercise on A4 paper. (a) Margins: 12 pitch 22–82, 10 pitch 12–72. (b) Double spacing. (c) Full punctuation. (d) Blocked paragraphs.

Metrication ← Sp caps

In certain instances some imperial measurements hv already ceased to be used in the UK. The EC want metric measurements to be used throughout the Community, but Britain is against a complete change.

When the changes* do come about, it wl mean th the mile, yd, foot + inch wl be replaced by the kilometre, metre + centimetre. The gram + kilogram wl supercede the ounce + pound for weighing goods. The fathom wl become 1 829 metres, while the gas therm wl be replaced by the joule. (Leave a space of at least 38 mm here, please.)

JOULE

But, for the time being, the pint wl continue to be used in pubs.

* This complete change wl not now take place until the 21st century.

WP15

Create a new document (filename METRIC) and key in document 5 for 10-pitch printout. When you have completed this task, proofread (screenread) carefully and correct if necessary. Print out original and store on disk under filename METRIC. Follow the instructions for text editing on page 182.

Each line or sentence in the lettered exercises should be typed three times and, if time permits, type each complete exercise once. Single spacing, with double between exercises. For **Skill measurement** follow instructions on page 28, and for **Record your progress** follow instructions on page 30. Left margin: 12 pitch 24, 10 pitch 15.

A Review alphabet keys

1 The freezer was stocked with pork, bread, six game and veal pies, and some quince jelly.

B Practise 1 *key—use A finger*

(NOTE If your typewriter does not have a figure 1 key, use small 'L'.)

2 We require 11 pairs size 11; also 11 pairs size 1.
3 Add up 11 plus 11 plus 11 plus 11 plus 11 plus 11.
4 On 11 August 11 girls and 11 boys hope to join us.
5 After 11 years, 11 of them will leave on 11 March.

C Practise 2 *key—use S finger*

6 sw2s sw2s s2ws s2ws s2s2s s2s2s s2sws s2sws 2s2ws.
7 22 sips 22 seas 22 skis 22 sons 22 spas 22 sets 2.
8 We need 2 grey, 2 blue, 2 red, and 22 orange ties.
9 The 12 girls and 12 boys won 122 games out of 212.

D Practise 3 *key—use D finger*

10 de3d de3d d3ed d3ed d3d3d d3d3d d3ded d3ded 3d3ed.
11 33 dots 33 dips 33 dogs 33 dads 33 dyes 33 duds 3.
12 Send 313 only to 33 Green Road and to 3 West Road.
13 Type the numbers: 3, 2, 1, 11, 12, 13, 32, 31, 23.

Skill measurement *23 wpm* *One minute* *Not more than one error*

SM6 If you feel some day that you would like a trip in 10
the country, perhaps you could drive out to a farm 20
to pick fruit. **(SI 1.09)** 23

SM7 Do you wish to take a holiday? Now is the time to 10
take one of our out-of-season vacations. Send for 20
our brochure. **(SI 1.26)** 23

1 | 2 | 3 | 4 | 5 | 6 | 7 | 8 | 9 | 10 |

Record your progress *One minute*

R4 The gavels which Liz Max saw last July are now out 10
of stock, and we would not be able to replace them 20
for some weeks - perhaps a month - when we hope to 30
receive a further quota. **(SI 1.23)** 35

1 | 2 | 3 | 4 | 5 | 6 | 7 | 8 | 9 | 10 |

Paragraphing

Paragraphs are used to separate the different subjects or sections. This breaks the writing into short passages to facilitate reading and understanding. There are three different forms of paragraphing, viz, indented, hanging and blocked.

Indented paragraphs

When using indented paragraphs, the first line of each paragraph is indented five spaces from the left margin. This indentation is made by setting a tab stop five spaces to the right of the point fixed for the left margin. When using indented paragraphs, two single or one double is turned up between paragraphs, whether typing in single or double spacing.

1 Type the following on A5 landscape paper. (a) Margins: 12 pitch 22–82, 10 pitch 12–72. (b) Single spacing, with double between each paragraph. (c) Set a tab stop at 27 (17) for the paragraph indentation.

Indent ——→ Your employer, and certain examining bodies, may ask you to use indented paragraphs. This means that, before you start typing, you must set a tab stop 5 spaces to the right of your left margin.

Return carriage twice on single

Indent ——→ Each time you start a new paragraph you should use the tab bar or key to move to the beginning of the first line.

Some word processors and software for computers have pre-set tab stops so that you do not have to set a tab for a standard paragraph indent.

Hanging paragraphs

When using hanging paragraphs, the second and subsequent lines of each paragraph start two spaces to the right of the first line. This type of paragraph is often used in display work to draw attention to particular points.

2 Type the following exercise on A5 landscape paper. (a) Margins: 12 pitch 22–82, 10 pitch 12–72. (b) Single spacing, with double between each paragraph. (c) Hanging paragraphs as shown.

If your hanging paragraph is long, you may wish to set a tab
Indent ——→ stop for the start of the first line and set your left margin for the beginning of the indented lines.

When you start a new paragraph, you should then use the mar-
Indent ——→ gin release key to move out to the tab stop. This will ensure that you do not forget that the second and subsequent lines are indented.

Blocked paragraphs

3 Type the following on A5 landscape paper. (a) Margins: Left 51 mm (2 inches), right 38 mm (1½ inches). (b) Make your own line-endings. (c) Single spacing, with double between paragraphs. (d) Block each paragraph at the left margin.

As you have already learnt, in blocked paragraphs all lines start at the same scale-point.

When single spacing is used, as in this exercise, you turn up 2 single spaces between the paragraphs.

However, when double spacing is used, you should turn up 2 double spaces between each paragraph.

Each line or sentence in the lettered exercises should be typed three times and, if time permits, type each complete exercise once. Single spacing, with double between exercises. For **Skill measurement** follow instructions on page 28, and for **Record your progress** follow instructions on page 30. Left margin: 12 pitch 24, 10 pitch 15.

A Review alphabet keys

1 The jam that he bought tasted of exotic fruit like quince, guava and pomegranate, and May ate it with zeal.

B Practise 4 *key—use F finger*

2 fr4f fr4f f4rf f4rf f4f4f f4f4f f4frf f4frf 4f4rf.
3 44 furs 44 fish 44 firs 44 feet 44 figs 44 fans 4.
4 The 4 men, 4 women, 24 boys and 4 girls go by car.
5 We ordered 434 sets and received 124 on 14 August.

C Practise 7 *key—use J finger*

6 ju7j ju7j j7uj j7uj j7j7j j7j7j j7juj j7juj 7j7uj.
7 77 jugs 77 jars 77 jigs 77 jets 77 jags 77 jaws 7.
8 The 7 boys and 77 girls sent 77 gifts to the fund.
9 Take 4 from 47, then add 27 plus 7 and you get 77.

D Practise 8 *key—use K finger*

10 ki8k ki8k k8ik k8ik k8k8k k8k8k k8kik kik8k 8k8ik.
11 88 keys 88 kits 88 kids 88 kinds 88 kilts 88 kings
12 Type 38, 83, 28, 848 and 482 with alternate hands.
13 The 8 men, 28 women, 8 boys and 78 girls are here.

Skill measurement *24 wpm* *One minute* *Not more than one error*

SM8 The account for May should now be paid, and I must 10
ask you to let me have your cheque for the sum due 20
as soon as you can. **(SI 1.04)** 24

SM9 When you leave the office at night you should make 10
sure that your machine is covered up and that your 20
desk is quite clear. **(SI 1.12)** 24

1 | 2 | 3 | 4 | 5 | 6 | 7 | 8 | 9 | 10 |

Record your progress *One minute*

R5 Our parents are fond of telling us that, when they 10
were quite young they were expected to work harder 20
than we do today; however, we will, no doubt, tell 30
our lazy children the same joyful tale. **(SI 1.29)** 38

1 | 2 | 3 | 4 | 5 | 6 | 7 | 8 | 9 | 10 |

Follow instructions given at top of page 42. Margins: 12 pitch 22–82, 10 pitch 12–72.

A Review alphabet keys

1 I saw the grey squirrel relax by the very old trees and then
jump with zest from one piece of bark to another.

B Language arts—agreement of subject and verb *(See explanation on page 181)*

2 Neither the lecturer nor the students are going to the park.
3 The typists, as well as the manager, are attending the game.
4 None of the travellers is willing to pay for the extra trip.
5 One of Ms Mitten's cars is not in use because it is damaged.

Skill measurement *30 wpm 5 minutes Not more than 5 errors*

SM38 When you apply for your first post, how should you look? Is 12
the prospective employer going to say to himself, "This per- 24
son is smart looking and I will be pleased to introduce her 36
to the office staff." Or will he feel that your clothes are 48
"way out", your hair is too startling and unkempt, and your 60
finger nails look dirty. Make certain that your appearance 72
is suitable for the job you are seeking, and forget about it 84
until after the interview. 89

At an interview you will be required to answer and ask ques- 101
tions. The interviewer will have your application form and 113
will perhaps ask you questions that you have answered on 124
paper; however, he wishes to have the information repeated 136
orally. When answering questions, speak clearly and do not 147
bite your words. **(SI 1.37)** 150

1 | 2 | 3 | 4 | 5 | 6 | 7 | 8 | 9 | 10 | 11 | 12 |

Record your progress *5 minutes*

R29 The interviewer will give you details about the business and 12
he will give you a chance to ask questions, so see that you 24
have one or 2 points in mind. You will certainly want to 35
know, for example, starting and finishing times, holidays, 47
salary, lunch breaks, etc. 52

The interviewer will usually indicate when the interview is 64
at an end. Say "thank you" and leave the room without undue 76
haste, and do not forget to take all your belongings with 88
you - it can be embarrassing if you have to return for an 99
item. On the way out, remember to thank the receptionist. 111

On the evening of the same day in which you had your inter- 123
view, write a short thank you note to the person who saw 135
you. This follow-up technique is important because it will 146
show that you have an interest in the prospects of working 157
for the organization. All persons present at an interview 169
are usually nervous. There is no reason to be frightened, 180
just treat the interviewer with respect. **(SI 1.39)** 188

1 | 2 | 3 | 4 | 5 | 6 | 7 | 8 | 9 | 10 | 11 | 12 |

Each line or sentence in the lettered exercises should be typed three times and, if time permits, type each complete exercise once. Single spacing, with double between exercises. For **Skill measurement** follow instructions on page 28, and for **Record your progress** follow instructions on page 30. Left margin: 12 pitch 24, 10 pitch 15.

A Review alphabet keys

1 The brightly coloured liquid was mixed in the jug, and given to the lazy patients for sickness.

B Practise **9** *key—use L finger*

```
2  lo9l lo9l l9ol l9ol l9l9l 99 laws 99 logs 99 lids.
3  Type 29, 39, 49, 927 and 939 with alternate hands.
4  Joe is 99, Bob is 89, Jim is 79, and George is 49.
```

C Practise **0** *key—use right little finger*

(If your machine does not have a 0 key, use capital 'O' and 'L' finger.)

```
5  101 201 301 401 701 801 901 10 left 10 look 10 lie
6  The 40 men, 70 women, 80 boys and 90 girls remain.
7  See the dates: 10 March, 20 July, 30 June, 10 May.
```

D Practise **5** *key—use F finger*

```
8  fr5f fr5f f5rf f5rf 55 fill 55 flit 55 fled 55 fit
9  5 firs, 15 furs, 25 fish, 35 figs, 45 fewer, 515 5
10 25 January 1525; 15 August 1535; 15 December 1545.
```

E Practise **6** *key—use J finger*

```
11 jy6j jy6j j6yj j6yj 66 jump 66 jerk 66 jest 66 jam
12 6 jars, 16 jets, 26 jabs, 36 jots, 46 jolts, 616 6
13 We need 656 green and 566 red by 16 February 1996.
```

Skill measurement 25 wpm One minute Not more than one error

```
SM10 I have just moved to my new house and, when I have   10
     put it straight, I would be glad if you could then   20
     spend a few days with me.  (SI 1.00)                 25

SM11 I am delighted to tell you that we have now joined   10
     the team.  We had hoped to do so last year, but we   20
     were then not old enough.  (SI 1.12)                 25

       1 | 2 | 3 | 4 | 5 | 6 | 7 | 8 | 9 | 10 |
```

Record your progress One minute

```
R6   I was sorry to find that my cheque - sent to Suzie   10
     on Monday - had not been received.  I think it has   20
     just gone astray in the post.  Shall I ask my bank   30
     to stop it now?  Please excuse the delay.  (SI 1.18) 38

       1 | 2 | 3 | 4 | 5 | 6 | 7 | 8 | 9 | 10 |
```

Document 5 Production target—15 minutes

CONDITIONS OF ADMISSION

ATTTENDANCE	Students are expected to be in their classes 5 minutes' before the scheduled starting time. Regular attendance* is required if satisfactory results are to be obtained.
STUDENTS' PROPERTY	The College cannot accept responsibility for personnal property. It is advisible not to bring items of value to the College.
FEES	The award of a place at the College is on the under-standing that the full course wil be completed, &, therefore, the payment of the fee, in full, is required before students commence there course of study. The fees for the present year are given below: Typist: Please leave 2" (51 mm) here for later insertion of fees.
ENTRY REQUIREMENTS	Prospective students should have at least a Pass Leaving Certificate.

* At least 75 per cent of any course.

Document 6 Production target—20 minutes

NOTICE TO STAFF

Examination Entry Lists

In addition to the individual entry forms, each class teacher must submit a list of candidates for each examination. The entry lists must contain the following information:

inset 5 spaces

(1) Examining Body concerned
(2) Type of Examination
(3) Date & time of examination
(4) Room req'd
(5) Group taking examination
(6) Name of each candidate in alphabetical order
(7) any special requirements

I should be glad if the above is strictly adhered to.

Each line or sentence in the lettered exercises should be typed three times and, if time permits, type each complete exercise once. Single spacing, with double between exercises. For **Skill measurement** follow instructions on page 28, and for **Record your progress** follow instructions on page 30. Left margin: 12 pitch 24, 10 pitch 15.

A Review alphabet keys

1 A small quiet boy who lives next door to Jack came out of the gate and went down the zigzag path.

Placement of certain characters

As already mentioned on previous pages, the placement of the hyphen and question mark varies with the make of the machine. This also applies to a few of the signs, symbols, and marks keys such as the oblique and quotation marks. When practising these keys, make sure you know whether or not you have to use the shift key, decide on the correct finger, and then practise the reach from the home key; then type the drills given.

B Practise quotation marks *No space after initial " no space before closing "*

2 "Go for 30 days." "Call at 12 noon." "Ring now."
3 "I am going," he said. "It is already very late."
4 Mary said, "Mr Bell is here." "Ring me tomorrow."

C Practise brackets (*One space before no space after*
) *No space before one space after*

5 (1 (2 (3 (4 (5 (6 (7 (8 (9) 10) 11) 12) 13) 14) 8)
6 (22) (23) (24) (25) (26) (27) (28) (29) (30) (31).
7 Mail: (a) 2 pens; (b) 3 pins; (c) 1 tie; (d) 1 hat

D Practise apostrophe *No space before or after in middle of a word*

8 It's Joe's job to clean Dad's car but he's unwell.
9 Don't do that; it's bad for Mary's dog; he's nice.
10 Bill's 2 vans are with John's 8 trucks at Reading.

Skill measurement *25 wpm* *1½ minutes* *Not more than 2 errors*

SM12 Just a year ago we said that you should be given a 10
trial as a clerk in sales and, as one of the staff 20
will leave next week, I would like you to take his 30
place. Let me know if this will suit you. **(SI 1.08)** 38

1 | 2 | 3 | 4 | 5 | 6 | 7 | 8 | 9 | 10 |

Record your progress *1½ minutes*

R7 Many thanks for your note about the dozen desks we 10
ordered. They are not required right away, but if 20
we have them on Thursday you may expect our remit- 30
tance quite soon. We will adjust our records when 40
we receive your invoice and the amount is paid. 49
(SI 1.29)

1 | 2 | 3 | 4 | 5 | 6 | 7 | 8 | 9 | 10 |

Cork Secretarial College

Principal: Patricia Kerry BA HDipEd CTG TDT

11 St Patrick's Hill
CORK

Telephone 021 507027

REPORT

Student Margaret O'Brien

Course Secretarial Studies Session 1992/1993

SUBJECT	Attendance hours		Marks %			Remarks
	Possible	Actual	Prep	Class	Exam	
COMMUNICATION	33	30	80	84	86	A high standard
SHORTHAND	110	107	82	79	75	Excellent work
TYPEWRITING	80	78	–	81	81	Excellent
SEC SERVICES	33	30	74	68	65	Good
BUSINESS ADMIN	33	30	62	67	60	Good
INFORMATION PROCESSING	33	30	-	78	70	Very good
ACCOUNTS	33	30	76	72	71	Very good standard

General Remarks Margaret has worked conscientiously during her first term and achieved excellent results. With continued effort she should reach a very high standard by the end of the course and be capable of obtaining an interesting and rewarding ~~sec~~ secretarial post.

Principal .... Date ....

Next term begins on 11 January 1993

TYPIST – Please check the attendance in the Data Files (filename CORK) + alter if necessary, page 183.

Follow instructions given on page 36. Margins: 12 pitch 24, 10 pitch 15.

A *Review alphabet keys*

1 The boy did just give a quick answer, but he could not find words to explain the amazing story.

Backspace key

Locate the backspace key on your machine. This is usually on either the top left or top right of the keyboard. When the backspace key is depressed, the carriage/carrier/cursor will move back one space at a time. On most electric and electronic machines the carriage/carrier/cursor will continue to move for as long as the backspace key is depressed.

Underscore key—underline function

Before underscoring a short word, backspace once for each letter and space in the word to be underscored. For longer words, or several words, use carriage release lever. After you finish underscoring, always tap space bar. Use shift lock when underscoring more than one character. A final punctuation mark may or may not be underscored. See last section of *Handbook, Solutions, and Resource Material* for examples of punctuation marks that are *not* underscored.

If you are using an electronic keyboard, follow instructions given for underscoring (underlining) in manufacturer's handbook. With word processors, it is not possible (on most systems) to underscore a heading, or words, in the normal way because a special underline function is available. In offices today, there is a tendency to use the word **underline** instead of the word **underscore**.

B *Practise underlining (underscore key)*

```
2 Please send them 29 only - not 9 - by air-freight.
3 John Brown, Mary Adams and Janet Kelly are coming.
```

C *Practise £ sign*

```
4 Buy 5 at £15, 8 at £68, 17 at £415 and 30 at £270.
5 £1, £2, £3, £4, £5, £6, £7, £8, £9, £10, £20, £30.
```

D *Practise ampersand* (&) *One space before and after*

```
6 Jones & Cutler Ltd, 67 & 68 North Street, Falkirk.
7 Mr & Mrs Weston, 18 & 19 Main Street, Cirencester.
```

E *Practise oblique* (/) *No space before or after*

```
8 I can/cannot be present.  I do/do not require tea.
9 Jim Minett will take an aural and/or written test.
```

Skill measurement *25 wpm* *2 minutes* *Not more than 2 errors*

```
SM13 There must be little imps who sleep until we begin   10
     to work and then they come to our office and start   20
     to harass and try us.  We must all try to keep our   30
     minds on the work we have to do, and avoid letting   40
     our thoughts move away from our immediate labours.   50
```
(SI 1.22)

1 | 2 | 3 | 4 | 5 | 6 | 7 | 8 | 9 | 10 |

Record your progress *2 minutes*

```
R8 There seems to be quite an amazing lack of simple,   10
   and easy-to-follow guides to operate the more com-   20
   plicated machines; in fact, we looked at 2 or 3 of   30
   the books and felt they made the operations seem a   40
   little hard - indeed, they were not.  We read just   50
   one foreign text that gave a lucid account of what   60
   had to be done.                                      63
```
(SI 1.30)

1 | 2 | 3 | 4 | 5 | 6 | 7 | 8 | 9 | 10 |

Document 2 Production target—12 minutes

MEMO (TYPIST – One top & one carbon copy, please)

To All Staff

From Ms P Kerry [Date 23.8.93

ABSENTEEISM & GENERAL BEHAVIOUR OF STUDENTS

With the new academic yr commencing, I feel we are all anxious not to have a repeat of the rather indifferent attitude of several students during last session.

I shd be very glad if teaching staff wd make sure that all students are def aware of our rules (& regulations). Be particularly firm if students are late.

I have been asked for a number of refs for last year's students, & I shd be glad if you wd let me have, as soon as possible, an up-to-date list of any appts that the students have been offered.

PK/Staff/PB

Document 3 Production target—20 minutes

CORK SECRETARIAL COLLEGE

Examinations – (APRIL) 1993

Name of student	Class	Subject
Anna Kennedy	B1	Typewriting – Stage II
Ann O'Hara	C4	European Studies – Intermediate
Catherine O'Leary	B1	Information Processing – Stage I
Bridie Joesbury	C2	Accounting – Intermediate
Mary Leam (LEAM)	B1	Typewriting – Stage III
June Flynn	B1	Information Processing – Stage I
Eamonn Devlin	C2	Accounting – Intermediate
Michael O'Dwyer	C2	European Studies – Intermediate

(TYPIST – Double spacing)

Follow instructions given on page 36. Margins: 12 pitch 24, 10 pitch 15.

A *Review alphabet keys*

1 The day dawned quiet and warm, and the lazy foxes
enjoyed a feast at the back of the undergrowth by
Valerie Peters' farm.

B *Practise at key (@)* *One space before and after, in continuous text*

2 f@f f@f d@d j@j 9 @ 10p; 8 @ 11p; 7 @ 12p; 3 @ 8p.
3 Please send 44 @ £5; 6 @ £7; 13 @ £8; and 28 @ £9.
4 Order 420 @ £12, 50 @ £5, 40 @ £6 and 5 @ £8 each.

Numeric keypads

Some machines with electronic keyboards have a numeric keypad, usually placed to the right of, and separate from, the alphabet keyboard. This keypad may be used in addition to, or instead of, the figure keys on the top row of the keyboard. When using the 10-key pad, employ the 4 5 6 as the home keys on which you place the J K L fingers. The fingers and thumb will then operate the keypad as follows:

J = 1 4 7 **K** = 2 5 8 **L** = decimal point 3 6 9
Thumb = 0 **Little finger** = enter, comma, minus

The layout of the keypad will differ from one machine to another. Study your keyboard and, if you have a keypad, note any differences from the layout above and the characters to which the suggested fingering applies.

C *Practise typing figures on the numeric keypad*

5 456 654 147 258 369 041 520 306 470 508 906 159 02
6 417 528 639 159 350 256 107 369 164 059 378 904 38
7 4.5 6.9 4.1 4.7 5.2 5.8 4,655 3,987 2,541 8,465 79

Skill measurement *25 wpm* *2½ minutes* *Not more than 3 errors*

SM14 We were all happy to hear that you are now back at 10
work, and we hope that your long rest by the lakes 20
will have restored you to good health. As soon as 30
you can, please call and see us. You will observe 40
that we have moved to a house quite near to Rugby, 50
and I am sending you a map of the area so that you 60
will find us. **(SI 1.11)** 62

1 | 2 | 3 | 4 | 5 | 6 | 7 | 8 | 9 | 10 |

Record your progress *2½ minutes*

R9 Have you ever thought of taking one of our out-of- 10
season holidays? A quiet winter break - January - 20
may be just what you would enjoy. In our brochure 30
you will find a wide choice of 122 cities to which 40
you can go. Write to: Sun Traveller Ltd, Leighton 50
Buzzard, and we will be pleased to send you one of 60
our up-to-date guide books telling you, in detail, 70
about our exotic holidays. **(SI 1.30)** 75

1 | 2 | 3 | 4 | 5 | 6 | 7 | 8 | 9 | 10 |

Ref PK/FT

23 August 1993

Typist – Take a carbon please – and don't forget the envelope

Mr Patrick Cassidy
12 Waterford St
CORK

Dear Mr ——

I am pleased to offer you a permanent part-time appt w us, to take effect from 1 Sept 1993, as a lecturer of Business Administration. [The hours wl be as follows:

Mondays and Fridays 0900 - 1230 hours
Tuesdays
Wednesdays
Thursdays

TYPIST – Wld you please enter the hrs here. You wl find them in the Data Files (filename P/T), page 184.

You wl be resp for teaching B— A— to 3 groups of twenty students, leading to a final examination at Stage II to be taken in June of ea yr.

Holidays wl be taken during the normal College vacation, + it wl be necy to give one full term's notice on either side of any termination of this appt.

In the advert for this post it was stated that the starting salary wd be £5 350 per annum, but in view of yr past experience I am pleased to be able to offer you £5 850 per annum. [I hope very much that you wl accept this invitation to join the staff of the College, + that you wl enjoy many happy yrs with us.

Yrs sinc

Principal

Standard sizes of paper

In the office you will have to use different sizes of paper. The standard sizes are known as the 'A' series and are shown below. The most common of these sizes are: A4, A5 and A6.

420 mm
297 mm
A3
420 mm
594 mm
A2
210 mm
148 mm
A5
210 mm
297 mm
A4
105 mm
74 mm
A7
105 mm
148 mm
A6

Sizes	25 mm or 2.5 cm = 1"
A2 420 × 594 mm	
A3 420 × 297 mm	
A4 297 × 210 mm (landscape)	$11\frac{3}{4}'' \times 8\frac{1}{4}''$ (approx)
A4 210 × 297 mm (portrait)	$8\frac{1}{4}'' \times 11\frac{3}{4}''$ (approx)
A5 210 × 148 mm (landscape)	$8\frac{1}{4}'' \times 5\frac{7}{8}''$ (approx)
A5 148 × 210 mm (portrait)	$5\frac{7}{8}'' \times 8\frac{1}{4}''$ (approx)
A6 148 × 105 mm	$5\frac{7}{8}'' \times 4\frac{1}{8}''$ (approx)

Vertical linespacing

6 single vertical lines = 25 mm or 2.5 cm (1 inch)

Number of single-spaced lines in the full length of A4 and A5 paper:

A4 landscape paper—50 single-spaced lines
A4 portrait paper—70 single-spaced lines
A5 landscape paper—35 single-spaced lines
A5 portrait paper—50 single-spaced lines

Horizontal spacing

The three most usual typefaces are:

10 characters to 25 mm or 2.5 cm (1 inch) – known as 10 pitch
12 characters to 25 mm or 2.5 cm (1 inch) – known as 12 pitch
15 characters to 25 mm or 2.5 cm (1 inch) – known as 15 pitch

Number of horizontal characters in full width of A4 and A5 paper

	10 pitch	**12 pitch**	**15 pitch**
A4 landscape	117 (centre point 58)	141 (centre point 70)	176 (centre point 88)
A4 portrait	82 (centre point 41)	100 (centre point 50)	124 (centre point 62)
A5 landscape	82 (centre point 41)	100 (centre point 50)	124 (centre point 62)
A5 portrait	59 (centre point 29)	70 (centre point 35)	88 (centre point 44)

Cork Secretarial College

OFFICE SERVICES—REQUEST FORM

This sheet contains instructions which must be complied with when typing the documents. Read the information carefully before starting, and refer back to it frequently.

Typist's log sheet

Originator Ms Patricia Kerry Principal Department — Date 23.8.93 Ext No 2

Typists operating a word processor, or electronic typewriter with appropriate function keys, should apply the following automatic facilities: top margin; carrier/cursor return; line-end hyphenation; underline OR bold print (embolden); error correction; centring; any other relevant applications.

Remember (a) to complete the details required at the bottom of the form; (b) to enter typing time per document in appropriate column; and (c) before submitting this **Log sheet** and your completed work, enter TOTAL TYPING TIME in the last column so that the Typist's time may be charged to the originator.

Document No	Type of document and instructions	Copies – Original plus	Input form¶	Typing time per document	Total typing time ▼
1	Letter to Mr Cassidy with an envelope	1 original + 1 carbon	MS		
2	Memo to Staff	1 original + 1 carbon	MS		
3	List of examination candidates	1 original	MS		
* 4	Completion of Report Form	1 original	MS		
5	Extract from the Conditions of Admission	1 original	AT		
6	Notice to Staff	1 original + 1 carbon	MS		
			TOTAL	TYPING TIME	

TYPIST – please complete:

Typist's name: Date received: Date completed:

Time received: Time completed:

If the typed documents cannot be returned within 24 hours, the office services supervisor should inform the originator. Any item that is urgent should be marked with an asterisk (*).

¶ T = Typescript AT = Amended Typescript MS = Manuscript SD = Shorthand Dictation AD = Audio Dictation

▼ To be charged to the originator's department.

Linespace selector

The linespace selector is a lever or knob that may be situated at the left- or right-hand end of the paper table or to the left or right of the keyboard. Most machines can be adjusted for single and double spacing and may also have the facility for $1\frac{1}{2}$, $2\frac{1}{2}$ and treble spacing. The selector controls the distance between the lines of typing. With single spacing (1) there is no clear space between lines of typing; with double spacing (2) there is **one** clear space between each line; with treble (3) spacing there are **two** clear spaces between each line.

6 single-line spaces equal 25 mm (1 inch)

25 mm

Single spacing (type on every line)	Double spacing (type on every second line)	Treble spacing (type on every third line)
I am	I am	I am
going	*(space)*	*(space)*
to	going	*(space)*
the	*(space)*	going
market	to	*(space)*
today	*(space)*	*(space)*

Blocked paragraphs

Paragraphs are used to break up the writing into short passages to facilitate reading and understanding. There are three different styles of paragraph but, for the time being, we will deal with the **blocked** paragraph where all lines start at the left margin.

When typing **blocked** paragraphs in **single** spacing, turn up two **single** spaces between each paragraph, ie, leave one blank space between each paragraph.

1 Type the following paragraphs on A5 landscape paper. (a) Margins: 12 pitch 22–82, 10 pitch 12–72. (b) Leave 25 mm (one inch) clear at the top of the page, ie, turn up 7 single spaces. (c) Single spacing.

We are sure you will have noticed that laser printers cut down on print costs and noise.

You can achieve a high quality finish in a wide variety of typestyles.

When typing **blocked** paragraphs in **double** spacing, turn up two **double** spaces between each paragraph, ie, leave three blank spaces between each paragraph.

2 Type the following paragraphs on A5 landscape paper. (a) Margins: 12 pitch 22–82, 10 pitch 12–72. (b) Leave 25 mm (one inch) clear at the top of the page, ie, turn up seven single spaces. (c) Double spacing.

As you have already learnt, when using blocked paragraphs

all lines start at the same scale-point. Return twice on double

When typing blocked paragraphs in double spacing, you should

turn up twice between paragraphs.

Amounts in figures

With sums of four figures or more, leave a space between the hundreds and thousands and a space between thousands and millions—example in exercise 6 on page 41. Please see **Variations in display**, in the last section of *Handbook, Solutions, and Resource Material*, for alternative methods.

See Practical Typing Exercises, Book One, page 1, for further exercises on

Fully-blocked letter with full punctuation and display

Letter display is exactly the same as given on pages 56–58 for open punctuation. However, when using full punctuation, note the following points:

(a) Full stop after the abbreviation Ref. but no punctuation in the reference.
(b) Note the punctuation and spacing in the 'For the attention of . . .' line, with no full stop at the end.*
(c) The points for typing the name and address of the addressee are the same as those for typing envelopes, given on page 144.
(d) Always type a comma after the salutation.
(e) Always type a comma after the complimentary close.
(f) Always type full stop after Enc./Encs.

* If the last word were abbreviated (Esq.), then a full stop would be necessary.

6 Type the following letter in fully-blocked style using full punctuation. (a) Use A4 letterhead paper (Kenkott Scotia PLC). (b) Suitable margins. (c) Follow the display. (d) Type a C6 envelope.

```
Our Ref. CPS/FAD

1st December 1993

FOR THE ATTENTION OF MRS. K. COX

F. L. Paget & Co. Ltd.,
34 Lincoln Road,
NEWARK,
Notts.      NG22 1AA

Dear Sirs,

EURO PLANNER FOR 1994

Now that the single European market is established, we are sure it
would be to your advantage to have a yearly planner that shows
European holidays and festivals, together with the relevant
country's flag, so that you can see where your continental contact
is likely to be available.

The planner shows all the European flags along its border and comes
with a selection of self-adhesive flagging sticks and a chart pen.
Prices are as follows:

Poster version     38 in. x 24 in.    £9.55
Mounted planner    38 in. x 24 in.   £15.95

Order this week, and you can have the planner before you close for
your Christmas vacation.  We enclose an order form.

Yours faithfully,

CHRISTOPHER P. SPOONER     Sales Manager     Enc.
```

Added points for full or open punctuation

Note these points when you type letters with either full or open punctuation, in blocked or semi-blocked style.

(a) Whether using full or open punctuation 'st', 'nd', 'th' may be used in dates. Similarly a comma may follow the month—eg, 21st August, 1993.
(b) If a date appears in the body of a letter, then it should be in the same form as that used at the head of the letter.
(c) Whether using full or open punctuation, the date may be typed on the same line as the reference and backspaced from the right margin.
(d) The words 'Our ref' may already appear in a printed letter heading. If this is the case, it is necessary to type the reference after it, irrespective of its position in the heading.
(e) The words 'Your ref' may also appear. This is the reference of the firm to whom you are writing, and if their reference is given, then it must be inserted.

See Practical Typing Exercises, Book One, page 51, for further exercises on

Fractions

3 Find the ½ key and the % key on your keyboard and make certain that you know whether or not you have to use the shift key. Type each of the following lines three times on A5 landscape paper. Margins: 12 pitch 22–82, 10 pitch 12–72.

```
;;; ½½½ ;;; ½½½ ;½; ;½; 1½; 2½; 3½; 4½; 5½; 6½; 7½; 8½; 90½;
;;; %%% ;;; %%% ;%; ;%; ½%; 2%; 3%; 4%; 5%; 6%; 7%; 8%; 19%;
```

NOTE In addition to the ½, most typewriters have keys with other fractions. Examine your machine to find what fractions it has. These are all typed with the ; finger. Some will require the use of the shift key. Practise the reaching movement from the home key to the fraction key you wish to type. Remember: ALWAYS return your finger to the home key.

Sloping fractions

When fractions are not provided on the typewriter, these should be typed by using ordinary figures, with the oblique, eg, 2 fifteenths = 2/15; 3 sixteenths = 3/16. Where a whole number comes before a 'made-up' fraction, leave a clear space (NOT a full stop) between the whole number and the fraction. Certain examining bodies allow the use of fractions already on the keyboard and sloping fractions to be used in the same exercise, other examining bodies do not, in which case use sloping fractions throughout.

4 Type the following on A5 landscape paper. (a) Double spacing. (b) Margins: 12 pitch 22–82, 10 pitch 12–72.

```
11¼, 12½, 13¾, 14⅛, 15⅜, 16⅝, 17⅞, 18¼, 19½, 20¾, 30⅛,
11 1/4, 12 1/2, 13 3/4, 14 1/8, 15 3/8, 16 5/8, 17 7/8,
```

Decimals

(a) Use full stop for decimal point. This is usually typed in the normal position of the full stop and not raised. NOTE In some countries the comma is used to indicate the decimal point.
(b) Do NOT leave a space before or after decimal point.
(c) No punctuation is required at the end of figures except at the end of a sentence.
(d) Always insert the number of decimal places required by using zero.
eg, 2 decimal places: type 86.40 not 86.4 3 decimal places: type 95.010 not 95.01
(e) With sums of four figures or more, leave a space between the hundreds and thousands and a space between thousands and millions. Please see **Variations in display**, last section of *Handbook, Solutions, and Resource Material*, for alternative methods.

5 Type the following sentences three times on A5 landscape paper. (a) Single spacing. (b) Margins: 12 pitch 22–82, 10 pitch 12–72.

```
Add up 12.54, 13.02, 24.60, 6.75, and 0.20 and you get 57.11.
The sheet measures 1.200 x 5.810 x 2.540 m; the gross weight
is approximately 50.802 kg and the net weight is 38.102 kg.
```

(For European Community currencies, see last section of *Handbook, Solutions, and Resource Material.*)

Sums of money in context

(a) If the sum comprises only pounds, type as follows: £5, £10 or £5.00, £10.00.
(b) If only pence, type: 10p, 97p.
NOTE No space between figures and letter p, and no full stop after p (unless, of course, it ends a sentence).
(c) With mixed amounts, ie, sums comprising pounds and pence, the decimal point and the £ symbol should always be used, but NOT the abbreviation p, eg, £7.20.
(d) If the sum contains a decimal point but no whole pounds, a nought should be typed after the £ symbol and before the point, eg, £0.97.

6 Type the following in double spacing on A5 landscape paper. (a) Double spacing. (b) Margins: 12 pitch 22–82, 10 pitch 12–72.

```
We have purchased goods to the value of £200.50, and we must
send our cheque for this amount; however, we still await a
credit note for £61.49 which means the cheque should be for
£139.01.  We offer a discount of 2½% on sums up to £9 999.99
and 3½% on sums from £10 000.00.
```

See Practical Typing Exercises, Book One, page 1, for further exercises on

Forms of address with full punctuation—Addressing envelopes

The guide to the addressing of envelopes, given on page 102, applies with the exception of inserting punctuation after abbreviations and at line-ends. It should be noted that Miss and Ms do not require a full stop. Examples:

Mr. M. James   Dr. O. Coleman   Messrs. W. O. Horne & Sons   Ms N. Gray

Mrs. W. Fallon, 24 St. John's Street, BOSTON, Lincs. PE21 6AA	E. P. Freeman, Esq., M.A., B.Sc., T. R. Beach & Co. Ltd., 2 Herne Bay Road, BANBURY, Oxon. OX16 8LB

Points to note:

(a) Full stop after an initial followed by one clear space.
(b) Comma at the end of each line except for the last line before the postcode, which is followed by a full stop.
(c) NO punctuation in postcode.
(d) Comma after surname, followed by one space before Esq.
(e) Full stop and NO space between the letters of a degree, but a comma and space between each group of letters.
(f) Notice abbreviation for Oxfordshire.

3 Type each of the following lines twice in single spacing. (a) Use margins of 12 pitch 20–80, 10 pitch 11–71. (b) Notice that there is NO full stop in the 24-hour clock.

Ms W. K. Fleming will see you at 10 a.m. or 2 p.m. tomorrow.
Address the letter to P. W. St. John-Lloyd, Esq., M.D., B.A.
Miss U. B. Wallace will meet Mrs. L. V. Stait at 1400 hours.

4 Address C6 size envelopes to the following. Use blocked style and full punctuation. Mark the envelope to Ms Hewitt 'CONFIDENTIAL', and the envelope to K. C. Brennan P.L.C. 'FOR THE ATTENTION OF MR. G. MADDEN'. Do not copy the single quotation marks.

Ms A. I. Hewitt, O.B.E., 17 Park Road, SWINDON. SN2 2NR
K. C. Brennan P.L.C., 3 High Street, SEASCALE, Cumbria. CA20 1PQ
M. Dominique Lemaitre, 20 Rue Breydel, 1060 BRUSSELS, Belgium.
Mr. J. and Mrs. K. Chisholm, 5 High Street, INVERNESS. IV2 4EX
Mme. Jacqueline Huby, Plateau due Kirchberg, PO Box 1431, LUXEMBOURG.
F. J. Jones p.l.c., Llangawsai, ABERYSTWYTH, Dyfed. SY23 1AA
Dr. Karl Wimmer, Gustav-Adolf-Str. 9, 400 DÜSSELDORF, Germany.

Half-space corrections

You can squeeze in an extra letter, eg, type four letters where there were originally three, or spread a word with a letter less than the incorrect word, eg, type a four-letter word where there were five letters before. Inserting a word with an extra letter:

(a) Erase incorrect word.
(b) Move carriage to second letter of the erased word.
(c) Depress backspace key, hold it down and type first letter of new word, release backspace key and tap space bar once; hold down backspace key, type second letter, and repeat process.

Inserting a word with a letter less:

(a) Erase incorrect word.
(b) Move carriage to third letter of the erased word.
(c) As in (c) opposite.

Alternatively: By means of the paper release lever, move the paper so that the printing point is half a space to the left of the erased word, or place printing point half a space to the right so that $1\frac{1}{2}$ spaces precede and follow the word.

Electric/electronic keyboards: Some of these keyboards have a half-space key, and some manual machines have a half-space mechanism on the space bar.

5 Type lines 1, 2, 3 and 4 exactly as shown; then squeeze the word **them** in each of the two blank spaces in line 2 and spread the word **her** in each of the two blank spaces in line 4. Use margins of 12 pitch 22–82, 10 pitch 12–72.

1 I told her that I will call. I told her that I will call.
2 I told   that I will call. I told   that I will call.
3 I told them that I will call. I told them that I will call.
4 I told   that I will call. I told   that I will call.

See Practical Typing Exercises, Book One, page 50, for further exercises on

Each line or sentence in the lettered exercises should be typed three times and, if time permits, type each complete exercise once. Single spacing, with double between exercises. For **Skill measurement** follow instructions on page 28, and for **Record your progress** follow instructions on page 30. Margins: 12 pitch 22–82, 10 pitch 12–72.

A Review alphabet keys

1 The bold pilot was unable to land the jet owing to extremely thick fog which quite covered the whole zone.

B Improve control of space bar

2 as is so or be in am if an me go my do he by us ask may you.
3 It is so. Ask me to go. You must be in time. I may do so.
4 Who is she? He can go home on 6 May. It is a 65-page book.

C Improve control of down reaches

5 Ac lack back rack hack jack track crack brace vacant accents
6 Ab cabs dabs tabs jabs able table gable sable labels enables
7 Ask Jack to bring back the labels for that one vacant table.

Spelling

Employers suggest that the greatest impediment to a typist is uncertainty about spelling. We all find difficulty in spelling certain words and, from now on, there will be spelling drills on each **Skill building** page. When typing these, look carefully at each word and note the sequence of the letters. Practise these drills as often as possible.

D Spelling skills *Correct the one misspelt word in each line. (Answer: page 181)*

8 view untill merge awful chaos quiet forty remit absorb centre
9 lose occur gauge audio among receive develop seperate accrue
10 I have received your cheque and will book the accomodation.

Skill measurement *25 wpm 3 minutes Not more than 3 errors*

SM15 We have not yet been able to send the goods you ordered last 12
week as they are not stock lines, but we shall do all we can 24
to let you have some of the goods, if not all, by Tuesday of 36
next week. We trust that you will excuse the delay in send- 48
ing your requirements, and that we may look forward to meet- 60
ing your requests more promptly in the future. We enclose a 72
new price-list. **(SI 1.21)** 75

1 | 2 | 3 | 4 | 5 | 6 | 7 | 8 | 9 | 10 | 11 | 12 |

Record your progress *3 minutes*

R10 Have you ever followed modern machine manuals in any detail? 12
They seem to be written in a complex language which contains 24
a great deal of jargon - quantity rather than quality with a 36
lack of easy-to-follow wording. I did read 3 books in which 48
the message was plain, and one told me how to produce clear, 60
dazzling graphics in a simple way. Students using this book 72
would find it easy to follow because there are many diagrams 84
and notes that are very clear. **(SI 1.37)** 90

1 | 2 | 3 | 4 | 5 | 6 | 7 | 8 | 9 | 10 | 11 | 12 |

(b) Used with figures only:

Open punctuation	*Full punctuation*		
No, Nos	No., Nos.	number(s)	NOTE It would seem preferable to add an s for the plural of yd and qr. This style is recommended by the *Oxford Dictionary for Writers and Editors;* however, the British Standards Institution gives both examples without the s. Follow the style used in the exercise being copied.
mph	m.p.h.	miles per hour	
am	a.m.	ante meridiem—before noon	
pm	p.m.	post meridiem—after noon	
in	in.	inch(es)	
ft	ft.	foot (feet)	
yd, yds	yd., yds.	yard(s)	
qr, qrs	qr., qrs.	quarter(s)	
g	g	gram(s)	
kg	kg	kilogram(s)	NOTE Punctuation is never used in metric abbreviations
mm	mm	millimetre(s)	
m	m	metre(s)	
km	km	kilometre(s)	

(c) Abbreviations always used:

Open punctuation	*Full punctuation*		
eg	e.g.	exempli gratia—for example	
etc	etc.	et cetera—and others	NOTE There is no space in the middle of an abbreviation
ie	i.e.	*id est*—that is	
NB	N.B.	*nota bene*—note well	
viz	viz.	*videlicet*—namely	
Esq	Esq.	Esquire	NOTE Miss is not an abbreviation and does not require a full stop; likewise Ms does not require a full stop
Messrs	Messrs.	Messieurs—Gentlemen	
Mr	Mr.		
Mrs	Mrs.		
Ms	Ms		

1 Type the following sentences on A5 landscape paper. (a) Note the use of abbreviations. (b) Margins: 12 pitch 22–82, 10 pitch 12–72. (c) Blocked paragraphs. (d) Single spacing, with double between each sentence. (e) Open punctuation.

```
Mr & Mrs A T Goulde were told to see Dr H Partridge at St Augustine's Hospital
at 3.00 pm.
The cars, motor bikes, vans, etc, were all parked in a small area which
measured only 600 sq ft.
Parker & Browne PLC is a large company, but F S Dodwell & Co Ltd is more well
known, although employing fewer staff.
Leave a top margin of 25 mm, and a left margin of 38 mm, when typing the report
for Ms J Farmer BSc.
```

2 Type the following sentences on A5 landscape paper. (a) Margins: 12 pitch 22–82, 10 pitch 12–72. (b) Blocked paragraphs. (c) Single spacing, with double between each sentence. (d) Full punctuation. (e) On completion, compare with the previous exercise.

NOTE One space after a full stop at the end of an abbreviation, unless it occurs at the end of a sentence when two spaces are left. No space after a medial full stop within an abbreviation.

```
Mr. & Mrs. A. T. Goulde were told to see Dr. H. Partridge at St. Augustine's
Hospital at 3.00 p.m.
The cars, motor bikes, vans, etc., were all parked in a small area which
measured only 600 sq. ft.
Parker & Browne P.L.C. is a large company, but F. S. Dodwell & Co. Ltd. is more
well known, although employing fewer staff.
Leave a top margin of 25 mm, and a left margin of 38 mm, when typing the report
for Ms J. Farmer, B.Sc.
```

See Practical Typing Exercises, Book One, page 50, for further exercises on

Display

Some types of matter such as notices, menus and advertisements are much more attractive if items are displayed on separate lines and good use is made of capital letters, small letters, the underscore and bold print.

In its simplest form, and to save time, decide on a *suitable* left and top margin depending on the length of the longest line and the actual number of lines to be typed. Then type each line at the left margin, leaving extra lines between items as required for emphasis.

Capitals

Important lines may be given prominence by using *spaced capitals*, ie, leave one space between each letter and three spaces between each word.

NB when using *closed capitals*, it is usual to leave only one space between each word.

Notice the use of spaced capitals, closed capitals and the underline to stress important lines in the exercises that follow.

Electronic keyboards

If you are using an *electronic machine*, you may be able to make use of the **bold** function key. This key is depressed before typing the chosen line, eg, **THE EUROPEAN COMMUNITY** in the exercise below. The line will then appear in a heavier print than the others in the exercise, and so be given prominence. To save time, you can also use the **automatic underline** feature if your electronic machine has this particular function.

The margins have been decided for you in the following two exercises. As the exercises contain only 12 lines each, a 51 mm (2 inch) top margin will make your completed exercise more pleasing to the eye.

1 Display the following notice on A5 portrait paper. (a) Leave 51 mm at the top of the page. (b) Left margin: 12 pitch 24, 10 pitch 18. (c) Copy the exercise line for line.

			Turn up 13 single spaces
1	Line 1	T H E S I N G L E M A R K E T	
2	Space	↓	Turn up 2 single spaces
3	Line 2	How will it affect you?	
4	Space	↓	Turn up 2 single spaces
5	Line 3	KEEP UP TO DATE	
6	Space	↓	Turn up 3 single spaces
7	Space		
8	Line 4	The United Kingdom and	Type these 3 lines in single spacing
9	Line 5	The Irish Republic	
10	Line 6	are members of -	
11	Space	↓	Turn up 2 single spaces
12	Line 7	THE EUROPEAN COMMUNITY	

Open punctuation

Up to this point in the book all the exercises have been displayed with open punctuation. This means that full stops have not been inserted after abbreviations, eg, Mrs F L Bunting MA JP, and business and personal letters have been typed with the omission of commas after each line of the address, and after the salutation and complimentary close. The modern trend is to omit punctuation in those cases as it simplifies and speeds up the work of the typist. However, punctuation is always inserted in sentences, so that the grammatical sense is clear.

Full punctuation

It is also acceptable to insert punctuation after abbreviations, eg, Mrs. F. L. Bunting, M.A., J.P., and after each line of an address, as well as after the salutation and complimentary close. Grammatical punctuation is always inserted. Open and full punctuation must NEVER be mixed: a document must be typed in either open or full punctuation. (See also last section of *Handbook, Solutions, and Resource Material*, for further information.)

Standard abbreviations

In typewritten work abbreviations should not, as a rule, be used. There are, however, a few standard abbreviations that are never typed in full, and others that may be used in certain circumstances. Study the following lists, so that you will know when not to use abbreviations and when it is permissible to use them. You must always be consistent in their use.

(a) Used in the cases indicated:

Open punctuation	*Full punctuation*	
Ltd	Ltd.	Limited. Abbreviation used only in names of private limited companies and companies limited by guarantee. The abbreviation may be used but it must be typed in full if that is how it appears in the printed letterhead or in the exercise being copied.
PLC, plc or Plc	P.L.C., p.l.c. or P.l.c.	Public Limited Company. It may be typed in full but is usually abbreviated. Follow the style used in the exercise being copied.
Co	Co.	Company. Abbreviation used only in names of companies. The abbreviation may be used but it must be typed in full if that is how it appears in the printed letterhead or in the exercise being copied.
OHMS	O.H.M.S.	On Her Majesty's Service. Usually abbreviated but occasionally typed in full. Follow the style used in the exercise being copied.
PS	PS.	Postscript. Abbreviation used only at the foot of a letter.
v	v.	Versus. May be abbreviated or typed in full. Follow the style used in the exercise being copied.
&	&	And, known as the 'ampersand'. Abbreviation used in names of firms, such as Smith & Brown, and in numbers, such as Nos 34 & 35 (Nos. 34 & 35).
@	@	At. Abbreviation used only in invoices, quotations and similar documents.
%	%	Per cent. May be abbreviated with figures, otherwise it is typed in full.
Bros	Bros.	Brothers. Abbreviation used only in the names of companies.
MEP	M.E.P.	Member of the European Parliament. May be abbreviated or typed in full. Follow the style used in the exercise being copied.

2 Type the following exercise on A5 portrait paper. (a) Leave 51 mm clear at the top of the page. (b) Left margin: 12 pitch 16, 10 pitch 11. (c) Copy the exercise line for line.

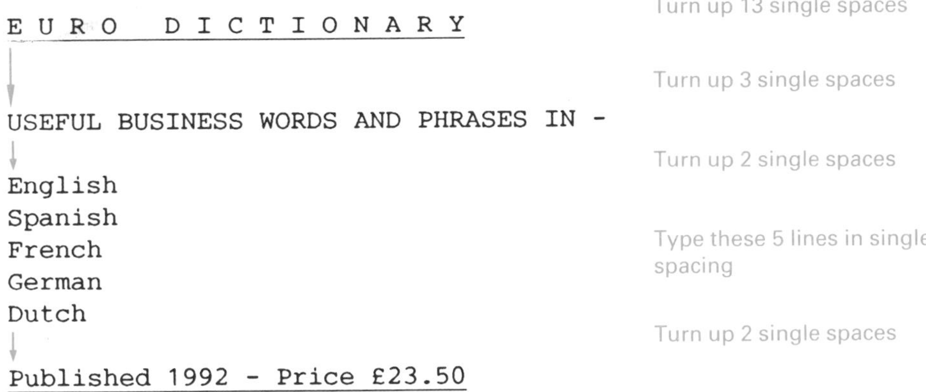

E U R O   D I C T I O N A R Y

USEFUL BUSINESS WORDS AND PHRASES IN -

English
Spanish
French
German
Dutch

Published 1992 - Price £23.50

Effective display

In certain cases a piece of display looks more attractive, and is more effective, when centred on the page. To do this, you will need to use the backspace key and follow the points given for horizontal centring on this page and vertical centring on the next page.

Backspace key

Refer to page 37 and locate the backspace key on your machine.

Horizontal centring—Blocked style

When centring a piece of display in the full width of the paper, take the following steps:

(a) See that the left edge of the paper is at 0 on the paper guide scale.
(b) Move margin stops to extreme left and right.
(c) Divide by two the total number of spaces between 0 and the scale point reached by the right-hand edge of paper; this gives the centre point of the paper.
(d) Bring carriage/carrier/cursor to the centre point.
(e) Locate the backspace key and backspace once for every two characters and spaces in the longest line. Ignore any odd letter left over.
(f) Set the left margin at the point reached.
(g) All lines in the exercise start at the left margin.

On electronic keyboards there is usually an automatic centring function which will centre the typed line when you press the appropriate key(s). To save time you can also use the automatic underline feature if your machine has this particular function.

3 Display the following notice on A5 landscape paper. (a) Leave 51 mm clear at the top of the page. (b) Centre the longest line horizontally. (c) Set the left margin and start all lines at this point.

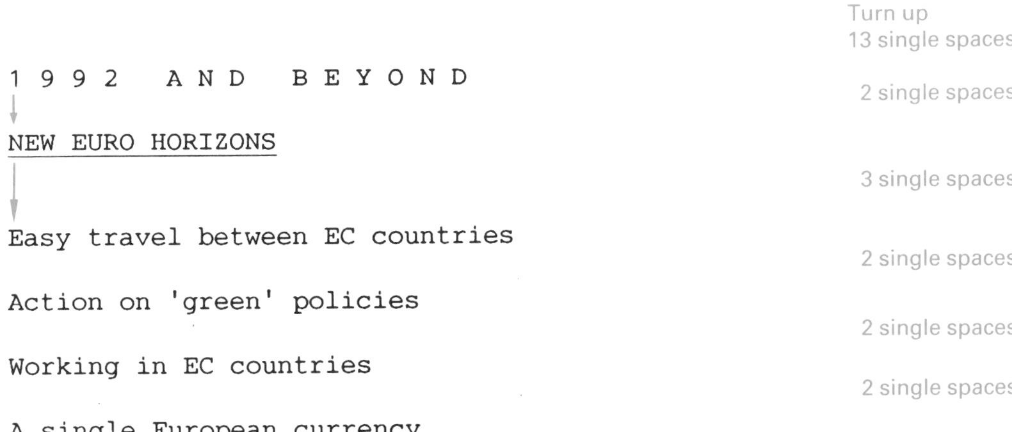

1 9 9 2   A N D   B E Y O N D

NEW EURO HORIZONS

Easy travel between EC countries

Action on 'green' policies

Working in EC countries

A single European currency

The left margin will be set at 12 pitch 34, 10 pitch 25.

Follow instructions given at top of page 42. Margins: 12 pitch 22–82, 10 pitch 12–72.

A Review alphabet keys

1 The thick haze over the lake meant that Jacques would not be expected to visit his good friends living nearby.

B Language arts—agreement of subject and verb
(See explanation on page 181)

2 The box of 12-pitch printwheels is no longer in that drawer.
3 Both the report and the letter are almost ready for posting.
4 Every name and address on the printout is being scrutinized.
5 Each boy and girl is ready to study the 'Electronic Office'.

Skill measurement *30 wpm* *4½ minutes* *Not more than 4 errors*

SM37 Before your employer leaves on a business trip, obtain from 12
her/him instructions as to what business or private letters 24
may be opened and what correspondence should be forwarded by 36
mail. If you decide to send on the actual letters, make a 47
copy of each as a safeguard against loss or damage in the 59
post. When posting, make sure that the envelope used is of 71
a suitable size and that it is addressed to the town your 83
employer will have reached by the time the letter arrives. 94

Mark the letter/package clearly TO AWAIT ARRIVAL, and state 106
your business address to which the letter should be returned 118
if not claimed within a certain time. You must also record 130
the date of posting mail. **(SI 1.35)** 135

1 | 2 | 3 | 4 | 5 | 6 | 7 | 8 | 9 | 10 | 11 | 12 |

Record your progress *4½ minutes*

R28 The storage medium used on a word processor (and some elec- 12
tronic typewriters) is referred to as a floppy disk or disk- 24
ette because it is made from flexible materials, as distinct 36
from hard disks which are much larger and used more in com- 48
puter memories. Floppy disks are usually 8 inch or 5¼ inch 60
in size (adequate for 120 and 75 A4 pages) and you can even 72
buy smaller ones known as minidisks. There are also single- 84
and double-density disks - the double-density disk will hold 96
more data. Disks are in a jacket-type cover. 105

When using a floppy disk, you will have a disk drive into 117
which you insert the disk. Inside the drive, the disk spins 129
at high speed and when keying in information, the data will 140
be transferred to the disk by a device called a head. This 151
head will also read data from the disk and transfer it to a 163
screen or thin window display. **(SI 1.38)** 169

1 | 2 | 3 | 4 | 5 | 6 | 7 | 8 | 9 | 10 | 11 | 12 |

Vertical centring

To centre matter vertically on a sheet of paper, take the following steps:
(a) Find the number of vertical single spaces on the paper.
(b) Count the number of lines and blank spaces between the lines in the exercise to be typed.
(c) Deduct (b) from (a).
(d) Divide answer in (c) by two to equalize top and bottom margins (ignore fractions).
(e) Insert paper with left edge at 0 on paper scale. See that the top edge of the paper is level with the alignment scale.
(f) Turn up the number of spaces arrived at in (d) PLUS ONE EXTRA SPACE.
NB Use your calculator as and when necessary.

Vertical centring using a VDU

If you have a VDU, use the reverse index (index up) to find the vertical starting point, in the following way: Move the cursor to the line for the vertical centre of the page.

A5 landscape—line 18; A5 portrait—line 25; A4 portrait—line 35.

TABLES IN DOUBLE SPACING

Press the **reverse index key** once for every line except the last one (ignore it).

TABLES IN SINGLE SPACING

Press the reverse index key once for every line and vertical space in the heading(s) and once for every two lines (including vertical spaces) in the body. If there is a single line left at the end, ignore it.

4 Display the following on A5 landscape paper. (a) Centre the notice vertically. The vertical spacing at the side of the notice and the calculation below are given as a guide. (b) Centre the longest line horizontally. (c) Set the left margin and start all lines at this point.

			Turn up
1	Line 1	P R E M I E R E T U I T I O N	
2	Space	↓	2 spaces
3	Line 2	offers	
4	Space	↓	3 spaces
5	Space		
6	Line 3	GERMAN/FRENCH/SPANISH LANGUAGE COURSES	2 spaces
7	Space	↓	
8	Line 4	Tailor-made to suit you	1 space
9	Line 5	Improve your career prospects	1 space
10	Line 6	Make the best of the Single Market	1 space
11	Line 7	For further information please telephone -	1 space
12	Line 8	081-602 0403	

The left margin will be set at 12 pitch 29, 10 pitch 20.

The calculations for the vertical centring in the above exercise are as follows:
(a) Number of lines on A5 landscape paper = 35
(b) Number of lines and spaces in exercise = 12
(c) Deduct (b) from (a) 35 − 12 = 23
(d) Divide answer in (c) by 2 for top and bottom margins (ignore fractions)
23 ÷ 2 = 11
(e) Turn up 12 single spaces and type the first line of the notice. As you wish to leave 11 clear spaces, it is necessary to turn up the extra space as you will type on the 12th line, so leaving 11 clear.

3 Type the following letter from Eastways Developments (UK) Ltd on A4 letterhead paper. (a) Margins: 12 pitch 22–82, 10 pitch 12–72. (b) Take a carbon copy. (c) Mark the letter PERSONAL.

Our ref MP/AC/102/(Yr initials)

(Insert tomorrow's date, then leave 10 lines clear for name & address to be inserted later.)

Dr (leave blank)

TRADE FAIR - LA FLECHE, FRANCE

We feel th the single European market presents us with our biggest challenge & an even bigger opportunity.

We are, therefore, taking part in a Trade Fair wh is being held in France in 4 months' time. [We require our stand at the fair to be staffed throughout the 10-day period with bilingual personnel who speak both French & German fluently.

I ~~understand~~ shd be glad if you wld let me hv details of any staff (, registered with yr agency,) who may be suitable. [I enclose full details of the T— F—.

Yrs sinc

MARKETING DIRECTOR

4 Type the following on A4 paper. (a) Single spacing. (b) Set a tab stop at 12 pitch 18, 10 pitch 15 for side headings. (c) Margins: 12 pitch 32–88, 10 pitch 29–72.

EUROPEAN FREE TRADE ASSOCIATION (EFTA) (Type side headings in the order indicated - but do not type the figures. Retain abbreviations.)

9-11 rue de Varembé 1211 Geneva 20 Switzerland

(2) OBJECTIVE EFTA's first objective was free trade (between its original member states). Its second objective was the creation of a single market, to include all western European countries, achieved through the free trade agreement.

(1) ESTABLISHED 3 May 1960

(3) MEMBER STATES Austria, Finland, Iceland, Norway, Switzerland and Sweden. In 1973 all the EFTA member states entered into a new relationship with the EC. Two - Denmark and the UK - withdrew from EFTA at the end of ~~December~~ November 1972 to become members of the EC on 1 January 1973.

(Leave 4 lines clear)

All EFTA and EC countries have co-operated in a successful attempt to simplify border formalities for trade in goods in Western Europe. lc

WP14

Create a new document (filename EFTA) and key in document 4 for 15-pitch printout. When you have completed this task, proofread (screenread) carefully and correct if necessary. Print out original and store on disk under filename EFTA. Follow the instructions for text editing on page 182.

Spaced capitals

To centre words that are to be typed in spaced capitals:
Say the letters and spaces in pairs, backspacing once for each complete pair, including once for the two extra spaces between words, eg, S space P space A space C space E space D space space space C space A space, etc. DO NOT backspace for the last letter of the final word.

S P A C E D   C A P I T A L S

Remember to leave three spaces between each word.

5 Display the following notice on A5 landscape paper. (a) Centre the whole notice vertically. (b) Centre the longest line horizontally.

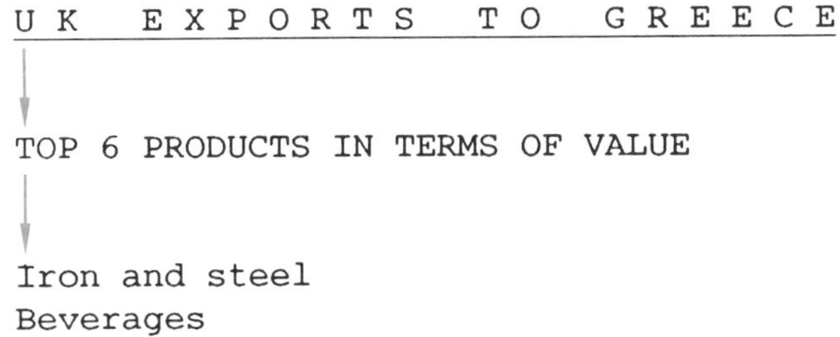

U K   E X P O R T S   T O   G R E E C E

Leave 2 clear spaces here, ie, turn up 3 single spaces

TOP 6 PRODUCTS IN TERMS OF VALUE

Leave 2 clear spaces here, ie, turn up 3 single spaces

Iron and steel
Beverages
Various manufactured goods
Road vehicles
Specialized machinery
Electrical machinery

6 Display the following notice on A5 portrait paper. (a) Centre the whole notice vertically. (b) Centre the longest line horizontally.

EC AND THE ENVIRONMENT

Leave 2 clear spaces here, ie, turn up 3 single spaces

C A M P A I G N I N G   I S S U E S

Leave 2 clear spaces here, ie, turn up 3 single spaces

Air pollution
Maintenance of woodlands
Sources of energy
Animal welfare
Greenhouse effect
Recycling of waste materials

7 Display exercise 1, on page 43, on A5 landscape paper. (a) Centre the whole notice vertically. (b) Centre the longest line horizontally.

8 Display exercise 2, on page 44, on A5 landscape paper. (a) Centre the whole notice vertically. (b) Centre the longest line horizontally.

Allocating space

In examinations and in business, you may be given instructions that will require you to leave a certain amount of blank space in a typewritten document for the insertion, at a later date, of further information. For example, you may be asked to leave room for the name and address of the addressee in a circular letter, to leave a specified top margin of, say, 51 mm (2 inches), or to leave a certain amount of space in the middle of a document for the later insertion of a diagram, photograph, etc.

In an examination, you will be told how much space to leave, either as a measurement, eg, leave 25 mm (one inch), or as a number of linespaces, eg, leave seven single lines clear.

It is important to remember that if an instruction states 'leave seven lines *clear*', you must turn up *one* extra space, ie, turn up eight single spaces and type on the eighth line, so leaving seven clear. If the instructions ask for a space of '*at least* 51 mm (2 inches)', it is wise to leave a little extra space rather than risk not leaving sufficient space. If the words 'at least' are not used, then the amount of space left must be exact.

2 Type the following on A4 paper. (a) Single spacing. (b) Margins: 12 pitch 22–82, 10 pitch 12–72.

(Leave a top margin of at least 51 mm.)

CHARLES DE GAULLE

1890 – 1970

Born in Lille in 1890, the second son of Henri de Gaulle, a teacher, Charles de Gaulle became a French General, Statesman + President of France.
(On ~~the~~ 7th April 1921 he married Yvonne Vendroux. They had a son + 2 daughters.

(Leave 10 single lines clear.)

During World War II de Gaulle (briefly) held the office of Under Secretary of State for War*, before escaping to England to organize French resistance as leader of the Free French Movement. He became President of France in Dec 1958 + was re-elected in 65. He opposed British entry to the EEC. // It is often said th there has not bn a leader of France since, with the charisma, power + authority of General Charles de Gaulle.

* During 1940.

Create a new document (filename GAUL) and key in document 2 for 12-pitch printout. When you have completed this task, proofread (screenread) carefully and correct if necessary. Print out original and store on disk under filename GAUL. Follow the instructions for text editing on page 182.

Following instructions given at top of page 42. Margins: 12 pitch 22–82, 10 pitch 12–72.

A Review alphabet keys

1 The exquisite butterflies flew past, and Kathy could see the amazing colours of jade, blue, and mauve on their wings.

B Build speed on fluency drills

2 Did for the key all dog why see you put car ask new her site
3 She did not see the new bus. Ask her for all the old shoes.
4 Tom has won the new car. Buy all the tea you can. See May.
5 Put out the cat and the dog now. You may see him for a day.

C Build speed on phrase drills

6 to me to go to ask to see to get to the to her to him to us.
7 I am to ask you to see if you can go to the game on Tuesday.
8 I will talk to him as soon as he is ready to go to the play.
9 In order to get to them, you must come to me for a road map.

D Improve control of up reaches

10 Ki kick kirk kite kind king skim skips taking asking napkin.
11 Aw awed laws saws paws yawn Shaw shawl crawls brawls straws.
12 He is taking the skips of straw to Crawley on Monday 3 June.

E Spelling skill *Correct the one misspelt word in each line. (Answer: page 181)*

13 guard recur queue pursue govern beleive tariff fulfil humour
14 modern cancell except access genius serial unique transferred
15 The video recorder was out on tempoary loan until Thursday.

Skill measurement *26 wpm One minute Not more than one error*

SM16 In spite of the rain all of us thought it had been an excel- 12
lent evening; but the guests could not travel till the storm 24
had passed. **(SI 1.15)** 26

1 | 2 | 3 | 4 | 5 | 6 | 7 | 8 | 9 | 10 | 11 | 12 |

Record your progress *One minute*

R11 Enclosed please find our price-lists. When you have studied 12
the range of goods, you will be amazed at the quality of the 24
vast majority of the articles. Our agent will keep in touch 36
and you may expect a visit. **(SI 1.31)** 41

1 | 2 | 3 | 4 | 5 | 6 | 7 | 8 | 9 | 10 | 11 | 12 |

Side headings

These headings are typed to the left of the set left margin. Side headings are usually typed in closed capitals with or without the underline, but lower case may also be used, with underlining.

The following steps should be taken:

(a) Set left and right margins.
(b) Type main heading and first paragraph (if any).
(c) From the left margin tap in once for each character and space in the longest line of the side headings, plus three extra spaces, and reset the left margin.
(d) Set a tab stop at the point where the left margin was originally set.
(e) To type the side headings, use the margin release and bring typing point to tab stop set in (d).

NOTE If you are using an electronic keyboard, you may have the facility for setting a second left margin, often referred to as an indent margin, instead of setting a tab stop.

1 Type the following on A4 paper. (a) Double spacing. (b) Margins: 12 pitch 28–88, 10 pitch 22–72. (c) Set a tab stop at 12 pitch 18, 10 pitch 12 for the side headings. (d) Correct the two circled errors.

WORKING IN THE EUROPEAN COMMUNITY

A British citizen can work in EC countrys without a work permit; all s/he needs is a valid passport. A visitors permit is not sufficient and the applicant needs a residence permit which should be obtained as soon as possible from the local authorities.

DENMARK It is difficult to find employment in Denmark unless you have a good knowledge of Danish, although most Danes do speak English.

BELGIUM It is not easy to find a job in Belgium because of a high unemployment rate. A knowledge of French is essential and Dutch an advantage. You must register at the local Town Hall within one week of arrival.

FRANCE A residence permit must be obtained from This is difficult to get unless you already hv a job arranged.

Please insert the information from the Data Files (filename WORK) on page 184.

Create a new document (filename WORK) and key in document 1 for 10-pitch printout. When you have completed this task, proofread (screenread) carefully and correct if necessary. Print out original and store on disk under filename WORK. Follow the instructions for text editing on page 182.

See Practical Typing Exercises, Book One, page 47, for further exercises on Side headings

Types of display headings

Main headings

The main heading, the title of a passage, is blocked at the left margin when using blocked display. Unless otherwise instructed, turn up seven single spaces, 25 mm (one inch), from the top edge of the paper before starting the main heading. It may be typed in:

(a) Closed capitals—leave one space between each word.
(b) Spaced capitals—leave one space between each letter and three spaces between each word.
(c) Lower case with initial capitals. To give greater emphasis, these headings should be underlined. The underline must not extend beyond the typing.
(d) Main headings may be underlined. Generally it is wise to follow the display indicated in the exercise to be copied.
(e) Bold print.

1 Type the following exercise on A5 landscape paper. (a) Single spacing. (b) Margins: 12 pitch 22–82, 10 pitch 12–72.

Turn up 7 single spaces

REPETITIVE STRAIN INJURY (RSI)

↓ Turn up 2 single spaces

Good posture is a very important habit to develop from the start of your typewriting training if you are to avoid strain. Make sure you are sitting comfortably, with your back supported and your feet flat on the floor.

↓ Turn up 2 single spaces

Always check that you are sitting centrally to the typewriter about a handspan away from the machine.

Subheadings

The main heading may be followed by a subheading which further clarifies the contents of the passage. Turn up two single spaces after typing the main heading and then type the subheading.

2 Type the following exercise on A5 landscape paper. (a) Single spacing. (b) Margin: 12 pitch 22–82, 10 pitch 12–72.

Turn up 7 single spaces

EUROPEAN ICE CREAM LEAGUE

↓ Turn up 2 single spaces

Do you like ice cream?

↓ Turn up 2 single spaces

Apparently our passion for ice cream far exceeds that of people living in hotter, sunnier climates. We eat twice as much as the Greeks and almost 3 times more than the Spanish. Only the Swedes and Danes eat more than the British.

↓ Turn up 2 single spaces

During 1990 ice cream consumption was 7.1 litres per head of the population.

See Practical Typing Exercises, Book One, page 4, for further exercises on

Follow instructions given at top of page 42. Margins: 12 pitch 22–82, 10 pitch 12–72.

A Review alphabet keys

1 The brightly coloured liquid was mixed in a jug and given to the lazy patient for sickness.

B Improve control of figure keys

2 aqla sw2s de3d fr4f fr5f hy6h ju7j ki8k lo9l ;p0; 1234 56789
3 The certificates were numbered 123/456/7890 and 489/267/134.
4 Find me invoices numbered: 9195, 19153, 59191, 27846, 72864.
5 24 May 1987, 30 June 1988, 17 July 1989, 15 May 1987, 6 June

C Language arts—agreement of subject and verb
(See explanation on page 181)

6 Keyboarding is the entering or keying in of text or numbers.
7 Function keys are special keys on most electronic keyboards.
8 You were our first employee when we started business in May.
9 He agrees with me, I agree with you, and they agree with us.

Skill measurement *30 wpm 4 minutes Not more than 4 errors*

SM36 Please note that as from 2 October there will be an increase 12
of 9% in air fares because of higher landing charges, a drop 24
in the value of sterling, and a surge in the price of fuel. 36

May we again remind you that you must comply with police and 48
immigration regulations at the points of arrival and depar- 60
ture and at any place along the route. Your journey may be 72
broken at most stops (except on package tours) with no extra 84
charge, provided you complete your journey within the dates 96
stated. As there are a number of formalities, the check-in 107
time quoted is the time you must register at the check-in 119
desk. **(SI 1.37)** 120

1 | 2 | 3 | 4 | 5 | 6 | 7 | 8 | 9 | 10 | 11 | 12 |

Record your progress *4 minutes*

R27 We were very glad to learn from your letter of 16 April that 12
the prospects we discussed when you visited us some 3 months 24
ago are now materializing. You inform us that you have pur- 36
chased a new truck for business purposes and that you intend 48
saving storage charges by housing it in your factory; doubt- 60
less you have calculated well and the truck will cut down on 72
your expenses. 75

Have your insurance brokers reviewed your policies since you 87
bought the truck? We do venture to suggest that you go over 99
your insurance cover with your brokers to make sure that you 111
have comprehensive protection. The fact that you have this 123
truck in your works may change the rates and may invalidate 135
the policies. **(SI 1.39)** 137

1 | 2 | 3 | 4 | 5 | 6 | 7 | 8 | 9 | 10 | 11 | 12 |

Paragraph headings

Apart from the main heading and the subheading at the beginning of a passage, paragraph headings are used to give emphasis to the first few words of a paragraph. In blocked style the paragraph heading starts at the left margin as in exercise 3 below. It may be typed in upper case, with or without underlining, or in lower case with underlining. The heading may be followed by a full stop and two spaces, or just the two spaces without the full stop, and may also run straight on into the following words of the paragraph but may be emphasized by using capitals, underlining, or bold print.

3 Type the following exercise on A5 portrait paper. (a) Single spacing. (b) Margins: 12 pitch 13–63, 10 pitch 6–56.
NOTE The figure in blue after the paragraph heading indicates the number of character spaces to be left and should not be typed.

Turn up 7 single spaces

TRAVELLING ABROAD

Turn up 2 single spaces

Duty-free Allowances

Turn up 2 single spaces

CUSTOMS CONTROLS 2 From 1 January 1993 customs checks were more or less removed. Spot checks will still be carried out to ensure that travellers are only bringing in to the country alcohol and tobacco products for personal use.

Turn up 2 single spaces

PERSONAL ALLOWANCES 2 One person is now allowed 120 bottles of wine, 10 litres of spirits, and 110 litres of beer, as well as 800 cigarettes, without being charged.

Blocked exercises typed in double spacing

NB If the text is typed in double spacing, it is wise, and easier for the reader, if an extra space, or spaces, is left after the headings. As stated on page 40, it may be easier for you to return twice on double, but three single spaces are equally acceptable.

4 Type the following exercise on A5 portrait paper. (a) Double spacing. (b) Margins: 12 pitch 13–63, 10 pitch 6–56.

Turn up 7 single spaces

T O W N   T W I N N I N G

EXCHANGE TRIPS

Turn up 2 double spaces

Town twinning has, over the years, given many people the opportunity of experiencing a culture and lifestyle very different from their own.

Turn up 2 double spaces

Young people, particularly, benefit enormously from these exchange trips.

In addition to the horizontal lines, a boxed table has vertical lines and the left and right sides may or may not be closed in by vertical lines. The vertical lines between the columns must be ruled exactly in the middle of each blank space. It is therefore advisable to leave an odd number of spaces between the columns—one for the vertical ruling and an equal number on either side of the ruling. If the outside verticals are to be ruled, the horizontal lines must extend two spaces to the left and right of the typed matter.

To rule the vertical lines, take the following steps:

(a) First set left margin and tab stops.
(b) From the last tab stop, tap space bar once for each character and space in the longest line of the last column plus two spaces, and set right margin at point reached.
(c) After typing main heading and subheading (if there is one), turn up two single spaces and return carriage to left margin.
(d) Press margin release key and backspace two. This gives you the starting point for the horizontal lines which will extend to the right margin.
(e) Move to first tab stop and backspace two; at this point make a pencil mark for the first vertical line.
(f) Move to the next tab stop and backspace two; at this point make a pencil mark for the second vertical line.
(g) Continue in the same way for any additional columns.
(h) When you have typed the last horizontal line, mark in pencil the bottom of each of the vertical lines.
(i) Horizontal lines may be ruled by underscore and the vertical lines in matching colour ink.
(j) Do not allow the vertical lines to extend above or below the horizontal lines: they must meet precisely.

NOTE When marking the top of the vertical lines, make a note of the scale points at which they have to be drawn so that when you have typed the bottom horizontal line, you will know exactly where to make the pencil marks.

7 Type the following table on A5 landscape paper. (a) Centre the table vertically and horizontally on the paper. (b) Leave three spaces between columns. (c) Rule horizontal lines by underscore and vertical lines in ink.

GROSS NATIONAL PRODUCT (GNP)

<u>Per capita</u>

Country	GNP ($)	Currency
The Netherlands	9 190	Guilder
Portugal	2 055	Escudo
Spain	4 237	Peseta
Italy		
Denmark	11 020	Krone

Typist - You will find the information for Italy in the Data Files, page 183, (filename GNP). Please insert it here.

8 Type the following table on A5 landscape paper. (a) Centre the table vertically and horizontally on the paper. (b) Leave three spaces between columns. (c) Rule horizontal lines by underscore and vertical lines in ink.

EUROPEAN ECONOMIC INDICATORS - 1991

	Inflation	Interest rates	Unemployment
	%	%	%
France	3.5	9.1	9.4
Germany	4.4	9.1	6.3
Spain	5.9	12.8	15.9

See Practical Typing Exercises, Book One, pages 45–46, for further exercises on

Shoulder headings

When this form of heading is used, it is typed at the left margin and may be in closed capitals, lower case with initial capitals, and/or bold print. Lower case headings should be underlined. The shoulder heading is preceded and followed by one blank line when using single spacing. When using double spacing, it is preceded by two or three blank lines and followed by one.

5 Type a copy of the following on A5 landscape paper. (a) Blocked paragraphs. (b) Single spacing. (c) Margins: 12 pitch 22–82, 10 pitch 12–72.

E U R O T U N N E L

Turn up 2 single spaces

The Channel Tunnel

Turn up 2 single spaces

COMPLETION

Turn up 2 single spaces

It is planned that the Channel Tunnel will be completed in June 1993. This will enable users to travel, in comfort, from the terminal in England to the terminal in France in approximately 35 minutes.

Turn up 2 single spaces

CONVENIENCE

Turn up 2 single spaces

It should be possible to take a train from London and arrive in Paris approximately 3½ hours later on the same train.

6 Type a copy of the following on A5 portrait paper. (a) Blocked paragraphs. (b) Double spacing. (c) Margins: 12 pitch 13–63, 10 pitch 6–56.

T H E   P R I N C E ' S   T R U S T

Turn up 1 double space

8 BEDFORD ROW, LONDON, WC1R 4BA

Turn up 2 double spaces

Grant Aid

Turn up 1 double space

The Prince's Trust has established a new form of grant for those under 26 and out of full-time education.

Turn up 2 double spaces

Inter-European Projects

Turn up 1 double space

Grants will be given for projects in the fields of crafts, design, communications, new technology, tourism, and the environment.

Turn up 2 double spaces

Amount

Turn up 1 double space

The grants range widely up to £10 000.

See Practical Typing Exercises, Book One, page 7, for further exercises on

Blocked tabulation—Horizontal ruling

A neat and pleasing appearance may be given to column work by ruling in ink or by the use of the underscore key. An 'open' table has no ruled lines, its main use is for displayed columns of items in the body of a letter or report. A 'ruled' table has the column headings separated from the column items by horizontal lines above and below the headings, and below the last line in the table.

When typing a ruled table proceed as follows:

(a) Find vertical starting point by calculating number of typed lines and spaces—remember to count the horizontal lines.
(b) In the usual way, backspace to find the left margin.
(c) From the last tab stop, tap space bar once for each character and space in the longest line of the last column, and set right margin at point reached.
(d) Type main heading and subheading (if there is one) at left margin. Turn up two single spaces and return carriage to left margin.
(e) Type underscore from margin to margin.
(f) Remember to turn up TWICE after and ONCE before a horizontal line.

5 Type the following table on A5 landscape paper. (a) Use blocked style and centre table vertically and horizontally on the paper. (b) Leave three spaces between columns. (c) Insert leader dots. (d) Rule by underscore.

Line 1	EUROPEAN HOLIDAYS		
Space			
Line 2	________________	________________	________________
Space			
Line 3	Country	Date	Holiday
Line 4	________________	________________	________________
Space			
Line 5	Belgium ...	11 November	Armistice Day
Line 6	Netherlands	30 April	Queen's Birthday
Line 7	Spain	25 July	St James's Day
Line 8	________________	________________	________________

NOTE Do NOT underline column headings in a ruled table

Blocked tabulation with columns of figures

When columns in a table contain figures, care must be taken to see that units come under units, tens under tens, etc. Where there are four or more figures, these are grouped in threes starting from the unit figure, a space being left between each group. When typing blocked tabulation, the £ symbol is placed above the first figure in the longest line.

6 Display the following table on A5 landscape paper in blocked style. (a) Centre vertically and horizontally on the paper. (b) Leave three spaces between columns and rule by underscore. (c) Insert leader dots.

TURNOVER

1990-1992

Goods	1990	1991	1992
	£	£	£
Computer supplies	1 985 240	995 985	1 172 248
Furniture	3 112 300	4 002 755	4 384 973
Accessories	998 275	992 831	883 467

Follow instructions given at top of page 42. Margins: 12 pitch 22–82, 10 pitch 12–72.

A Review alphabet keys

1 The examination was very difficult for the lazy boy who just
managed to complete the first question; but unfortunately he
did not gain many marks.

B Review hyphen key

2 full-time, up-to-date, blue-grey, 48-page, re-cover, co-opt.
3 Full-time students wore pin-striped blue-grey ties. He considered that the up-to-date 248-page document was now ready.

C Build accuracy on punctuation review

4 "Is John - John Mann, not John Green – here, please?" "No."
5 I think (in fact I'm sure) that Mrs Laing will arrive today.
6 Send me the documents immediately; I cannot wait any longer.
7 Call me tomorrow. May I borrow 3 or 4 books? Ask Mrs Tait.
8 We require: 2 daisywheels, 6 carbon ribbons, 10 small disks.

D Improve control of out reaches

9 Ga game gape gave gates gales garlic galley baggage Algarve.
10 Up upon sups cups upset soups couple duplex couplet superior
11 The superior baggage belongs to the couple going to Reigate.

E Spelling skill *Correct the one misspelt word in each line. (Answer: page 181)*

12 quay basic weird losing prefer mislaid necessery acknowledge
13 paid weigh truley height eighth ascends recommend sufficient
14 I will definitely recommend that they alter this stationary.

Skill measurement *26 wpm* *1½ minutes* *Not more than 2 errors*

SM17 As a good typist you must be fast, accurate, and able to set 12
out all kinds of documents. In your first post there may be 24
some forms of layout that are not clear. If that is so, you 36
may need help. **(SI 1.18)** 39

1 | 2 | 3 | 4 | 5 | 6 | 7 | 8 | 9 | 10 | 11 | 12 |

Record your progress *1½ minutes*

R12 Dear Hazel, It is exactly 6 months since you moved from this 12
Sales Office to join our Accounts Section; therefore, as you 24
now qualify for a transfer and your work is highly regarded, 36
we would be happy to discuss the future with you. May I see 48
you one day soon? **(SI 1.31)** 51

1 | 2 | 3 | 4 | 5 | 6 | 7 | 8 | 9 | 10 | 11 | 12 |

Leader dots

(a) Leader dots (full stops) are used to guide the eye from one column to another. There are four methods of grouping but, for the moment, we will use only continuous leader dots.

(b) Leader dots must be typed at the same time as you type the horizontal line to which they apply.

(c) There must always be one clear space between the last word and the first dot and between the last dot and the vertical line, ie, leader dots must never be typed close up to the preceding or following word or line. No word or letter must be allowed to extend beyond the last leader dot, although leader dots may extend beyond the last word.

(d) Leader dots must always finish at the same point on every line, although the longest line may not have any leader dots—all dots on the other lines finish at the last letter of the longest line.

(e) In the exercises below, the leader dots finish at the last letter of the longest line and, to ensure that you do not type them beyond this point, tab in to the tab stop *after* the leader dots and backspace once for each space between columns, plus one. Then type one full stop. This will be the last leader dot. The others can be filled in when you have completed the details up to this point. Remember to leave one space before typing the first leader dot.

3 Type the following on A5 portrait paper. (a) Centre vertically and horizontally. (b) Insert leader dots between first and second columns. (c) Retain all abbreviations.

MEMBERS OF THE EUROPEAN PARLIAMENT (MEPs)*

Elected every 5 years
Parliament held in Strasbourg

NUMBER OF MEPs PER COUNTRY ← (underline)

Country	Number
Belgium	24
Denmark	16
Germany	81
France	81
Greece	24
The Republic of Ireland	15

(TYPIST: Double spacing for the table, please.)

* 434 Members

4 Type the following on A5 landscape paper. (a) Centre vertically and horizontally. (b) Insert leader dots.

SINGLE MARKET MEASURES (TYPIST – Retain all abbreviations)

National Legislation

Description	Ref No	Date (1)
Food for particular nutritional uses	89/398	16/5/91
Official control of foodstuffs	89/397	20/6/91
Lawnmower noise (2)	88/180	1/7/91
Flavourings	88/388	22/6/91
Fruit juices	89/394	14/6/91

(Double spacing)

(1) Date of implementation
(2) Cylinder motors

Create a new document (filename LEG) and key in document 4 for 15-pitch printout. When you have completed this task, proofread (screenread) carefully and correct if necessary. Print out original and store on disk under filename LEG. Follow the instructions for text editing on page 182.

See Practical Typing Exercises, Book One, page 43, for further exercises on

Personal letters

As the name implies, these are written by you to personal friends and it is acceptable practice today to type them, except in very personal circumstances such as a special birthday or anniversary. If you are not using stationery with your home address printed on it, then type on a plain sheet of paper and place your address about 13 mm (half an inch) from the top of the page and block each line at the left margin. After the last line of your address, turn up two single spaces and type the date. After the date, turn up two singles and type the salutation; turn up two singles and start the first paragraph. From the example below, you will see that all lines start at the left margin—this is called **fully-blocked**, or **blocked**, style.

An example is given below in **fully-blocked** style. It is also in **open punctuation**, which means, that there is no punctuation in the sender's address, date or salutation (Dear Collette), nor in the complimentary close (Yours sincerely). When the recipient is not familiar with your handwriting, it is a good plan to type your name five single-line spaces below the complimentary close. If you wish to give your personal letter a more intimate tone, handwrite the salutation (Dear George, Mary, etc) and the complimentary close (Sincerely, Love, Kindest regards, etc) and add a handwritten friendly message at the end.

Certain **formal personal letters** will be a little more reserved. When writing to a person much older than yourself, or to whom you owe respect, or with whom you are not on familiar terms, the salutation and complimentary close would be more formal.

1 Type the following formal personal letter on plain A5 portrait paper. (a) Use margins of 12 pitch 13–63, 10 pitch 5–56. (b) Leave one clear space between the two halves of the postcode. (c) Follow the layout and capitalization precisely.

Turn up 4 single spaces

Sender's home address

27 Bridge Street
FOLKESTONE
Kent
CT20 1BR

Turn up 2 single spaces

22 January 1993

Turn up 2 single spaces

Dear Collette

Turn up 2 single spaces

I was very pleased to hear from my daughter, Lucy, that you have invited her to stay with you and your daughter, Monique, at your home in France for 2 weeks during the summer school holiday.

Turn up 2 single spaces

Lucy is taking her GCE 'A' Level examination in French next year and it will be a great help to her to be able to speak French while staying with you. I do hope Monique will be able to visit us next year.

Turn up 2 single spaces

Yours sincerely

Turn up 5 single spaces

EMMA ROGERS

Blocked tabulation with single-line column headings

Refer to Unit 38, pages 79 to 82 for the method to be used when arranging items in columns.

Footnotes

Refer to Unit 46, page 120, for the method to be used when typing footnotes.
NOTE It is not usual to type a line above the footnote when it occurs in a table.

1 Type the following on A5 landscape paper. (a) Centre the whole table vertically and horizontally. (b) Leave three spaces between columns. (c) Follow the linespacing shown.

F A S T   F A C T S

below,/ If you require information on any of the products listed fax us on 021-247 0102.

Item No	Fax No	Software*	Notes
2030	101	Spreadsheets	
2031	106	Presentation Graphics	
2032	103	Desktop Publishing - DTP)	Free training given
2033	105	Windows Software)	
2034	104	Electronic Mail)	
2035	102	Databases	

trs/ * For information on Hardware, contact 021-247 1002

2 Type the following on A4 paper. (a) Centre the whole table vertically and horizontally. (b) Leave three spaces between columns. (c) Follow the linespacing shown.

INTERNATIONAL DIALLING CODES

All UK customers have access to International Direct Dialling (IDD) and dial direct to numbers on most exchanges in 200 countries worldwide.*

Country	IDD Code from UK	IDD Code to UK
France	010 33	19 (p) 44‡
Belgium	010 36	00 (p) 44
Italy	010 39 }	00 44
Luxembourg	010 352 }	
Greece	010 30 }	
Portugal	010 351 }	
Spain	010 34	07 (p) 44

TYPIST: Please check the IDD Code from the UK to Belgium. You will find it in the Telephone Directory.

current/ * Details of international telephone charges can be obtained from the International Operator - 155.

‡ (p) indicates a pause in dialling is necessary whilst waiting for a second tone.

See Practical Typing Exercises, Book One, pages 41–42, for further exercises on

Personal business letter

The personal business letter, which you write to an organization or individual about a personal business matter, is displayed in the same way as the formal personal letter on the previous page, but with one addition: the name and address of the addressee (the organization or person to whom you are writing) is inserted and starts on the second single-line space after the date; then turn up two spaces and type the salutation. When typing her name at the end, a lady may, if she wishes, add the word Mrs, Miss, or Ms (in brackets) after her name.

2 Type the following personal business letter on plain A5 portrait paper. (a) Use margins of 12 pitch 13–63, 10 pitch 6–56. (b) Type the letter in fully-blocked style with open punctuation. (c) Follow layout and capitalization precisely.

Turn up 4 single spaces

Sender's home address

67 Brayton Lane
Eglinton
GLASGOW
G41 5QE

Turn up 2 single spaces

26 January 1993

Turn up 2 single spaces

Name and address of addressee

Kenkott Scotia PLC
Byrnes Terrace
Langside
GLASGOW
G41 3DI

Turn up 2 single spaces

Dear Sirs

Turn up 2 single spaces

I am returning a pair of slippers that was bought for me as a present at Christmas. Unfortunately, the slippers are marked only in the continental size of 39 which, I understand, is size 5½ to 6. As I am size 5 (British measurement), they are, consequently, too large.

I should be glad, therefore, if you would please exchange them for the correct size.

Turn up 2 single spaces

Yours faithfully

Turn up 5 single spaces

Camilla Abbott (Mrs)

Turn up 2 single spaces

Enc

3 Type the following letter on a sheet of plain A5 portrait paper. Use margins of 12 pitch 13–63, 10 pitch 6–56. The letter is from Mrs Camilla Abbott to Kenkott Scotia PLC; therefore, apart from the date, which should be 17 February 1993, follow layout and wording in the letter above as far as the salutation, then type the following:

I wrote to you on 26 January returning a pair of slippers and asking for a replacement pair, in a size 5.

So far I have not even had an acknowledgement of my letter. I look forward to hearing from you by return.

Type the complimentary close and Mrs Abbott's name as in the letter in exercise 2 above.

See Practical Typing Exercises, Book One, page 8, for further exercises on Personal business letters

Follow instructions given at top of page 42. Margins: 12 pitch 22–82, 10 pitch 12–72.

A Review alphabet keys

1 The pretty girl gave a cry of terror as those ravens quickly seized the jewels from the box.

B Improve control of double-letter words

2 programmes possible running supply arrive proof agrees added
3 difficult football baggage accept excess rubber attend carry
4 Is it possible to supply a proof of the football programmes?
5 We agree that it was difficult to accept the excess baggage.

C Improve control of jump reaches

6 cr cry crop crush crown creep crash secret concrete decrease
7 ni nib nice niece night ninth niche united finished animated
8 Before nightfall I finished mixing the concrete we required.
9 My niece told me that the United Club held a secret meeting.

D Language arts—use of apostrophe *(See explanation on page 181)*

10 Mary's mother spent 2 weeks' holiday at her niece's cottage.
11 It's time that the bird was released from its new enclosure.
12 Remember that the word 'accommodation' has 2 c's and 2 m's.
13 She said, 'I don't think we will have time to call tonight.'

Skill measurement 30 wpm 3½ minutes Not more than 4 errors

SM35 You get basic tax relief on most mortgages by paying less to 12
the society who lent you the money, so no allowance is made 24
in your code. If you pay higher rate tax, your code will be 36
adjusted to give the extra relief due. If you pay interest 48
in full on mortgages or other loans for such things as home 60
improvements, an estimate of the amount of interest payable 72
will be given in your code. If you have a mortgage on prop- 84
erty that you let for a commercial rent (during 6 months of 95
each year) interest will be allowed as a deduction. **(SI 1.33)** 105

1 | 2 | 3 | 4 | 5 | 6 | 7 | 8 | 9 | 10 | 11 | 12 |

Record your progress 3½ minutes

R26 The number of guide cards used and their arrangement depend 12
on the filing system; however, the purpose of the guide card 24
is the same in all systems: to guide the eye when filing and 36
finding papers, and to support the folders. Guide cards can 48
be bought in all standard sizes, as well as for special sys- 60
tems such as fingerprint, medical, and insurance classifica- 72
tions. Most guide cards have a tab along the top edge, and 84
the space contains a plain and clear reference to the folder 96
behind. It is important that this reference should be easy 107
to read, and the marker show the exact order of the folders. 119
These cards, quite rightly, justify their existence. **(SI 1.36)** 129

1 | 2 | 3 | 4 | 5 | 6 | 7 | 8 | 9 | 10 | 11 | 12 |

Letters are ambassadors and advertisements for the organization that sends them; therefore, you must ensure that your letters are well displayed and faultlessly typed. Businesses have a variety of forms of display, and the examples that follow are in fully-blocked style with open punctuation, which you used in the letters on the previous pages.

A business organization will always have paper with a printed letterhead and you should turn up a minimum of two single-line spaces after the last line of the printed heading before starting to type. The originator (writer or author) of a business letter will also have a reference at the top and this, in its simplest form, consists of the initials of the writer followed by an oblique and the typist's initials. It is also accepted practice, but by no means essential, to type the originator's name five single spaces after the complimentary close, with her/his designation (official position) typed underneath on the next line.

4 Type the following letter on A4 letterhead paper which will be found in the *Handbook, Solutions, and Resource Material.* (a) Use margins of 12 pitch 22–82, 10 pitch 12–72. (b) Follow the layout and capitalization given.

Printed heading

KENKOTT SCOTIA PLC

Registered Office: Byrnes Terrace Langside GLASGOW G41 3DI

Registered Number: 76558 (Scotland) Telephone: 041-486 2907 Telex: 23398 FAX: 041-486 4843

Turn up 2 single spaces

Our Ref FE/BWP

3 February 1993

Mr Stuart Hyde
Hotel Continental
Main Street
GLASGOW
G10 9PG

Dear Mr Hyde

Thank you for your letter dated 28 January in which you stated that you wished to call at our Glasgow offices and discuss the possibility of purchasing some of our British made furniture.

If convenient to you, Glen Mackintosh, our Sales Manager, would be free to see you on Tuesday 1 March at 1100 hours. He would be pleased to show you our products and offer his advice. I hope you will be able to join us for lunch on that day.

Please let us know if the suggested date and time are convenient to you.

Yours sincerely

Turn up 5 single spaces

F EMERSON
Sales Director

LOS ARENALES DEL SOL
EL ALTET (ALICANTE PROVINCE) SPAIN

Typist – please retype neatly, correcting the 5 errors.

Spain has many attractive coasts, but among the most beautiful is the Costa Blanca - "The White Coast" - and just south of Alicante you will find the finest beach of all at Los Arenales del Sol: the dunes in the sun!

1 There is a broad arc of golden sand stretching around the bay towards Alicante just 10 killometres (approximately 6 miles) away.

2 Los Arenales has remained unspoiled and strict controls by the Spanish goverment make sure that it will stay that way.

3 There is no hotels, but there are 3 supermarkets and a number of smaller shops such as a farmacia (chemist), a butcher and a great many cafés and restaurants.

4 Barlovento Playa is a residential developement seperated from the beach by the coast road only. There are 2 blocks of apartments* and 10 bungalows built on naturally terraced ground.

---

* The majority of buildings are 6-storey blocks of flats.

Document 6 *Production target—10 minutes*

HAYLOCK + FELLOWS EUROPE
24 Main Street Newport Shropshire

TELEPHONE – Newport (0952) 655128

BARLOVENTO PLAYA – SPAIN

a private housing estate:

FLATS AND BUNGALOWS ← spaced caps

Swimming Pool ↑ Rooftop Garden
leave 3 clear spaces

Prices from £30 000

Follow instructions given at top of page 42. Margins: 12 pitch 22–82, 10 pitch 12–72.

A Review alphabet keys

1 An extract from the magazine on the technique of painting in oils was requested by the majority of folk who were revising art.

B Improve control of shift key

2 Dear Sir, Yours faithfully, Mr J Brown, New York, Hong Kong.
3 Dear Mr Brown, Dear Mrs Green, Miss R Grey, Miss Jean R Dua.
4 Advanced Word Processing and the Electronic Office, by Joyce
5 and Derek Stananought is available from McGraw-Hill Book Co.

Figures

In a great many instances there are no spaces or commas in a group of four or more figures (see page 40—**Amounts in figures**). Examples of these are: reference numbers, telephone numbers and telephone codes, overseas postcodes, street numbers, the year, invoice and account numbers, insurance policy numbers, cheque numbers, etc.

C Improve control of figure keys

6 ewe 323 woe 293 our 974 rye 463 you 697 tour 5974 writ 2485.
7 Type 1 and 2 and 3 and 4 and 15 and 16 and 17 and 80 and 90.
8 Drill: 10, 29, 38, 47, 56, 123, 456, 789, 010, 343, 678, 86.
9 Accounts: 00-11-2345, 00-12-6789, 00-13-5858, 00-14-2679-80.

D Improve control of jump reaches

10 Ve five live jive dive even vein pave have rave valve events
11 On lone zone cone tone hone bone fond only once bonus lesson
12 Five of these events have a once only bonus for the winners.

E Spelling skill *Correct the one misspelt word in each line. (Answer: page 181)*

13 cheque usable curser buffet format liaison referred business
14 debtor wholly reigns hungry choose develope exercise received
15 Choose 2 of the exercises referred to by my liason officer.

Skill measurement *26 wpm* *2 minutes* *Not more than 2 errors*

SM18 Last May we had a chance to buy a large stock of fine cotton 12
sheets, and we are now selling these at a reduced price. If 24
your own stock of sheets is low, now is the chance to obtain 36
some of these goods at half price or less. Send an order by 48
July at the latest. **(SI 1.13)** 52

1 | 2 | 3 | 4 | 5 | 6 | 7 | 8 | 9 | 10 | 11 | 12 |

Record your progress *2 minutes*

R13 As requested, I give below the pay scales objected to at our 12
last 2 meetings. May I say that I am still quite puzzled by 24
the large increases suggested, and I feel that the new rates 36
should not be made effective at the present time. May I ask 48
you not to inform your staff before we next meet. **(SI 1.26)** 58

1 | 2 | 3 | 4 | 5 | 6 | 7 | 8 | 9 | 10 | 11 | 12 |

Document 3 Production target—25 minutes

FACSIMILE MESSAGE
Please advise immediately if transmission is incomplete or unclear

(Typist - leave one space clear)

To Fax No 010 34 65 688077 From John Brown

Name Antonio Santamaria Date Today's

SUBJECT AGENCIES*

(Please enter their address. You will find it in the Data Files (filename FAX) on page 183.)

Your fax dated Yesterday's date

Our agencies are as follows:

NAME	ADDRESS	TELEPHONE
DUBOIS & CIE		+ 33 61 94 12 15
KUNZE & WILDT	Berliner Str 89 5000 COLOGNE 90 Germany	+ 49 221 74 38 39 59
TORTORELLA Spa	Corso Europa 11 Modena 18012 Italy	+ 39 59 71 82 93

* Appointments recently made

Document 4 Production target—15 minutes

From Nigel Grant-Gough
To Richard Williams
Date

BARLOVENTO PLAYA

Mr & Mrs J Clark of Newport, Shropshire, hv. reserved apartment 6A in block 2 on the Barlovento site. I hv. quoted them £83 333 (this is based on today's exchange rate of 180 pesetas to the £ sterling) but if they offer less, I think Llopia, SA may be prepared to drop to £80 000. [As I sh. be in Bristol for a conference next week, I leave the decisions to you; however, remember to check the exchange rate before quoting in sterling! [I am attaching all the relevant papers.

NGG/yr initials

1 Type the following fully-blocked letter in open punctuation, from Kenkott Scotia PLC, on A4 letterhead paper. (See *Handbook, Solutions, and Resource Material.*) (a) Margins: 12 pitch 22–82, 10 pitch 12–72. (b) At this elementary stage in your learning process, keep to the spacing and layout indicated.
NB For an explanation of the numbered items see pages 59 and 60.

1 Reference	Our ref PP/BWW	
		Turn up 2 single spaces
2 Date	22 February 1993	
		Turn up 2 single spaces
4 Name and address of addressee	Mr C Archer P F Archer PLC Rosebank Industrial Estate Kirkintilloch GLASGOW G66 1JY	
		Turn up 2 single spaces
5 Salutation	Dear Sir	
		Turn up 2 single spaces
7 Body of letter	As suppliers of office equipment we do know that some com- panies may not be aware of the new legal requirements for the installation and operation of office machinery.	
		Turn up 2 single spaces
	We are taking the liberty of enclosing a leaflet which gives brief details of these EC Directives. If you would like a member of our staff to visit you and give further informa- tion, please let me know.	
		Turn up 2 single spaces
8 Complimentary close	Yours faithfully	Turn up 5 single spaces
10 Signatory	A TOMLINSON	Turn up 1 single space
11 Designation	Chief Executive	
		Turn up minimum of 2 single spaces
12 Enclosure	Enc	

2 Type the following fully-blocked letter in open punctuation, from Kenkott Scotia PLC, on A4 letterhead paper. (See *Handbook, Solutions, and Resource Material.*) (a) Margins: 12 pitch 22–82, 10 pitch 12–72. (b) The details, as far as the salutation, are exactly as those given in the letter above. (c) After typing the salutation, turn up two single spaces and type the following paragraphs.

I refer to my letter mailed to you this morning.

We have received, by this afternoon's post, further EC
Directives covering the use of office machinery, and are
enclosing these.

Obviously it would be wise to take professional advice on
these new regulations. We shall be pleased to help you.

(d) The complimentary close, etc, is the same as in the letter above.

See Practical Typing Exercises, Book One, page 10, for further exercises on

TYPIST – PLEASE INSERT THE HANDWRITTEN DETAILS ON TO A SKELETON FORM.

HAYLOCK & FELLOWS EUROPE
Estate Agents
24 Main Street NEWPORT Shropshire United Kingdom TF10 5JH

APPLICATION FOR OVERSEAS PROPERTY

Name of applicant John CLARK .... ~~Mrs~~/Mr/~~Miss/Ms~~*

Hilary CLARK .... Mrs/~~Mr/Miss/Ms~~*

Present address Please take from document 1 ....

.... Postcode ....

Telephone number: Home 0952 820120 Business ....

Address of property you wish to buy Avenida Madrid 14

Los Arenales del Sol EL ALTET (Alicante Province)

SPAIN

Type of property you wish to buy apartment – 3 bedrooms and

2 bathrooms

.... Price quoted £83 333

Name and address of your bank National Bank 12 Main Street

NEWPORT Shropshire TF10 7BW

I/We will pay in sterling/pesetas* (Typist – delete I and the oblique. The Clarks wil pay in sterling)

Signature(s) ....

Date Today's date

* Delete as applicable
The information supplied above is for general guidance only and does not form part of any legal contract

3 Type the following fully-blocked letter in open punctuation, from Kenkott Scotia PLC, on A5 letterhead paper. (a) Margins: 12 pitch 13–63, 10 pitch 6–56. (b) Insert today's date. NB For an explanation of item number 6, see page 60.

NOTE Use of lower case for typist's initials

Our ref BD/ofh

Turn up 2 single spaces

Ms R Panting
Paxwell Press
Bank Avenue
NEWTON ABBOT
Devon
TW12 5NA

Turn up 2 single spaces

Dear Ms Panting

Turn up 2 single spaces

6 Subject heading

RECYCLED PAPER

Turn up 2 single spaces

We wish to order further supplies of stationery from you, but feel that we should this year use recycled paper.

Consequently, before we send you our usual order, can you forward quotes for A4 and A5 letterhead paper, as well as envelopes, using recycled paper.

Yours sincerely

BARBARA DOWLING (MRS)
Office Manager

4 Type the following letter from Kenkott Scotia PLC on A5 letterhead paper. (a) Margins: 12 pitch 13–63, 10 pitch 6–56. (b) Insert today's date and enclosure notation.

Ref PR/Acc/9281

Mr E R Jacklaus JP
13 Church Avenue
COLCHESTER
Essex
CO4 5BE

Dear Mr Jacklaus

ACCOUNT NO 02864

We wish to acknowledge receipt of your cheque for £153.95 to cover the amount outstanding on your Account No 02864.

As requested, we enclose our latest catalogue, and look forward to your continued custom.

Yours sincerely

NOTE Remember to type the enclosure notation

ACCOUNTS DEPARTMENT

See Practical Typing Exercises, Book One, page 11, for further exercises on

Ref NG-G/*yr initials*

Today's date

Typist - carbon copy + envelope, please. I hv indicated those abbreviations to be typed in full by inserting a full stop after them.

Mr J and Mrs H Clark
22 Wyndham St.
NEWPORT
Shropshire
TF10 7BW

Dear Mr & Mrs C——

Thank you for calling to see me about buying an apartment on the Spanish Costa Blanca and for giving me such a clear picture of yr. requirements.

We are agents for Llopia, SA of Alicante and give below details of a residential estate now being built in the sea-side resort of Los Arenales del Sol which is 10 km (approx. 6 miles) south of the city of Alicante.

Inset 5 spaces

1 This residential development is known as Barlovento Playa.

2 There are 10 bungalows *apartments* and 2 blocks of apartments - ea. block has 12 ~~flats~~, and the front balcony of ea. ~~apartment~~ faces the sea. *DS*

I hope that the information given on the encl. sheets will clarify the explanation I gave you earlier today. *NP* [I shd. be glad if you wd. both sign the encl. application form and return it to me as soon as you can.

Yrs. sinc.

NIGEL GRANT-GOUGH
Overseas Dept.

5 Type the following letter from Kenkott Scotia PLC on A4 letterhead paper. (a) Margins: 12 pitch 22–84, 10 pitch 12–74.

NB For an explanation of the numbered items, see pages 59 and 60.

Ref RAB/4PU/MA

Turn up 2 single spaces

8 March 1993

Turn up 2 single spaces

3 Special mark FOR THE ATTENTION OF NICHOLAS VAN SERTIMA

Turn up 2 single spaces

P Van Sertima & Sons
22 Main Road
GLASGOW
G32 5LL

Dear Sirs

12 ASH DRIVE DUMBARTON

Thank you for your letter of 3 March, in which you complain about the quality of the work carried out at your offices. Please accept our sincere apologies.

Our foreman has inspected the work and agrees that your complaints are entirely justified. We will make good all the defective work within the next few days, and regret the inconvenience you have been caused.

I wish to confirm that our workmen will be at your office premises in Western Road, Glasgow, on Monday, 15 March, at 0830 hours, to commence the decorating and repair work you wish to be carried out there.

I am enclosing a specification of the work to be done and assure you that it will be completed as quickly and as efficiently as possible.

Yours faithfully

Turn up 1 single space

9 Name of organization KENKOTT SCOTIA PLC

Roberta A Bushell (Ms)
BRANCH MANAGER

Enc

See Practical Typing Exercises, Book One, page 12, for further exercises on

HAYLOCK & FELLOWS EUROPE

This sheet contains instructions that must be complied with when typing the documents. Read the information carefully before starting, and refer back to it frequently.

OFFICE SERVICES—REQUEST FORM

Typist's log sheet

Originator NIGEL GRANT-GOUGH Department Lettings Date Today's Ext No 34

Typists operating a word processor, or electronic typewriter with appropriate function keys, should apply the following automatic facilities: top margin; carrier/cursor return; line-end hyphenation; underline OR bold print (embolden); error correction; centring; any other relevant applications.

Remember (a) to complete the details required at the bottom of the form; (b) to enter typing time per document in appropriate column; and (c) before submitting this **Log sheet** and your completed work, enter TOTAL TYPING TIME in the last column so that the Typist's time may be charged to the originator.

Document No	Type of document and instructions	Copies – Original plus	Input form¶	Typing time per document	Total typing time ¥
* 1	Letter - 22 Wyndham St - and envelope	1 original + 1 carbon	AT		
2	Application for overseas property form for completion	1 original	MS		
3	Fax message. Form for completion	1 original	AT		
4	Memo + envelope	1 original	MS		
5	Article w. numbered items	1 original	T		
6	Notice	1 original	MS		
			TOTAL	TYPING TIME	

TYPIST – please complete:

Typist's name: Date received: Date completed:

Time received: Time completed:

If the typed documents cannot be returned within 24 hours, office services supervisor should inform the originator. Any item that is urgent should be marked with an asterisk (*).

¶ T = Typescript AT = Amended Typescript MS = Manuscript SD = Shorthand Dictation AD = Audio Dictation
¥ To be charged to the originator's department.

Open punctuation

1 No punctuation is inserted in the reference, date, name and address of addressee, or the salutation.
2 In the body of the letter the points mentioned on page 28 apply.
3 No punctuation is inserted in the complimentary close, or in any of the wording that may follow it.

Printed letterhead

Letters are usually typed on the printed letterhead paper of the company that is sending the letter. Depending on the display of the letterhead and the length of the letter itself, it is usual to turn up anything from two to nine single spaces after the last line of the printed heading before commencing the letter.

Some organizations provide plain paper for business documents. The letterhead is stored on a disk and copied on to a sheet of paper as and when the heading is required.
NOTE Suitably printed letterheads and forms for this and other units are in the *Handbook, Solutions, and Resource Material* and may be photocopied.

Fully blocked

Every line in the letter begins at the left margin, which may be lined up with the start of the printed letterhead. If it is a short letter, the left margin may be anything from 25 mm to 51 mm (1 inch to 2 inches).

Linespacing

The example given on page 61 is suggested as a neat, compact style, pleasing to the eye. Note the linespacing between each item in the letter. There must always be *at least* one clear linespace between each individual part.

Parts of the letter

1 *REFERENCE*—Our ref, Your ref
   (a) Type at the left margin or in the space provided on the headed paper.
   (b) In their simplest forms they consist of the originator's/author's and operator's initials, eg, AMD/ACM.
   (c) Many documents are stored (filed) on disks and, therefore, a disk number plus type and number of the document serve as a reference. For example: D12/L31/JB/TH as a reference would mean that the document is on Disk 12; L31 tells us that it is a letter numbered 31; JB are the author's initials and TH are the initials of the operator.

2 *DATE*
   (a) Use the style that your employer prefers, but it is more usual to type it in the order of day, month, year, eg, 10 October 1993.
   (b) Even when using fully-blocked style of letter display, some employers prefer the date to be typed at the right margin for ease of reference.

3 *SPECIAL MARKS*, eg, FOR THE ATTENTION OF, URGENT, PRIVATE, PERSONAL
   (a) Usually typed in capitals with or without the underline, and/or in bold print.
   (b) All special marks are typed two single spaces above the name and address of the addressee. In a letter, for the attention of a particular person may be typed above *or* below the name and address, but it is placed ABOVE on the envelope; therefore, as the special marks MUST ALWAYS be typed on the envelope, and the operator usually copies the details from the letter, we suggest that for the attention of is typed above the name and address of the addressee.

   When a letter is addressed to a business organization and marked for the attention of a particular person, eg, Mrs E Holiday, the salutation MUST be **Dear Sirs**. If the writer wishes the salutation to be **Dear Mrs Holiday**, the attention line should not be used, and **Mrs E Holiday** should be typed on the line preceding the name of the organization. The result of the present informality when writing business letters, since they are addressed to individuals, is that the salutation **Dear Sirs** is seldom used, thus avoiding the implication that members of the organization consist of only male persons. In business, the operator should follow the housestyle, and in an examination, follow the suggestions given in the typewriting syllabus for the particular examining body.

5 Type the following circular letter on A4 letterhead paper (Kenkott Scotia PLC). (a) Use margins of 12 pitch 22–82, 10 pitch 12–72. (b) Turn up 10 single spaces so that the date and the name and address of the addressee may be inserted before a letter is sent out. (c) Take a carbon copy.

Our Ref VIL/APA.824

Dear Sir/Madam

Self-Catering Holidays ← CAPS

For the first-time holiday maker, or even those who regularly choose self-catering as (there) style, here are some tips which you may find useful when staying in your holiday home.

Guide to Villas and Apartments

Most of our properties (is) second homes and will, therefore, vary widely according to the tastes of their owners.

(a) Nearly all villas have swimming pools, so be extra careful about safety, particularly if you have toddlers travelling with you.

trs/

(b) ~~Full~~ Detailed house notes are given on the workings of the hot water system, etc. If something should go wrong, advice and guidance may be obtained from the house managers or representatives.

(c) Most areas suffer from water shortages, particularly the Algarve, Lanzarote, Costa del Sol, Corfu and Paxos. Supplies may be cut off for short or long periods of the day, so use water sparingly.

Yours faithfully
KENKOTT SCOTIA PLC

Terry Richards
TRAVEL ADVISER

WP10 Create a new document (filename TRAV) and key in document 5 for 10-pitch printout. When you have completed this task, proofread (screenread) carefully and correct if necessary. Print out original and one copy and store on disk under filename TRAV. Follow the instructions for text editing on page 182.

6 File the carbon copy of the above letter. Send the top copy to:

Mrs P O'Connor 47 Main Street
CRAIGAVON Co Armagh BT66 5AG.
Insert today's date + delete the word 'Sir'.

4 *NAME AND ADDRESS OF ADDRESSEE* (INSIDE ADDRESS)

(a) Single spacing.
(b) Each item preferably on a separate line.
(c) It is usual to type the name of the post town in capital letters and the Post Office prefer it in this style when typing the address on the envelope.
(d) The postcode is always typed in BLOCK CAPITALS. Do not use full stops or any punctuation marks between or after the characters. Leave one clear space between the two halves of the code.

WINDOW/APERTURE ENVELOPES

A great many organizations now use envelopes from which a panel has been cut out at the front; they are known as window/aperture envelopes. The object of the window envelopes is threefold:

–it saves time in typing the name and address on both letter and envelope;
–it avoids the possibility of error in copying the address on to the envelope;
–it eliminates the almost impossible task of typing envelopes on certain printout machines where an envelope feeder is not fitted.

The name and the address of the addressee must be typed so that, when the document is folded, the position of the address will coincide with the cut-out portion on the envelope. To help the typist, the position of the cut-out is shown on the headed paper by marks in the corners of a rectangle or by a ruled box. Window envelopes usually have a transparent cover over the cut-out part; aperture envelopes do not. Any special marks (for the attention of, urgent, etc) should be typed, in the box, two spaces above the name and address and must be visible when the folded sheet is placed in the envelope.

5 *SALUTATION*
As with all other items, the salutation is typed at the left margin with one clear linespace above and below it and no punctuation.

6 *SUBJECT HEADING*
This may be typed in upper or lower case, but is easier to read and more clear to the reader if typed in all capitals or bold print. If it is typed in lower case with initial capitals, the subject heading must be underlined.

7 *BODY OF LETTER*

(a) Usually typed in single spacing with double between the paragraphs.
(b) Short letters may be typed in double spacing if preferred.

8 *COMPLIMENTARY CLOSE* (SUBSCRIPTION)
As with all other items, typed at left margin when using fully-blocked style of display. Only the first word has an initial capital.

9 *NAME OF ORGANIZATION SENDING THE LETTER*
This may be typed as part of the complimentary close.

(a) May be typed in upper or lower case, but capitals are preferable for clarity.
(b) Never underline.
NOTE The practice of typing the organization's name after the complimentary close is less popular with the authors of today's business letters as these are much less formal and more personal. In any case, the name was really only inserted after Yours faithfully, never after Yours sincerely.
(c) If the name of the organization has to be put in, turn up one single space only after the complimentary close.
(d) ALWAYS follow the layout/instructions given to you by your employer/examiner.

10 *NAME OF SIGNATORY*

(a) Turn up five single spaces after the complimentary close (or name of organization if inserted) before typing the name of the person who will sign the letter.
(b) A lady may wish to insert her title (Mrs/Miss/Ms), usually after her name in brackets.

11 *DESIGNATION*

(a) After the name of the signatory, turn up one single space and type the designation (official position of the person signing the letter).
(b) May be typed in upper or lower case.

12 *ENCLOSURE*

(a) The inclusion of papers or documents in a letter must be indicated in some way, the most usual being the abbreviation Enc (Encs or Enc(2) if there are more than one).
(b) This abbreviation will not always appear on the examination paper and will rarely be dictated in the office. It is the responsibility of the typist to note if an enclosure is mentioned in the body of the letter and, if it is, to make sure that the abbreviation is typed at the foot of the letter.

For other styles of business letters, see last section of *Handbook, Solutions, and Resource Material*.

Circular letters

Circulars, or circular letters, are letters of the same contents which are sent to a number of customers or clients. The original is usually typed on a master sheet (stencil or offset litho) and a quantity is 'run off'. Alternatively, a circular letter may be stored on a disk and individual letters produced on a word processor.

Reference—in usual position.

Date—typed in various ways; eg, 21 July 1993
July 1993 (month and year only)
Date as postmark (these words are typed in the position where you normally type the date).

Follow instructions or layout.

Name and address of addressee

(a) Space may be left for this and in that case the details are typed on individual sheets after they have been 'run off'. When preparing the master (or draft), turn up eight single spaces after the date (leaving seven clear) before typing the salutation.

(b) Very often the name and address of addressee are not inserted and, if this is so, no space need be left when the master is prepared. Turn up two single spaces after the date.

Salutation

(a) Dear . . . the remainder of the salutation is typed in when the name and address are inserted.

(b) Dear Sir, Dear Madam, Dear Sir(s), Dear Sir/Madam.

Signature

The author may or may not sign the letter. If he or she is signing, type the complimentary close, etc, in the usual way. Should the author not wish to sign, type Yours faithfully and the company's name* in the usual position, turn up two single spaces and type the name of the signatory, then turn up two single spaces and type the designation.

* If the company's name is not being inserted, turn up two single spaces after Yours faithfully and type the name of the signatory, then turn up two single spaces and type the designation.

4 Type the following letter on A4 letterhead paper (Kenkott Scotia PLC). (a) Use margins of 12 pitch 22–82, 10 pitch 12–72. (b) Leave three clear vertical spaces so that the date may be inserted whenever a letter is sent to a customer.

Our Ref JF/Air/4028/ma

Dear Customer

CHARTER FLIGHTS

If a number of executives from your company fly on a regular basis, time and money could be saved if you charter an aircraft.

We have over 200 aircraft available, including helicopters and executive jets. Our representative will advise you on the choice of aircraft, taking into account the number of passengers, distance to be flown and operating hours, and produce a quote within 24 hours.

I enclose an illustrated brochure giving full details.

Yours faithfully

JONATHAN FAIRFIELD

Operations Manager

Enc

6 Type the following fully-blocked letter in open punctuation, from Kenkott Scotia PLC, on A4 letterhead paper. Margins: 12 pitch 22–84, 10 pitch 12–74.

Our ref JF/ES

Your ref YRT/22/FG

17 March 1993

URGENT

Mr Robert T Higham
47 Mount Road
Bridgetown
GLASGOW
G40 1BU

Dear Sir

ENVIRONMENTAL MANAGEMENT

My company is concerned about the EC Directive which deals with ways of improving standards of environmental performance throughout the European Community.

For example, we feel we may be able to improve on our methods of waste disposal. Also the visual impact that our factory premises have on the surrounding area, as well as any nuisance the large juggernauts may cause to local residents.

I understand that you may be able to give us some help and advice on this matter, and I should be very glad if you could contact me as soon as possible.

I enclose an illustrated brochure which gives a detailed description of the activities of our company.

Yours faithfully
KENKOTT SCOTIA PLC

JACK FINISTON
European Operations Director

Enc

NOTE This exercise contains all the parts of a business letter. Keep your copy and refer to it when necessary.

See Practical Typing Exercises, Book One, page 13, for further exercises on

2 Type the following exercise on A4 paper. (a) Margins: 12 pitch 20–82, 10 pitch 10–72. (b) Single spacing. (c) Arabic figures in blue indicate the number of spaces to be left after the roman numeral, and are not to be typed. (d) Read the passage through before starting to type and correct the three circled errors.

The Training and Enterprise Council ← CAPS

The Training and Enterprise Council (TEC) is responsible for improving job training and helping businesses to develope, grow and compete in the Single European Market.

The TEC helps employers by -

trs/ (i)4 Providing expert advice on training and new business start-ups; providing free acsess to a wide range of quality training material.

(ii)3 Providing a help line on training and staff development issues.

lc/ (iii)2 Holding regular managment seminars on a wide range of Practical Business topics. /lc

The TEC helps students, including adults, by -

(i)4 Providing a free guide to training courses throughout the country.

(ii)3 Providing free, specially-developed courses and help for those returning to work after a long absence.

TYPIST - You wl find items (iii) & (iv) in the Data Files (filename TEC), page 184. Please type them here.

3 Type the following on A5 portrait paper. (a) Margins: 12 pitch 13–63, 10 pitch 6–56. (b) Single spacing with double between each item.

Please correct the 2 circled errors.

GREEN ISSUES ← Sp Caps

The EC is very aware of the effects of pollution on the world in which we live, and is legislating on various issues.

I4 ORGANIC FARMING

There is a small, but growing, market for food produced without the aid of artificial fertilizers or pesticides.

II3 WASTE RECYCLING

trs/ Community funds is available for research into the treatment and recycling of paper, glass and industrial waste.

uc/ III2 Noise

Noise is a pollutant and maximum levels have been established by the EC in the case of certain new machinery.

IV3 ATMOSPHERIC POLUTION

H Lead free petrol reduces the amount of pollution in the atmosphere.

See Practical Typing Exercises, Book One, page 38, for further exercises on

Follow instructions given at top of page 42. Margins: 12 pitch 22–82, 10 pitch 12–72.

A Review alphabet keys

1 The breakfast Jackson requested was excellent even though it was cooked for him in a frying pan over a brazier.

B Improve skill on fluency drill

2 she her his him are not has had any our who did but was see.
3 they that week know time will days this here your food when.
4 They know that this food must have been left here some days.
5 Your team hope that they will have much more time this week.

C Build speed on phrases

6 to me, to go, to do, if it, if he, if we, do we, do it, out.
7 and the, for the, may the, can the, you are, you can, it is.
8 If you are late, you can get the last train to go from town.
9 If he calls, do we want him to do the work for the firm now?

D Improve control of in reaches

10 Ar are art ark lark dark park arch larch tartar barter March
11 Ou out our sour dour pour tour ounce pounce bounced trounced
12 It was dark in the park and the rain poured on the tourists.

E Spelling skill *Correct the one misspelt word in each line. (Answer: page 181)*

13 medium input argues omitted expenses priviledges inconvenient
14 diary depot misuse mislaid harassed comitees advertisement
15 My advertisment about this year's diaries had been omitted.

Skill measurement *27 wpm One minute Not more than one error*

SM19 The day was sunny but cool. After we had rested and had our 12
snack, we packed our bags and set out for the distant cliffs 24
some 2 miles off. **(SI 1.15)** 27

1 | 2 | 3 | 4 | 5 | 6 | 7 | 8 | 9 | 10 | 11 | 12 |

Record your progress *One minute*

R14 A thick haze covered the headland, and the wind, now at gale 12
force, was sharp and biting. I walked on and in a long time 24
I judged I had done only 3 miles. Anxious and quite worried 36
I sat down for a short time. **(SI 1.12)** 42

1 | 2 | 3 | 4 | 5 | 6 | 7 | 8 | 9 | 10 | 11 | 12 |

Roman numerals

Use of roman numerals

(a) For numbering tables or paragraphs instead of using ordinary (arabic) figures, eg, Chapter IX, Table XIII.

(b) Sometimes to express the year, eg, 1993—MCMXCIII.

(c) For designation of monarchs, forms and class numbers, eg, George VI, Form V, Class IX.

(d) Small roman numerals are used for numbering prefaces of books, subparagraphs or subsections.

Examples of roman numerals

Study the following table. Note the seven symbols, I (one), V (five), X (ten), L (fifty), C (one hundred), D (five hundred) and M (one thousand). Note also that when a smaller numeral precedes a larger one, it is subtracted, eg, IX = 9; but when a small numeral follows a larger one, it is added to it, eg, XI = 11.

Roman numerals may be typed in upper or lower case. It is important to remember to use a capital or small I (i) to represent the figure one.

Arabic	Capital roman	Small roman	Arabic	Capital roman	Small roman
1	I	i	20	XX	xx
2	II	ii	30	XXX	xxx
3	III	iii	40	XL	xl
4	IV	iv	50	L	l
5	V	v	60	LX	lx
6	VI	vi	70	LXX	lxx
7	VII	vii	80	LXXX	lxxx
8	VIII	viii	90	XC	xc
9	IX	ix	100	C	c
10	X	x	1 000	M	m

NOTE In the above example the roman numerals are blocked at the left.

1 Type the following exercise on A5 landscape paper. (a) Margins: 12 pitch 22–82, 10 pitch 12–72. (b) Double spacing.

Refer to Section IX, Chapter II, Page 340, Paragraph 2(iii).

Read parts XVI, XVII, and XVIII, subsections ii, vi, and ix.

The boys in Forms VI and IX will take Stages I, II, and III.

Charles II, Henry VIII, George IV, James VI, and Edward III.

Enumerations using roman numerals

When roman numerals are used for enumerations, they may be blocked at the left (as is usual when typing in blocked style), eg,

(i)[4] Title of Book Leave four spaces after right bracket.
(ii)[3] Name of Author Leave three spaces after right bracket.
(iii)[2] Publisher Leave two spaces after right bracket.

Correction of errors

Correct the error as soon as you know you have made a mistake and read through the whole exercise when you have finished typing it and while the paper is still in the machine, in case there is an error you had not noticed before.

There are various methods that may be used to correct errors:

Rubber

(a) Turn up the paper so that the error is on top of the platen or paper table.
(b) Press the paper tightly against the cylinder or paper table to prevent slipping.
(c) Erase the error by rubbing gently up and down, blowing away rubber dust as you do so. (Too much pressure may cause a hole.)
(d) If you are using a new or heavily inked ribbon, erase first with a soft rubber and then with a typewriter eraser.
(e) Turn paper back to writing line and insert correct letter or letters.
(f) Always use a clean rubber.

NOTE If the typewriter has a carriage/carrier, move it to the extreme right or left to prevent rubber dust from falling into the mechanism of the machine.

Correction paper

These specially coated strips of paper are placed in front of the printing point over the error on the original and between the carbon paper(s) and the copy sheet(s). The incorrect character(s) is (are) typed again through the correction paper(s) which will cover up or lift off the incorrect character(s). Remove the coated strips and type the correct character(s).

Correction fluid

Correction fluid is produced in various shades to match the typing paper and is applied with a small brush. The incorrect letter is obliterated and when the fluid is dry, the correct letter may be typed over the top. The liquid may be spirit- or water-based. If the spirit-based liquid is used, it is necessary to add thinner to the bottle as, after a time, the original liquid tends to thicken. Spirit-based liquid dries more quickly than water-based. Avoid unsightly blobs. Use tissue paper to wipe the brush.

Correction ribbon

Some electric typewriters and most electronic typewriters are fitted with a correction ribbon. When making a correction with a correction ribbon, it is necessary to:

(a) Backspace to the error.
(b) Press the correction key—the error is then removed.
(c) Type the correct letter(s).

Correction on electronic equipment

Electronic typewriters are equipped with a memory and may have a narrow window so that automatic corrections can be made.

To make a correction on a word processor/computer, one may use the automatic overstrike, delete or erase functions.

Most electronic keyboards are now fitted with a relocate key which, when depressed, returns the carrier to the last character/space typed before the correction was made.

Author's errors

When writing the original text from which the keyboard operator will copy, the author may unwittingly make mistakes, and it is the operator's responsibility to correct these when keyboarding. In practice exercises we draw attention to the words by circling them. See page 83 for information about **Integrated Production Typing Projects**.

Proofreading

The most competent keyboard operator makes an error occasionally, but the error does not appear in the letter or document placed on the employer's desk for signature. Why? Because the operator has carefully proofread the work before it has been taken from the machine; the error has been detected and it has been corrected.

Follow instructions given at top of page 42. Margins: 12 pitch 22–82, 10 pitch 12–72.

A Review alphabet keys

1 Don't try to fix electrical equipment yourself. You may not
realize just how very dangerous this could be.

B Practise common letter combinations

2 it additional committee entitled definite credit remit visit
3 or transport effort report inform story order work word form
4 Your committee is entitled to free transport for the visits.
5 Make a definite effort to prepare an additional credit note.

C Improve control of up reaches

6 at bat hat cat sat that swat chat water elated patter lately
7 ju jug jut jury June Judy jump juice junior justice justify.
8 We were elated to see that June and Judy Judd were not late.
9 Pat Justin gave me a jug of water to quench my great thirst.

D Language arts—use of apostrophe *(See explanation on page 181)*

10 The man's computer terminal is on a desk in the main office.
11 The men's computer terminals were attached to the mainframe.
12 The child's personal computer was not really very expensive.
13 The children's personal computers were bought at cut prices.

Skill measurement *30 wpm* *3 minutes* *Not more than 3 errors*

SM34 When travelling in an aeroplane, make sure that none of your 12
hand luggage obstructs the aisle or seat areas. It should 24
be stored in the overhead lockers or under the seat in front 36
of you. Enjoy your flight! Sit back, relax, and make your- 48
self comfortable - the cabin staff will be pleased to attend 60
to your needs. Hot or cold meals will be served during the 72
flight, depending on the time of day and length of flight. 83
Radio and tape players may be used. **(SI 1.27)** 90

1 | 2 | 3 | 4 | 5 | 6 | 7 | 8 | 9 | 10 | 11 | 12 |

Record your progress *3 minutes*

R25 A wide range of tax-free goods is available on the aircraft, 12
and a list of the products, with prices and comparative UK 24
retail prices, will be found in the seat pocket. Your cabin 36
staff will let you know in good time as to when the tax-free 48
products will be on sale. For your guidance a list of items 60
you can hear on the audio channels is in the pocket - adjust 72
the sound to suit your needs, but keep the volume low. Some 84
flights have a film and you should select a suitable channel 96
to listen to the sound-track and channel 2 for quality jazz. 108
Your headset should be placed in the seat pocket before you 120
leave the aircraft. **(SI 1.27)** 124

1 | 2 | 3 | 4 | 5 | 6 | 7 | 8 | 9 | 10 | 11 | 12 |

Screenreading

While proofreading has always been an integral part of the typist's training, it is now doubly important because, if you wish to operate a word processing machine, your ability to check quickly and correct errors in typing, spelling, grammar, etc, is even more meaningful. Documents prepared on a word processing machine are often used over and over again, and you can well imagine the disastrous results if you typed the wrong figures, were careless in checking your finished work, and your original error is then repeated hundreds of times. When checking soft copy on the VDU screen, it can be helpful to use the cursor as a guide as you move it across the screen; a less time-consuming aid is to have the base of the screen for the line you are checking and using the vertical scroll to move the text up one line at a time. Adjusting the brightness of the soft copy can also be helpful. If a number of copies are required, it is wise to print one copy and proofread it before printing the final, or further, copies.

1 In the exercise below, the sentences in COLUMN ONE have been repeated in COLUMN TWO. Those in column one are correct, but in each sentence in column two there is a typing error. Compare the sentences and see how quickly you can spot the errors. Then type the sentences correctly.

	COLUMN ONE		COLUMN TWO
1	Thank you for your letter.	1	Thank you for your letter.
2	Please book the accommodation.	2	Please book the accomodation.
3	Our cheque for £221.00 is here.	3	Our cheque for £212.00 is here.
4	Ask to see that painting.	4	Ask to see the painting.
5	The book is on your desk.	5	The book is on your Desk.
6	His name is Mr B Edwardes.	6	His name is Mr B Edwards.
7	Call in to see me on 12 May.	7	Call in to see me on 12 May
8	He took 3 years to write the book.	8	He took 3 year to write the book.
9	Send me £20.00.	9	Send me £20.00p.

Further exercises on proofreading are on pages 178–180.

Typing from manuscript copy

You will have to type letters or documents from handwritten drafts. Take particular care to produce a correct copy. Before typing, first read the manuscript through to see that you understand it. Some words or letters, not very clear in one part, may be repeated in another part more clearly. Check the completed document and correct any errors *before* removing the paper from the machine.

2 Type the following paragraph on A5 landscape paper. (a) Read the whole passage through before you start to type. (b) From the top edge of the paper turn up seven single spaces. (c) Margins: 12 pitch 22–82, 10 pitch 12–72. (d) Single spacing. (e) Keep to the lines as in the copy. (f) Correct the three circled errors.

THE EUROPEAN COMMUNITY

The European Community is a group of 12 countrys bound
together by 3 international treaties, of which the most
important is the Treaty of Rome.

The Treaty of Rome was signed in 1957 by Belgium, France,
Italy, Luxembourg, Netherlands and Germany. They was
joined in 1973 by Denmark, Ireland and the United kingdom,
in 1981 by Greece and in 1986 by Portugal and Spain.

4 Type the following exercise on A4 paper. (a) Margins: 12 pitch 22–82, 10 pitch 12–72. (b) Single spacing for the main part.

EUROPEAN COMMISSION DIRECTIVE

VDU and Computer Operators[1]

the UK in/ The directive, which became law in 1992, sets out the minimum health and safety requirements for VDU and computer users.

WORKSTATIONS

New workstations installed after 31 December 1992 must meet minimum regulations laid down and work stations already in use have to be adapted by 1995.[2] (Please check date in Data Files (filename VDU) on page 184)

REQUIREMENTS

uc/ NP/ Operators will be entitled to a free eyesight test prior to using a vdu + regularly thereafter, + free glasses if these are req'd for use when operating the VDU. // The directive specifies th the desk must hv –

(a) a large, low-reflection surface;

(b) a document holder;

(c) adequate space for change of posture + comfort.

(Double spacing between ea. item.)

The work chair is req'd to be stable with adjustable backrest, height + tilt, + adjustable seat height facilities. (A footrest must be supplied if needed.)

1 Health + Safety Regulations.

2 Employers who fail to comply may be liable to expensive litigation.

Create a new document (filename VDU) and key in document 4 for 10-pitch printout. When you have completed this task, proofread (screenread) carefully and correct if necessary. Print out original and one copy and store on disk under filename VDU. Follow the instructions for text editing on page 182.

3 Type the following paragraphs on A4 paper. (a) Read the paragraphs through carefully before you start to type. (b) From the top edge of the paper turn up seven single spaces. (c) Margins: 12 pitch 22–82, 10 pitch 12–72. (d) Double spacing. (e) Keep to the lines of the copy and correct any typing errors BEFORE removing paper from the machine. (f) Correct the circled errors.

PROOFREADING TYPEWRITTEN DOCUMENTS

An Important Technique

It is essential to proofread (cheque for errors) a document
before you remove the page from the machine, because it is
not easy to realign the typing when the page is reinserted.
When proofreading, bare in mind the following types of
errors: typographical errors – you struck the wrong key;
word substitution – FROM for FORM, YOU for YOUR, etc;
figures not typed in correct sequence; inconsistencies in
use of capitals, in spelling, in spacing, etc.

4 Type the following exercise on A4 paper. (a) Read the paragraphs through carefully before you start to type. (b) From the top edge of the paper turn up seven single spaces. (c) Margins: 12 pitch 22–82, 10 pitch 12–72. (d) Double spacing. (e) Keep to the lines as in the copy and correct any typing errors BEFORE removing paper from the machine. (f) Correct the circled errors.

FURTHER PROOFREADING HINTS

Not only do you have to look for typing errors, you also
have to read for sense; therefore, it is often necesary
to read a document twice – once for typing errors and
once for sense.

Useful Tips

Use the paper bail as a guide as you read each line, and
make yourself focus on each letter of each word (with a
VDU screen, use the cursor and scroll key). You will not
find your typing errors if you just scan the page, and you
must give special attention to numbers and words that sound
alike or look alike.
When the material contains statistical date and/or has to
be duplicated or printed in some form, ask a colleague to
help – one of you reading the original allowed while the
other follows the copy.

Typewriting theory and conventions

Over the years certain conventions with regard to display and layout of typewritten documents have become accepted practice. While some examining bodies and employers do not worry unduly about layout as long as the document is clean, attractive and correct (no typing, spelling or grammatical errors), we do suggest that you use the 'theory'/conventions given in this textbook as a guide. In exercise 2 on page 40, it is necessary to leave at least two clear spaces between paragraphs typed in double spacing; however, it would not be 'wrong' if you left three clear, but it would be ridiculous if you left six. When you are familiar with the conventions and standards suggested in this textbook, then you can adjust the layout of a document to suit the contents, your employer or the examiner.

1 Footnotes are used:
  (a) To identify a reference, or person, quoted in the body of a report.
  (b) For explanations that may help or interest a reader.
  (c) To give the source of a quotation cited in a report.

2 Each footnote is:
  (a) Preceded by the reference mark which corresponds to the reference mark in the text.
  (b) Typed in single spacing.

3 The reference mark may be a figure or letter, with or without brackets, asterisk, dagger or double dagger.

In the text
  (a) It is typed as a superscript.
  (b) NO space is left between it and the previous character.

In the footnote
  (a) It is usually typed as a superscript, but may be typed on the same line as the rest of the text. If the asterisk key on the typewriter is used, it will automatically be raised as a superscript. Therefore, any other reference mark in the footnote must be typed as a superscript.
  (b) ONE space is left between the reference mark and the first word.

4 The footnote is:
  (a) Usually placed on the same page on which the corresponding reference appears in the body of the text.
  (b) Typed in SINGLE spacing, with double between each footnote. If the main body of the text is typed in double spacing, the footnote is still typed in single spacing.
  (c) May be separated from the main text by a horizontal line, typed from margin to margin. The horizontal line is typed by using the underline, at least ONE single space after the last line of the text, and the footnote is typed on the second single space below the horizontal line.

NOTE When the footnote has to be typed at the bottom of the first page, care must be taken to leave enough space at the bottom of the page for the footnote and, if a continuation page is needed, a clear space of 25 mm (one inch) should be left after the footnote at the bottom of the page.

Some electronic/word processing machines have a superscript facility which raises the character above the line.

3 Type the following exercise on A4 paper. (a) Margins: 12 pitch 22–82, 10 pitch 12–72. (b) Double spacing, except for the footnote which must be typed in single spacing.

P E T   P A S S P O R T S

Officials in Brussels would like to see vaccination certificates or "pet passports" for cats and dogs arriving in Britain from the Continent.* [The British Government is against any change ~~at all~~ in the traditional laws, because of the fear of the spread of rabies to Britain. The Commission ~~believes~~ understands that Denmark, Portugal and Holland have been cleared of rabies as 60% of the fox population has been vaccinated.‡

NP/ ㄱ ✓

TYPIST – Please enter the year here. You will find it on the Data Files (filename PET) on page 184

---

* This would mean that quarantine would no longer be necessary.

‡ An EC-funded programme began in ✓ to vaccinate foxes against rabies; but the countries still heavily affected are France and Germany.

Create a new document (filename PET) and key in document 3 for 10-pitch printout. When you have completed this task, proofread (screenread) carefully and correct if necessary. Print out original and store on disk under filename PET. Retrieve the document and follow the instructions for text editing on page 182.

We have reserved this unit for consolidation so that you have an opportunity to apply the practices and procedures introduced in the previous units thus enabling you to revise where necessary, or practise keyboard techniques and drills in order to type more accurately or more quickly.

Data files

This is the first occasion you have been asked to use the **Data files** (mentioned in the Preface). Follow instructions and check carefully.

Production target

The examiner, and your employer, will be interested in how many documents you type in a given time; therefore, in addition to accuracy and acceptable layout, we have set a Production target time for each exercise. At first you will reach this target only after concentrated practice.

If you make an error, stop and correct it. Of course, the more errors you make, the more time you waste (!) in making corrections. When you have typed the complete exercise, check the whole document carefully and correct any errors you may find BEFORE removing the paper from the typewriter or printing the document from the screen. At the top of each page, type the date and the Production target.

Production target—10 minutes

1 Type the following on A5 portrait paper.
  (a) Leave 25 mm (one inch) clear at the top of the page.
  (b) Double spacing.
  (c) Margins: 12 pitch 13–63, 10 pitch 6–56.

S P O T L I G H T   S P A I N

THE SPANISH MARKET

Spain is an exciting market with plenty of scope for companies who wish to do business there.

Prepare any trade literature in Spanish. Remember that Spaniards are sometimes slow in answering letters, so telephone calls and visits are more effective, but you will need Spanish to get past the receptionist; book your appointment well in advance.

Working hours are different and the lunch period - 2.00 to 4.00 pm - is sacred. The working day ends at 8.00 pm, but Spaniards will often talk business over dinner until midnight. Buena suerte!

TYPIST: Please check the times in the Data Files (filename SPAIN) page 184, + alter if necessary.

1 Type a copy of the following exercise on A4 paper. (a) Make all the necessary corrections. (b) Margins: 12 pitch 22–82, 10 pitch 12–72. (c) Double spacing.

A N I M A L   W E L F A R E

Transport of Animals

(a) Health An EC directive stated that, as from 1 January 1993, all

trs/ animals must be fit to travel and that they must be watered, fed

run on/ and tested at appropriate intervals on long journeys.

stet/ The transporter ~~has to~~ must provide an itinerary for journeys of over 24 hours.

Distance

(b) For certain animals there is a limit on the distance they can be taken.

(c) Arrival Animals must be inspected when they arrive at their place of destination.

2 Type a copy of the following on A5 portrait paper. (a) Make all the necessary corrections. (b) Margins: 12 pitch 13–63, 10 pitch 6–56. (c) Single spacing.

EC HYGIENE REGULATIONS

Transport of Food

The EC hygiene rules ~~state~~ stipulate just how food may be sold, stored, transported / trs
and displayed.

The maximum temperature at which food must be transported and stored is now 8 °C. It was 10 °C. From April 1993 it drops to 5 °C.

Butchers and others must not use wooden blocks for cutting up food -
NP/ stainless steel must be used instead. Corner shops and garages are no longer allowed to sell sandwiches and snacks unless they have a chill
run on/ cabinet and receive the food in a container. refrigerated

Those who previously used the back of their ~~lorries,~~ cars or vans with no temperature control to carry food to shows, sports events, etc, must now use refrigerated transport.

WP7

Create a new document (filename FOOD) and key in document 2 for 12-pitch printout. When you have completed this task, proofread (screenread) carefully and correct if necessary. Print out original and store on disk under filename FOOD. Follow the instructions for text editing on page 182.

Production target—25 minutes

2 Type the following on A4 letterhead paper (Kenkott Scotia PLC). (a) Margins: 12 pitch 22–82, 10 pitch 12–72.

Ref TPB/ib

14 April 1993

Mrs Louise Kidd BA(Hons)
17 Paisley Road
HAMILTON
Lanarkshire ML3 8NA

Dear Mrs Kidd

THE SPANISH MARKET

As a shareholder in our company, I was pleased to receive your letter enquiring about our need to export our goods to Spain.

Spain is one of the fastest growing economies in Europe, and has the potential for much more economic development. In 1992 world attention was focused on Spain because the Olympic Games were held in Barcelona, and Expo '92 in Seville.

There are great export opportunities for UK manufacturers. Spain has progressively removed barriers caused by differ-ing requirements from those of other Member States.

We need to compete in this growing market if we are to expand as a company.

Yours sincerely

Toby P Barrymore
Head of Marketing and Sales

Production target—6 minutes

3 Display the following notice on A5 landscape paper. (a) Centre the whole notice vertically. (b) Centre the longest line horizontally.

<u>V A C A N C Y</u>

SECRETARY required to work for
the European Marketing Manager

Word Processing skills essential
<u>Salary</u> - c£8 500

Apply quoting ref 31209/Sec/Euro

Proofreaders' marks

When amendments have to be made in typewritten or handwritten work of which fair copy is to be typed, these may be indicated in the original copy by proofreaders' marks. To avoid confusion, the mark may also be placed in the margin against the line in which the correction is to be made. The Royal Society of Arts use only the stet signs, ie, (✓), in the margin, but other examining bodies may use any or all of the examples that follow.

Mark which may be in margin	*Meaning*	*Mark in text*	
lc	Lower case = small letter(s)	— /	under letter(s) to be altered or struck through letter(s)
uc or CAPS	Upper case—capital letter(s)	═ /	under letter(s) to be altered or struck through letter(s)*
♂ (delete sign)	Delete (take out)	/	through letter(s) or word(s)
NP or //	New paragraph	// or [	placed before the first word of a new paragraph
Stet or (✓)	Let it stand, ie, type the word(s) that has been crossed out and has a dotted or broken line underneath	----	under word(s) struck out
Run on	No new paragraph required. Carry straight on	⟵⟶	
⋏	Caret—insert letter, word(s) omitted	⋏	placed where the omission occurs
⌒	Close up—less space	⌒	between letters or words
trs	Transpose, ie, change order of words or letters as marked	⟲ ∽	between letters or words, sometimes numbered
#	Insert space	⋏	
‖	Straighten margin		
ital.	Italics	—	(Underscore)
⊙	Insert full stop	⋏	
;/	Insert semi-colon	⋏	
(:)	Insert colon	⋏	
,/	Insert comma	⋏	
' (apostrophe mark)	Insert apostrophe	⋏	
H	Insert hyphen	⋏	
|—|	Insert dash	⋏	
" "	Insert quotation marks	⋏	
(⋏)⋏	Insert brackets	⋏	

PONTYPOOL — If a word is not clear in the text, it may have been written in the margin in capitals. The word should be typed in lower case, or as indicated in the original script.

* Double underscore underneath words usually means that such words are to be typed in unspaced capitals. Treble underscore underneath words usually means that such words are to be typed in spaced capitals (one space between each letter, and three spaces between words).

Production target—10 minutes

4 Type the following on A5 landscape paper. (a) Read the passage through before starting to type. (b) From the top edge of the paper turn up seven single spaces. (c) Margins: 12 pitch 22–82, 10 pitch 12–72. (d) Double spacing. (e) Keep to the lines in the copy.

CAR NUMBER PLATES

<u>EC standards</u>

<u>Car number plates</u> are to be harmonized to EC standards.
Plates in the 12 member countries are to become a standard
size, shape and colour under the proposals being prepared by
the European Commission.

<u>The new-style</u>, light-reflecting plates will be yellow and
white. They will carry the 12-star European flag and a
letter denoting the country in which the car is registered.

Production target—15 minutes

5 Type the following on A5 portrait paper. (a) Read the passage through before starting to type and correct the three circled errors. (b) From the top edge of the paper turn up seven single spaces. (c) Margins: 12 pitch 13–63, 10 pitch 6–56. (d) Single spacing. (e) Keep to the lines as in the copy.

<u>DRIVING LICENCES</u>

Britain is one of the few countries in the world
~~which~~ that does not have photographs on driving
licences. Northern Ireland has had them since
the twenties.

PHOTOGRAPH (LICENSES)

To bring Britain ~~the~~ into line with other EC countries
driving licences will carry a photograph of the
holder starting with new drivers in 1993. Other
drivers will be asked to return their old document
—with a photograph which will be used on the new
licence. It is hoped that all 37 million drivers
will have photographs on (there) licences by the
year 2000.

COMPUTER IMAGE

A computer image of every (drivers) face will be
stored at the Driver and Vehicle Licensing Agency
in Swansea.

Follow instructions given at top of page 42. Margins: 12 pitch 22–82, 10 pitch 12–72.

A Review alphabet keys

1 When we walked among the foxgloves and bluebells on that hot
day in June, the crazy paving looked quite attractive.

B Improve control of down reaches

2 va vat vase vary vane oval rival canvas invade vacant valley

3 nk ink rank wink monk junk crank banker drinks unkind blanks

4 The vacant banker's house is near the taxi rank in Bankvale.

5 She did not charge VAT on the vase which was of great value.

C Language arts—use of apostrophe *(See explanation on page 181)*

6 The typist's workstation consisted of a screen and keyboard.

7 The typists' workstations were well laid out, and very tidy.

8 Our supervisor's office is at the end of the first corridor.

9 Their supervisors' offices were located on the fourth floor.

Skill measurement *30 wpm* *2½ minutes* *Not more than 3 errors*

SM33 The Chairman of the Board tells me that Tom Younger has been 12
badly hurt in an accident on the M5, and points out that Tom 24
will not be at work for at least 18 months. You are aware, 36
no doubt, of the fact that he has a large number of speaking 48
engagements in many different cities, and these will have to 60
be cancelled at once unless we are able to engage someone to 72
take over from him. **(SI 1.25)** 75

1 | 2 | 3 | 4 | 5 | 6 | 7 | 8 | 9 | 10 | 11 | 12 |

Speed building

Speed is built up more easily on short, simple exercises and, as we have now reached 2½ minutes at 30 wpm, and will continue at 30 wpm with increased lengths of timing, we suggest that you use the earlier **Skill measurement** exercises as practice material for speed building. For example, to increase your speed from 30 wpm to 35 wpm, use SM12 on page 36. As a guide, we suggest that if you have more than one error for each minute typed, then you should strive for greater accuracy. With less than one error for each minute typed, you may wish to build your speed by using short exercises of low syllabic intensity.

Record your progress *2½ minutes*

R24 When you arrive, you should follow the clearly marked black- 12
on-yellow 'arrivals' signs to immigration. If you are going 24
to take an onward flight, follow the signs to the 'Transfer 36
Desk'. After clearing immigration, wait in the lounge until 48
your flight number appears on the TV screen indicating which 60
carousel in the Baggage Hall to go to. Just place your bag- 72
gage on one of the unique, free-of-charge trolleys and go on 84
through customs to the exit zone on the terminal concourse. 96
(SI 1.35)

1 | 2 | 3 | 4 | 5 | 6 | 7 | 8 | 9 | 10 | 11 | 12 |

Follow instructions given at top of page 42. Margins: 12 pitch 22–82, 10 pitch 12–72.

A Review alphabet keys

1 The fox came quietly into the open, and enjoyed walking over the field which was bathed in hazy sunshine.

B Improve control of hyphen key

2 day-to-day, up-to-date, self-made, 1901-1972, three-quarters
3 air-to-air, take-off, re-create, re-elected, bird's-eye view
4 Two-thirds of the citizens had up-to-the-minute information.
5 Mr Evans-Gray said he would call at the do-it-yourself shop.

C Improve control of figures

6 1234 5678 9012 3456 7890 0102 9394 8586 7654 8902 1092 34878
7 My office telephone number is 0203 465234 and my home number is 0321 479857. Note the dates 1914-1918; 1939-1945. These numbers were in your notebook: 01-467 7302, and 01-234 3668.

D Improve control of adjacent keys

8 oi toil boil soil foil join voice noise coins choice adjoins
9 rt tart part dart cart sort forts sport mirth berths sported
10 The many voices joined in cheering the sporting darts teams.

E Spelling skill *Correct the one misspelt word in each line. (Answer: page 181)*

11 relying useless dismissed benifited acknowledge manufacturer
12 minutes cursory Wedesday dependent approximate appointments
13 We should benefit from the manufacture's sale on Wednesday.

Skill measurement *27 wpm* *1½ minutes* *Not more than 2 errors*

SM20 At the moment, there is no guide to help us to judge how far 12
we are from the roadside or from the car in front of us. We 24
know that a device is being made that will help us gauge how 36
far away we may be. **(SI 1.22)** 40

1 | 2 | 3 | 4 | 5 | 6 | 7 | 8 | 9 | 10 | 11 | 12 |

Record your progress *1½ minutes*

R15 Have you ever been to a large airport just to watch the end- 12
less movement of people and planes? You can see hundreds of 24
folk getting on and off these exciting jets, and it makes me 36
wonder how such unique planes zoom so gently into the air or 48
land without skidding. **(SI 1.27)** 52

1 | 2 | 3 | 4 | 5 | 6 | 7 | 8 | 9 | 10 | 11 | 12 |

4 Type each of the following lines three times on A5 landscape paper. (a) Single spacing. (b) Margins: 12 pitch 20–80, 10 pitch 18–78.

```
From afar there came to our ears the call "Cuckoo!  Cuckoo!"
They had spent $300 on presents and came home with only 90¢.
The asterisk (*) is used for a reference mark in a footnote.
250 ÷ 5 + 50 ÷ 4 = 25; 25 x 5 - 15 ÷ 2 = 55; $125 ÷ 5 = $25.
```

Brace

The brace is used by printers for joining up two or more lines. To represent the brace in typing, use continuous brackets as shown in exercises 5 and 6 below.

5 Type the following on A5 portrait paper. (a) Centre horizontally and vertically. (b) Double spacing except for the bracketed items which should be in single spacing. (c) Leave three spaces between columns.

```
FLIGHT TIMES - AIRBUS

London to Paris          Paris to London

0715) Not Sundays        1745
0915)
1045)                    1800) Saturdays only
                         1900)
1115                     2000)

1245                     1845

0945) Saturdays only     1945) Not Sundays
1145)                    2045)
```

Handwritten or printer's bracket

This has to be replaced by the round brackets, used in exercise 5 above. Where lines of unequal length are bracketed together, the brackets are typed immediately after the last characters in the longest line. All brackets in any one group are typed at the same scale point.

6 Type the following on A5 landscape paper. (a) Use the same linespacing as shown in the exercise. (b) Margins: 12 pitch 22–82, 10 pitch 12–72. (c) Leave five spaces between the columns. (d) Replace the handwritten bracket with round brackets.

```
SPACING BEFORE AND AFTER PUNCTUATION

Full stop              Two spaces at end of sentence.

Comma     }
Semicolon }            No space before, one space after.
Colon     }

Dash                   One space before and one space after.

Hyphen                 No space before and no space after.

Exclamation sign)      No space before, 2 spaces after at end
Question mark   )      of sentence.
```

NB It is permissible to type the single-line text against any of the 3 lines to which it refers

See Practical Typing Exercises, Book One, page 34, for further exercises on

Typing measurements

When typing measurements, note the following:

(a) The letter 'x' (lower case) is used for the word 'by', eg, 10 mm x 97 mm (space before and after the 'x').
(b) ONE space is left after the numbers and before the unit of measurement, eg, 210 (space) mm; 2 (space) ft 6 (space) in.
(c) Groups of figures should not be separated at line-ends.
(d) Most abbreviations do not take an 's' in the plural, eg, 6 in; 6 lb; 2 mm; 4 kg.
(e) With OPEN PUNCTUATION, there is no full stop after any abbreviation, unless at the end of a sentence.

1 Type each of the following lines three times on A5 landscape paper. (a) Margins: 12 pitch 22–82, 10 pitch 12–72. (b) Pay particular attention to the spacing in the measurements.

```
My rug measures 82 cm x 76 cm; and the other, 65 cm x 44 cm.
The carpets were all 6 ft 6 in x 5 ft 7 in or 16 ft x 15 ft.
Send me 5 lb of carrots, 2 oz of pepper, and 500 g of sugar.
```

Use of words and figures

(a) Use words instead of figures for number one on its own and for numbers at the beginning of a sentence. But if number one is part of a list of figures, it should be typed as a figure, eg, 'Follow the instructions 1, 2 and 3. Use figures in all other cases.
(b) With sums of four figures or more, leave a space between the hundreds and thousands and a space between the thousands and millions. (Please see **Variations in display**, in *Handbook, Solutions, and Resource Material* for alternative methods.)

NOTE TO WORD PROCESSOR AND VDU OPERATORS From this point in the textbook you will find various exercises with specific instructions for word processor and VDU operators. It is understood that the basic procedures of word processing will have been achieved at this stage and that you are able to start up the equipment; create a new file; use the pre-stored margins; key in text; proofread and correct the document on screen; print the document, store it on disk and close down (log off) the equipment.

2 Type the following exercise on A5 landscape paper. (a) Margins: 12 pitch 22–82, 10 pitch 12–72. (b) Turn up seven single spaces from the top of the paper. (c) Double spacing. (d) Read the passage through before starting to type. (e) Follow the line-endings given in the exercise. (f) Note the use of words and figures.

EUROPEAN CHILD BENEFIT - 1991
Families with 3 children are best off in Luxembourg where
child benefit (CB) is 4 times the UK rate; but worst off
in Spain where they receive 20 times less.

In France there is no benefit for one child but rates rise
sharply for 2 or more. A French couple with 2 children,
aged 5 and 8, receive £57.92 a month (ie, approximately
£695.04 per annum), and £177.36 a month (ie, approximately
£2 128.32 per annum) for 3 children, aged 10, 13 and 15.

Create a new document (filename POST) and key in document 2 above, using the pre-set margins, for 12-pitch printout. Embolden the main heading. When you have completed this task, proofread (screenread) carefully and correct if necessary. Print out original and store on disk under filename POST.

When you have completed exercise WP1, complete the **Record sheet**, a copy of which is in the *Handbook, Solutions, and Resource Material.* There are 22 word processing exercises in this text. Remember to fill in the **Record sheet** for each word processing exercise you complete.

Superscripts (Superior or raised characters)

A superscript is a character that is typed half a space above the line of typing. To type a superscript, turn the paper down half a space and type the character(s) to be raised; then return to the original typing line. If your machine does not have half spacing, use the interliner. In the exercise below, notice the degree sign. On its own it is typed immediately after the figure, but when followed by C (Centigrade/Celcius) or F (Fahrenheit), there is a space between the figures and the degree sign but no space between the degree sign and the letter C or F. Use lower case o for the degree sign, unless your keyboard has a degree sign on it, eg, 10 °C. Superscripts are used for typing degrees and mathematical formulae, eg, $a^2 - b^2$.

Subscripts (Inferior or lowered characters)

A subscript is a character that is typed half a space below the line of typing. To type a subscript, turn the paper up half a space and type the character(s) to be lowered; then return to the original typing line. If your machine does not have half spacing, use the interliner, eg, H_2O, $C_{12}H_{22}O_{11}$. Subscripts are used for typing chemical formulae.

2 Type the following lines three times each. (a) A5 landscape paper. (b) Double spacing. (c) Margins: 12 pitch 22–82, 10 pitch 12–72.

> Subscripts are used in typing H_2SO_4, $CaCO_3$, N_2O and CO_2.
>
> Superscripts are used for typing the degree sign 4 °C.
>
> A right angle equals 90°; 1° equals 60', and 1' equals 60".
>
> At 10 am the temperature was 4 °C; at 2 pm it was 20 °C.
>
> $ax + b^2 = a^2 - bx$. $a^2 (a - x) + abx = b^2 (a - b)$. $x^2 - a^2$.

NOTE For variations in methods of displaying the degree sign, please see last section of *Handbook, Solutions, and Resource Material.*

Accents

When a typewriter is used for a great deal of foreign correspondence, the keys are usually fitted with the necessary accents. However, when accents are used only occasionally, the following are put in by hand in the same coloured ink as the ribbon.

acute grave circumflex tilde

Usually typed as special characters are:

diaeresis and umlaut = quotation marks typed over letter, eg, Düsseldorf
cedilla = letter c, backspace and comma, eg, Alençon

3 Type the following on A5 landscape paper. (a) Double spacing. (b) Margins: 12 pitch 20–85, 10 pitch 11–76. (c) Take one carbon copy. (d) Insert the accents on the top and carbon copy.

> Franz Nüsslein, 18 Münchnerstrasse, Düsseldorf, Germany.
>
> André Brésilien, 25 av Gallieni, Alençon, France.
>
> Señor Juan Garcia, Edificio Phoenix del Mar, Alicante, Spain.

Some word processors and word processing software have special symbols, such as accent marks, that can be inserted during typing.

See Practical Typing Exercises, Book One, page 33, for further exercises on

Some examples of longhand abbreviations

In a rough draft certain longhand words may have been abbreviated, but these must be typed in full and spelt correctly. Some of these abbreviations are given below.

Abbreviation	*Word in full*	*Abbreviation*	*Word in full*	*Abbreviation*	*Word in full*
ack	acknowledge	dept(s)	department(s)	ref(s)	reference(s)
accom	accommodation	exp	experience	sec(s)	secretary(ies)
a/c(s)	account(s)	ffly	faithfully	resp	responsible
advert(s)	advertisement(s)	fr	from	sh	shall
amts	amount(s)	gntee(s)	guarantee(s)	shd	should
approx	approximately	hv	have	sinc	sincerely
appt(s)	appointment(s)	immed	immediate(ly)	togr	together
bel	believe	mfr(s)	manufacturer(s)	th	that
bn	been	necy	necessary	thru/thro'	through
co(s)	company(ies)	opp(s)	opportunity(ies)	w	with
cttee(s)	committee(s)	rec(s)	receive(s)/ receipt(s)	wh	which
dr	dear			wl	will
def	definite(ly)	recom	recommend	yr(s)	your(s) year(s)

Days of the week and months of the year—The usual longhand abbreviations are used, eg, Mon, Wed, Thurs, Jan, Feb, Sept, Dec.

3 After studying the above abbreviations, read the following passage to see that you understand it; then type a copy on A5 landscape paper. (a) All abbreviations to be typed in full, except BT and UK. (b) Margins: 12 pitch 22–82, 10 pitch 12–72. (c) Single spacing. (d) Follow the line-endings in the copy.

BT CHARGECARD

Chargecard holders can make calls from virtually any phone
in the UK without the need for small change, the amt
charged per call being the same as other users. The card
itself is free; you wl only pay when you use yr chargecard. Every call wl be individually listed on a separate
BT Chargecard statement. If it is necy to make calls
outside the office on behalf of the co or dept,
you can use yr card & charge the calls to your co's
a/c.

4 Type the following exercise on A5 landscape paper. (a) Margins: 12 pitch 22–82, 10 pitch 12–72. (b) Single spacing. (c) Follow the line-endings. (d) Abbreviations in full, except EC.

ACCOMMODATION TO LET

If you hv the opp to let accom, you may
find it worthwhile. Make sure you arrange appts to
interview prospective tenants & I recom th you
obtain refs if poss.
Decide whether you wd like to offer a room togr w
meals or perhaps you wd prefer yr guests to look after
themselves. Exp wl tell you wh method suits you
best. It may be necy to hv certain house rules th
yr tenants shd abide by.
You wl not be able to gntee th yr tenants wl be
suitable; perhaps you could let accom to students
fr one of the EC countries & so help to improve yr
knowledge of languages.

Special signs, symbols and marks

A variety of words (sign, symbol, mark) is used when referring to the characters on this page. One speaks of punctuation marks, the brace symbol and the £ sign. The word symbol is employed mainly for mathematical and scientific formulae and in computer terminology.

Degree	Small o, raised half a space.	6°
Feet	Apostrophe typed after the figure(s).	8'
Inches	Double quotation marks typed immediately after figure(s).	7"
Minus	To show subtraction—hyphen with space either side.	6 - 4 = 2
Minutes	Apostrophe typed immediately after figure(s).	10'
Multiplication	Small x with a space either side.	4 x 5
Seconds	Double quotation marks typed immediately after figure(s).	9"
To	Hyphen	21-25
Hash	In USA and Canada used before numbers When used after a number, it means weight (pounds). Must not be used for sterling sign.	#27

Constructing special signs, symbols and marks

Some characters, not provided on the keyboard, can be typed by combining two characters, ie, by typing one character, backspacing and then typing the second character, or by typing one character and then the second one immediately afterwards. In a few cases the interliner must be used to allow the characters to be raised or lowered.

Asterisk	Small x and hyphen.	∗
Brace	Continuous brackets typed one underneath the other. (See exercise on page 116.)	( ) ( ) ( )
Cent	Small c, backspace and type oblique (slash).	¢
Dagger	Capital I, backspace and type hyphen.	†
Division	Hyphen, backspace and type colon.	÷
Dollar	Capital S, backspace and type oblique.	$
Double Dagger	Capital I raised half a space, backspace and type another capital I slightly below; or capital I and equation sign.	‡
Equation	Two hyphens—one slightly above the other.	=
Exclamation	Apostrophe, backspace and type full stop.	!
Plus	Hyphen and lowered apostrophe.	+
Square brackets	Oblique and underscore—see explanation below	[ ]

On modern typewriters many of the above characters are provided. On others it is difficult to type the division or plus as combined characters. Where this is the case, it would be wise to insert these in matching-colour ink.

When the **asterisk** has to be typed in the body of the text (exercise 4 on page 116), it is typed as a superscript (raised character). Before typing the combination asterisk, turn the cylinder one half space towards you, type small x, backspace and type hyphen; then turn back to normal typing line. Where the asterisk is already fitted, DO NOT lower the paper before typing, as the sign on the typeface is already raised.

To type a **square bracket** take the following steps:

Left bracket:
(a) Type oblique sign.
(b) Backspace one and type underscore.
(c) Turn cylinder back one full linespace and type underscore.
(d) Turn cylinder up one full linespace, backspace once and continue with typing up to the right bracket.

Right bracket:
(a) Type oblique sign.
(b) Backspace two and type underscore.
(c) Turn cylinder back one full linespace and type underscore.
(d) Turn cylinder up one single space, tap space bar once, and continue typing.

1 Type each of the following lines three times. (a) Double spacing. (b) Margins: 12 pitch 22–82, 10 pitch 12–72.

[756 ÷ 12 = 63] [12 x 5 = 60] [200 ÷ 2 = 100] [10 + 15 = 25]

[20 + 6 ÷ 2 = 13] [200 x 2 ÷ 4 + 30 = 130] [40 + 6 ÷ 2 = 23]

Follow instructions given at top of page 42. Margins: 12 pitch 22–82, 10 pitch 12–72.

A Review alphabet keys

1 The male patient lay back quietly in the oxygen tent dozing,
just after his operation for a broken hip was over.

B Build speed on word family drill

2 nip lip hip gip rip tip dip sip van can ban ran pan fan man.
3 bold cold fold hold gold sold told full dull hull bull pull.
4 The man told us that he ran to stop the van as it moved off.
5 He sold a full can of ice-cold orange to that happy old man.

C Improve control of symbols and punctuation marks

6 "2" 3 is/was 4 @ £5 6 & 7 '8' 9 (9 - 8) Mr & Mrs one's £1023
7 They asked, 'Will you both come to Jim's party on 14 March?'
8 Mr & Mrs J Burgess (address below) paid £34 for the antique.
9 He/she requires 20 only @ £5 each, and 18 only @ £5.50 each.

D Improve control of adjacent reaches

10 po port spot pole pond pose upon sport spoil oppose suppose.
11 we west sweet sweep Crewe tower power fewer between western.
12 Many porters at Crewe Station were very popular with people.

E Spelling skill *Correct the one misspelt word in each line. (Answer: page 181)*

13 woollen sherriffs difference catalogues references compliment
14 usually achieved receivable absorption committees gauranteed
15 The comittees require references for all recent applicants.

Skill measurement *27 wpm 2 minutes Not more than 2 errors*

SM21 He said that if you want a garden then you will have to do a 12
great deal of work, but in these days you can buy many tools 24
which will be helpful for the heavy work, and thus save time 36
and effort. You would not need to employ hired help, and so 48
you could then save some money. **(SI 1.13)** 54

1 | 2 | 3 | 4 | 5 | 6 | 7 | 8 | 9 | 10 | 11 | 12 |

Record your progress *2 minutes*

R16 She exhaled deeply as they crossed the frozen lake and moved 12
swiftly past the hole lined with jagged ice. The sleds were 24
light and the 6 dogs well rested; consequently, there was no 36
need to think about a stop until we were in the next hamlet. 48
Then a sudden squall brought more snow and the track's mark- 60
ings were lost. **(SI 1.22)** 63

1 | 2 | 3 | 4 | 5 | 6 | 7 | 8 | 9 | 10 | 11 | 12 |

Follow instructions given at top of page 42. Margins: 12 pitch 22–82, 10 pitch 12–72.

A Review alphabet keys

1 The size of the paper requested by the teacher was important
as it made a difference to the vertical and horizontal spacing of the exercises, but the marking was adjusted.

B Improve control of figure keys

2 wet 235 let 934 get 535 his 682 did 383 lid 983 jar 714 1468
3 pat 015 out 975 are 143 sir 284 how 692 you 697 has 612 2579
4 Orders Nos 2981/88 and 2995/88 were sent on 3 November 1988.
5 Cheque No 021048 is for £536.97 and No 021069 for £5 634.78.

C Improve control of punctuation and symbol keys

6 61* 2" 3% 4 @ £5 6 & 7 '8' (9 - 0) "No" "Yes" 3/8 - 1/8 & Co
7 She said, "No, I will not call and see Brady & Co tomorrow."
8 My cheque for £5.29 has been cancelled. Here is another for
£55.29. The final total (£2 876.54) should read £22 876.54.

D Build accuracy on suffix drill

9 -able payable suitable reliable dutiable desirable available
10 -ible legible sensible terrible feasible divisible indelible
11 It is feasible that the available news is not very reliable.

E Spelling skill *Correct the one misspelt word in each line. (Answer: page 181)*

12 ensueing pitiful debited totally conceit pagination aggregate
13 ceiling forfeit eigths leisure precede repetition aggravate
14 Jack's conceit and arogance were really pitiful to witness.

Skill measurement *30 wpm 2 minutes Not more than 2 errors*

SM32 Some large offices have a pool of typists who share the work 12
to be done, but we do not know whether or not this is a good 24
plan. It is a matter upon which each firm should make a de- 36
cision based on the pressure of work and the number of staff 48
employed as typists. You may prefer a job in a typing pool. 60
(SI 1.22)

1 | 2 | 3 | 4 | 5 | 6 | 7 | 8 | 9 | 10 | 11 | 12 |

Record your progress *2 minutes*

R23 In September 1985, 9 000 people were killed in an earthquake 12
in Mexico City. Also, in June 1986 slight damage was caused 24
by a weak tremor which recorded as 5.4 on the Richter scale. 36
In March 1986, an earthquake struck southern Turkey and some 48
14 people were injured in 4 villages as houses fell. We are 60
lucky in Great Britain as there are only one or 2 zones that 72
have slight earth tremors. **(SI 1.32)** 77

1 | 2 | 3 | 4 | 5 | 6 | 7 | 8 | 9 | 10 | 11 | 12 |

Securing an acceptable right margin

Up to this stage in the book you have always returned the carriage/carrier/cursor at the same point as the line-ends in the exercise from which you have been copying. This is not usually possible, of course, and in a great many exercises you will have to decide on your own line-endings and also see that you do not have an untidy right margin. If you are using a manual or electric typewriter, a bell will ring to warn you that you are nearing the right margin.

Most electronic keyboards have normal carrier return, justified right margin and automatic return. This automatic return is referred to as automatic word wraparound. Some have devices which indicate that you are approaching the right margin and some do not. Consult the handbook that accompanies your machine.

Before you can practise making your own line-endings, it is necessary for you to become accustomed to listening for an audible signal (margin bell, etc) that warns you that you are nearing the end of the typing line. On your own typewriter, find out how many spaces there are after you hear the margin bell or warning device before you reach the set right margin. If you are using an electronic keyboard, we suggest that you do not utilize the automatic carrier return for the time being. Find out how the normal return works and what audible signal, if any, there is.

1 Type the following on A5 landscape paper and note the instructions in the text. (a) Use single spacing. (b) Margins: 12 pitch 22–82, 10 pitch 12–72. (c) Listen for the audible signal, but follow the copy line for line.

RIGHT MARGIN AUDIBLE-WARNING DEVICE

Five to 10 spaces from the right margin a bell or other signal on your machine will warn you that you are almost at the
end of the writing line. It is necessary to train yourself
to listen for this signal, and to re-act as follows:

If the bell/device signals at the beginning of a new word of
more than 5-10 letters, divide the word at the first available point.

If the bell/device signals at the end of a word, do not type
a further word on that line unless it has less than 5-10
characters (or 2 words such as 'for it' or 'I am', etc) or
unless the new word can be divided at an appropriate point.

It is not obligatory to divide a word; we do it to avoid
having an unsightly right margin.

Margin-release key

If at the right margin you cannot complete a word, the carriage/carrier can be unlocked by pressing the margin-release key (usually found at the top right or left of the keyboard). The word can then be completed. The margin-release key will release the left margin as well as the right one.

2 Type each of the following sentences exactly as it appears, using the margin-release key when necessary. (a) Use A5 landscape paper. (b) Double spacing. (c) Margins: 12 pitch 22–82, 10 pitch 12–72.

Hard copy is the name given to the text when it is printed out on paper.

Soft copy is the name applied to the data displayed on the VDU screen.

Text-editing is making changes to text after it has been keyed in.

Document 4 *Production target—12 minutes*

URGENT

FROM Rachel Lansdale Headmistress
TO Timothy Row Environmental Officer
DATE (Insert date)

"GREEN" FAIR

As you wl realize it is a matter of some urgency th we decide on the final programme for our "Green" Fair to be held in the school grounds on Wed 13 Oct at 1400 hrs.

Wd you please come to my study after school on Fri with as many ideas & details as possible. I understand classes 3A, 4A & 5A wl be helping to co-ordinate details.

RL/ (Yr initials here)

Document 5 *Production target—15 minutes*

STAFF NOTICE (TYPIST - A5 paper)

UNDERSTANDING "GREEN" ISSUES

A lecture is to be given in
the Main Hall
on (insert date & time here from Data Files (filename LEC) on page 184)
by Prof Donald Turvey MSc

TOPICS will include -

Acid rain - air, sea & land pollution
Wildlife
The greenhouse effect & the ozone layer
Organic farming
(single spacing here)

* * * * *

COFFEE AND BISCUITS FREE

Guide for dividing words at line-ends

In order to avoid having a wide gap (without any typing) on any one line at the right margin, you may feel it desirable to divide a long word. Always type the hyphen at the end of the line before typing the remaining part of the word on the next line. Here are a few hints to help you when you feel you have to divide a word.

Divide

(a) According to the pronunciation,
eg, prop-erty, not pro-perty
chil-dren, not child-ren

(b) According to syllables,
eg, per-fect, under-stand

(c) After a prefix, or before a suffix,
eg, com-bine, wait-ing

(d) Between double consonants,
eg, excel-lent, neces-sary

(e) Words already hyphenated at the hyphen,
eg, pre-eminent, self-taught

Do not divide

(a) Words of one syllable or their plurals,
eg, niece, nieces, case, cases

(b) At a point which would bring two letters only to the second line,
eg, waited, not wait-ed

(c) After an initial one letter syllable,
eg, again, not a-gain

(d) Sums of money, figures, dates or abbreviations,
eg, £10 000, UNESCO

(e) On more than three consecutive lines

(f) Proper nouns unless absolutely essential

3 Copy each of the following lines once for practice and then once for accuracy. (a) Use A5 landscape paper. (b) Margins: 12 pitch 22–82, 10 pitch 12–72. (c) Single spacing. (d) Note where the word is divided and where and why division is not possible.

```
sten-cil, pad-lock, mur-mur, pen-cil, prac-tise, elec-trical
com-ply, con-sent, dis-agree, sec-tion, trust-ing, pay-ments
cab-bage, stut-ter, neces-sity, suf-fix, sup-pose, sup-plied
self-support, re-entrance, dinner-time, chil-dren, prob-lems
case, cases, box, boxes, dose, doses, quickly, wrecked, NATO
unit, awaits, adores, 2 km, £250 400, 2 May 1993, Winchester
```

4 Type the following on A4 paper. If you feel that the right margin will be unsightly, then divide words at the line-ends. (a) Margins: 12 pitch 22–82, 10 pitch 12–72. (b) Double spacing.

EUROPE 2000

It may be that by the year 2000, many of you could be living and working in Community countries other than the United Kingdom. This will mean that - if the laws governing voting are changed - you will be free to vote, either in the United Kingdom, or in your "adopted" country.

By the end of this century, the Economic Community could consist of 20 or more member states, whereas in 1991 there were only 12.

In the year 2000, opportunities will be much wider for everyone, and Europe will have a much greater influence on world affairs.

Create a new document (filename EURO) and key in document 4 above for 12-pitch print-out. Use the pre-stored margins and embolden the main heading. When you have completed this task, proofread (screenread) carefully and correct if necessary. Print out original and store on disk under filename EURO.

TYPIST - A4 paper, double spacing
Find + correct the
4 word errors, please

G R E E N   I S S U E S

<u>Mountains of Waste</u>

All pupils should read the following notice carefully.

TIN CANS

Over 7 billion cans of drink is thrown away in Britain each year. If they were placed end to end, they would reach further than the moon! Almost half of them are aluminium and could be recycled. <u>Put your can in the bin provided in the school canteen.</u>

PACKAGING

Every <u>DAY,</u> Britain produces enough rubbish to fill Trafalger Square right up to the top of Nelson's Column! <u>Put your rubbish in the skips provided.</u>

ENERGY

If we save energy, it will help to modify the 'greenhouse effect'. Please - (double quotes, please)

Inset 25 mm

close all doors

turn the heating down if the classroom is to hot rather than opening windows (Single spacing for this item)

turn of lights in unused classrooms

don't leave taps dripping in cloakrooms.

GENERAL

Did you know that every year the average family throws out -

47 kilos of plastics

32 kilos of metal

54 kilos of food

74 kilos of glass

Single spacing here but before you type the items please check that the amounts are correct from the Data Files (filename GREEN) page 184.

RL/Green/4/EH

Follow instructions given at the top of page 42. Margins: 12 pitch 22–82, 10 pitch 12–72.

A Review alphabet keys

1 Mike was so full of zeal for the project but exaggerated his
abilities very much, and they were not quite up to the task.

B Practise line-end division

2 able, mail-able, read-able, suit-able, sens-ible, flex-ible.
3 so-cial, par-tial, ini-tial, finan-cial, spe-cial, pala-tial
4 pro-mote, pro-vided, per-mit, per-fume, pur-suit, pur-suant.
5 dis-may, dis-miss, dis-patch, dis-place, dis-grace, des-pair

C Speed up carriage/carrier/cursor return

6 I will.
I will go.
They may go today.
Ask them to go with you.

D Improve control of consecutive strokes

7 my enemy mammy myriad myself mystery gloomy clammy mystique.
8 ft lift soft loft left cleft bereft drifter crofter swiftly.
9 There was mystique, and mystery, around the crofter's house.

E Spelling skill *Correct the one misspelt word in each line. (Answer: page 181)*

10 movable pastime synonym justify through inconveneince eighth
11 arguing believe pitiful proceed receipt unecessarily ascent
12 The unnecessary inconvenience was hard to beleive or justify.

Skill measurement *28 wpm One minute Not more than one error*

SM22 Each year there are some new typewriters for you to use, and 12
you must know about them so that you are up to date when you 24
wish to change jobs. **(SI 1.11)** 28

SM23 A computer is now being made that will store voice patterns. 12
It will know your voice when you speak to it, and it will be 24
able to reply to you. **(SI 1.21)** 28

1 | 2 | 3 | 4 | 5 | 6 | 7 | 8 | 9 | 10 | 11 | 12 |

Record your progress *One minute*

R17 From our magazine you will see that we have spent many years 12
fitting all kinds of carpets - all our staff are specialists 24
and quietly complete their jobs. In truth, they are experts 36
who have spent their lives in this trade. **(SI 1.25)** 44

1 | 2 | 3 | 4 | 5 | 6 | 7 | 8 | 9 | 10 | 11 | 12 |

TYPIST – One carbon copy + an envelope please.

RL/264/ (Insert yr initials here)

(Type date + name + address of addressee here)

Dr Sir

SAVING ENERGY

Now th we are resp for our own budget, we feel th there are many ways where we cld save money + also be more caring of our environment.

I understand th you hv notes on energy saving for schools, wh you issue free, + that you carry out energy surveys, wh wd help us to be more energy efficient. I also believe th you issue, either free or at a discount, low-energy fluorescent light bulbs, wh use only one-fifth of the energy that standard bulbs use, + last 8 times longer. trs

During the school yr we are planning various environmental projects, including –

(Inset 5 spaces)

1 Enhancing the school grounds.
2 Use of recycled paper.
3 Organizing a "green" fair at the school.
4 Pollution control.

I look forward to hearing from you.

Yrs ffly

Rachel Lansdale (Mrs)
Headmistress

Variable linespacer

The variable linespacer is found on the left or right cylinder knob. By pressing this in, the cylinder can be moved to any position desired. Its purpose is to ensure that you have proper alignment of the details to be typed on dotted lines, ruled lines or when inserting details in a form letter or memo.

Memoranda (memorandums)

A message from one person to another in the same firm, or from the Head Office to a Branch Office, or to an agent, is often in the form of a memorandum—usually referred to as a 'memo'. Memoranda (the plural 'memorandums' is now widely accepted) may be typed on any of the usual sizes of paper. The layout of the printed headings may vary from organization to organization. There is no salutation or complimentary close in a memo.

Important points to remember when typing memos on headed forms:

(a) Margins: 12 pitch 13–90, 10 pitch 11–75. Margins may vary depending on the size of the form and the length of the message.

(b) The information to be inserted after 'To', 'From', 'Ref' and 'Date' may be aligned vertically as shown in the exercises that follow. Use variable linespacer to ensure the correct alignment of insertions, and start the information two character spaces after 'From'.

(c) Date: correct order—day, month, year. The month is not usually typed in figures.

(d) Some memos have a subject heading which gives the reader information about the contents of the memo. The heading is typed two single spaces below the last line of the printed headings, ie, turn up two single spaces.

(e) If there is no subject heading, start the body of the memo two single spaces after the last line of the printed headings.

(f) The body of the memo is usually typed in single spacing, with double between paragraphs.

(g) After the last line of the body, turn up two single spaces and type the reference. This is usually the dictator's and typist's initials which identify the department or person dictating the memo.

(h) If an enclosure is mentioned in the body of the memo, this must be indicated by typing Enc (or Encs if more than one enclosure) at the left margin. After the reference, turn up at least two single spaces before typing Enc or Encs.

(See *Handbook, Solutions, and Resource Material* for **Variations in display** of memos.)

NOTE A memo with printed headings is given in the *Handbook, Solutions, and Resource Material* and may be copied.

Ordinal numbers

(a) These numbers denote order of sequence, eg, 1st, 2nd or first, second.

(b) Words or figures may be used: follow the script and be consistent, ie, either words *or* figures. NOTE In exercise 1 below use figures for '5th floor'.

1 Type the following memo on a printed A5 memo form. (a) Follow the instructions given above. (b) Margins: 12 pitch 13–90, 10 pitch 11–75. (c) Make your own line-endings.

MEMORANDUM

From Nicholas Turrell Personnel Department

To All Staff

↓ Turn up 2 single spaces

Date 1 June 1993

↓ Turn up 2 single spaces

LANGUAGE CLASSES

↓ Turn up 2 single spaces

Language classes in French, German and Spanish will be held each Monday and Wednesday from 1200 hours in Conference Room 4 on the 5th floor in our main building in Firth Street. It is hoped that as many of you as possible will attend for any of the sessions which will last for 30 minutes each, and make use of the audio machines available. I am enclosing full details of these classes with this memo.

Turn up 2 single spaces

NT/rt

Turn up 2 single spaces

Enc

RECYLCED PAPER AND ENVELOPES

When new stationery is required please order from

GREENWAYS
Station Lane Industrial Estate
Avenue 4
Mill Hill Lane
Durham
DH1 3LB

P R I C E - L I S T

	White	Coloured
	£	£
PAPER (A4 210 mm x 297 mm)		
500 sheets - bond	14.18	13.99
500 sheets - bank	7.10	6.95
ENVELOPES (per 1000)		
89 mm x 152 mm	31.94	31.00
114 mm x 154 mm	33.32	32.50
108 mm x 219 mm	43.16	42.40

Made from 50% straw fibre and 50% recycled paper.

FAST DELIVERY SERVICE

RL/Paper/93

September 1993

2 Use printed A5 memo form. (a) Margins: 12 pitch 13–90, 10 pitch 11–75. (b) Make your own line-endings.

MEMORANDUM

From Lucy Carter Marketing Director

To Martin Abbot Chief Administrator

Date 4 June 1993

As you know I have to meet Monsieur Jean Chuilon in London on Tuesday 15 June to discuss the expansion of our Branch in Lyons.

Would you please come to my office on Thursday 10 June at 1500 hours, so that we can discuss final details. I am enclosing the relevant files.

LC/EMP

Encs

3 Use printed A5 memo form. (a) Margins: 12 pitch 13–90, 10 pitch 11–75. (b) Make your own line-endings.

MEMORANDUM

From Kim Ballard Finance Department

To All Staff

Date 8 June 1993

KILOMETRES INTO MILES

I understand there has been some difficulty with staff wishing to convert from kilometres into miles after travelling in Europe on business for the company and wishing to claim travelling expenses.

Unscientifically, without a doubt, we always multiply the kilometres by 6 and ignore (more or less) the last figure. Thus: 50 km x 6 equals 300 which equals 30 miles; or, 5 km x 6 equals 3 miles. I know it is more accurate to multiply by 5 and divide by 8, ie, 50 km x 5 equals 250 divided by 8 gives a little over 31 miles, but at the moment the finance department is following the first method.

KB/FW

4 Use printed A5 memo form. (a) Margins: 12 pitch 13–90, 10 pitch 11–75. (b) Make your own line-endings.

MEMORANDUM

From Edward Bourne Technical Director

To Mark Crowther Office Manager

Date (Today's)

TYPIST – Please insert the following heading: OPTICAL DISKS – RECORD STORAGE

Further to our conversation abt the problems with the safe storage of our many records, I understand th it is possible to use an optical disk with certain computer systems. It seems th the speed of access is greatly increased & the workload much reduced.

Please look into this & report back to me as soon as possible.

EB/(Yr initials)

See Practical Typing Exercises, Book One, page 17, for further exercises on

ST MARY'S SCHOOL

OFFICE SERVICES—REQUEST FORM

This sheet contains instructions that must be complied with when typing the documents. Read the information carefully before starting, and refer back to it frequently.

Typist's log sheet

Originator RACHEL LANSDALE (Mrs)   Department HEADMISTRESS   Date 21 Sept. 93   Ext No 230

Typists operating a word processor, or electronic typewriter with appropriate function keys, should apply the following automatic facilities: top margin; carrier/cursor return; line-end hyphenation; underline OR bold print (embolden); error correction; centring; any other relevant applications.

Remember (a) to complete the details required at the bottom of the form; (b) to enter typing time per document in the appropriate column; and (c) before submitting this **Log sheet** and your completed work, enter TOTAL TYPING TIME in the last column so that the Typist's time may be charged to the originator.

Document No	Type of document and instructions	Copies – Original plus	Input form¶	Typing time per document	Total typing time ¥
1	Price-List	1 original	T		
2	Letter + envelope to Environmental Officer Durham County Council County Hall Mill Hill Lane DURHAM DH4 6RE	1 original + 1 carbon	MS		
3	Notice about "green" issues	1 original	AT		
* 4	An urgent memo	1 original + 1 carbon	MS		
5	Staff notice	1 original	MS		
			TOTAL	TYPING TIME	

TYPIST – please complete:

Typist's name: Date received: Date completed:

Time received: Time completed:

If the typed documents cannot be returned within 24 hours, the office services supervisor should inform the originator. Any item that is urgent should be marked with an asterisk (*).

¶ T = Typescript   AT = Amended Typescript   MS = Manuscript   SD = Shorthand Dictation   AD = Audio Dictation

¥ To be charged to the originator's department.

Follow instructions given at top of page 42. Margins: 12 pitch 22–82, 10 pitch 12–72.

A *Review alphabet keys*

1 The azure blue sky was quite a breathtaking event for Trixie
to see, but it lasted just a few moments as the storm clouds
blew up and covered the sun.

B *Improve control of vowel keys*

2 locate unusual receiving suggestion examination distribution
3 assume anxious financial sufficient explanation requirements
4 Your suggestion has been received and we are anxious to have
an explanation of your quite unusual financial requirements.

C *Build accuracy on common prefix drill*

5 pro- procure profess process protect promote prolong profile
6 con- contain confirm condemn conceal confess consist content
7 Promise that you will not prolong the process. Also confirm
that Connie will not conceal the contents of that container.

D *Improve control of consecutive strokes*

8 ny any many rainy nylon canny granny anyhow anybody anything
9 gr ogre great grown agree angry grade hungry grumble vagrant
10 It was agreed that we should try to grow a good grade grape.

E *Spelling skill* *Correct the one misspelt word in each line. (Answer: page 181)*

11 forceful privilege admissable manufacturer immediately local
12 withold perceived absorption uncontrolled opportunity aloud
13 It was admissible for us to withhold the check until today.

Skill measurement *28 wpm* *2 minutes* *Not more than 2 errors*

SM24 When you eat your Brazil nuts at Christmas do you ever think 12
of the men who pick them and of the risks they run to do so? 24
One of the risks is the falling of nuts from the trees which 36
grow to a very great height. What we usually call nuts are, 48
in fact, really the seeds from the tree. **(SI 1.20)** 56

1 | 2 | 3 | 4 | 5 | 6 | 7 | 8 | 9 | 10 | 11 | 12 |

Record your progress *2 minutes*

R18 Different kinds of wild plants do not grow in the same place 12
because they need the soil and conditions to suit them, just 24
as you have your likes and dislikes. If you acquire a plant 36
which excels in a warm, dry place, it is prone to die if you 48
move it to a zone which is cold and damp. It is possible to 60
alter its habits over a period of time. **(SI 1.20)** 68

1 | 2 | 3 | 4 | 5 | 6 | 7 | 8 | 9 | 10 | 11 | 12 |

Column display in fully-blocked letters

When the matter is to be displayed in columns, three spaces should be left between the longest line of one column and the start of the next. The first column starts at the left margin and tab stops are set for each of the other columns as explained on page 80 (d–h).

6 Type the following letter from Eastways Developments (UK) Ltd on A4 letterhead paper. (a) Margins: 12 pitch 22–82, 10 pitch 12–72. (b) Take a carbon copy. (c) Type a C6 envelope. (d) Mark the letter and envelope PERSONAL. (e) Insert a subject heading GERMAN REFRESHER COURSES.

CS/RY 1 September 1993

Mrs Rose Haddow
26 Jesson Avenue
SWANSEA
West Glamorgan
SA8 2PQ

TYPIST – Would you please check the dates for the courses in the Data Files (filename SEC) p184.

Dear Mrs Haddow

I am pleased to hear that you wish to accept the vacancy offered to you for the post of bilingual secretary to our General Manager, Timothy Bowen. As stated in my previous letter, it will be necessary for you to attend the following German refresher courses, on the dates given, before taking up your appointment.

GR1/1	Room A1	Floor 3	1 day	Thursday 16 September
GR1/2	Room A1	Floor 3	1 day	Thursday 24 September
GR1/3	Room B2	Floor 4	1 day	Thursday 30 September

The courses will be held at the local Technical College in Clarendon Street. If you are unable to attend on any of these dates, I should be glad if you would let me know immediately.

Yours sincerely

Cecilia Spooner
Personnel Department

7 Type the following letter from Eastways Developments (UK) Ltd on A5 letterhead paper. (a) Margins: 12 pitch 13–63, 10 pitch 6–56. (b) Take one carbon copy. (c) Type a C6 envelope. (d) Date: 2 September 1993. (e) The details, as far as the subject heading and the complimentary close are exactly as those given in the letter above.

I refer to my letter of 1 Sept.

Unfortunately, the German Refresher Course on 30 Sept has bn cancelled. I shd be glad, therefore, if you wd attend the course detailed below on th date.

The Expert Language College Room 15 0900-1630

I am enclosing a map wh gives the address & location of the Language College.

Tabulation

Arrangement of items in columns

You may be required to arrange items in column form in such a way that they are horizontally centred on the page, with equal spaces between the columns and with equal margins. This can be done easily by means of the backspacing method you have already used in display work.

Tabulator key

All typewriters have three tabulator controls which you should locate on your machine as their positions vary on the different makes.

(a) A tab set key to fix the tab stops.
(b) A tab clear key to clear the tab stops.
(c) A tab bar or key to move the carriage/carrier/cursor to wherever a tab stop is set.

Preliminary steps for arranging items in columns

(a) Move margin stops to extreme left and right.
(b) Clear all previous tab stops that may be set already. On most machines this can be done by pressing the clear key while returning the carriage/carrier. On other machines there are special devices for this purpose.
(c) Insert paper seeing that the left edge is at 0.
(d) Set the left margin and tab stops.
(e) Test your tab stop settings by returning the carriage/carrier/cursor and then depressing the tab bar or key.

Typing the table

(a) Type the main heading at the left margin.
(b) Turn up two single (one double) spaces.
(c) At left margin type first item in first column.
(d) Tabulate to the second column and type first item; then tabulate to each of the remaining columns and type the first item.
(e) Continue in the same way with the rest of the table.

NOTE It is essential that you complete each horizontal line before starting the next line.

1 Carrying out the instructions given above, type the following table on A5 landscape paper. (a) Start the heading on the 14th single space from the top of the paper. (b) Set the left margin at the point given; the figures in brackets are for 10 pitch. (c) Set the tab stops as shown. (d) Double spacing.

Left margin: 24(15)

1st tab: 34(25)
2nd tab: 44(35)
3rd tab: 58(49)

COUNTRIES OF THE EUROPEAN COMMUNITY

Turn up one double

Twelve Member States - 1991

Turn up one double

Belgium	Germany	Luxembourg	Republic of Ireland
Denmark	Greece	Netherlands	Spain
France	Italy	Portugal	United Kingdom

Simple display in fully-blocked letters

Emphasis may be given to important facts in a letter by displaying these so that they catch the eye of the reader. In fully-blocked style, this display starts at the left margin, one clear space being left above and below, as in the specimen letter that follows.

5 Type the following letter from Eastways Developments (UK) Ltd on A4 letterhead paper. (a) Margins: 12 pitch 22–82, 10 pitch 12–72. (b) Take one carbon copy. (c) Fold letter to fit into a window envelope.

Our ref SGB/PT/389 18 August 1993

Cunningham Books PLC
26 High Street
Redhill
HEREFORD
HR2 7HG

NOTE The date has been typed on the same line as the reference and ends level with the right margin. To do this, backspace, from the right margin, once for every character and space in the date. Some organizations prefer to have the date typed in this position. Follow housestyle or layout of input from which you are copying.

Dear Sirs

SINGLE MARKET

If you have the following 2 books in stock, I should be glad if you would forward them, on approval.

Turn up 2 single spaces

Selling to Europe by Deacon Paget-Smith - £14.95
Getting into the European Market by V Moresby - £29.50

Turn up 2 single spaces

I understand that the books may be returned to you within 10 days if they do not contain the information required.

Yours faithfully

TYPIST – Please insert the Marketing Manager's name & designation here – SAMUEL GRAHAM BALL

Create a new document (filename BOOK) and key in document 5 for 10-pitch printout. When you have completed this task, proofread (screenread) carefully and correct if necessary. Print out original and one copy and store on disk under filename BOOK. Follow the instructions for text editing on page 182.

Standard margins

In the next (page 108) and subsequent **Integrated production typing projects**, very few instructions will be given about margins, and layout of documents. You should decide what you consider to be the most suitable margins for the length of document and type of display. One important point to remember is that the right margin is **never** wider than the left margin unless you are given special instructions.

In this book, to make the typing look balanced and attractive, we have nearly always chosen the same length of typing line for both 12 and 10 pitch (one exception being the memoranda); thus margins of 12 pitch 22–82, 10 pitch 12–72, means that you have a 60-space typing line, and if you are using A5 portrait paper with margins of 12 pitch 13–63, 10 pitch 6–56, you are typing with a 50-space line.

If no margin settings are given for an exercise, the following suggestions will be helpful:

A5 portrait	Typing line 50 spaces	12 pitch 13–63	10 pitch 6–56
A4 and A5 landscape	Typing line 60 spaces	12 pitch 22–82	10 pitch 12–72
	Typing line 70 spaces	12 pitch 18–88	10 pitch—not suitable
Memoranda		12 pitch 13–90	10 pitch 11–75

If you are given specific measurements (millimetres/inches) for margins—say, 25 mm (one inch) on the left and 13 mm (half an inch) on the right (12 pitch 13–90, 10 pitch 11–75) on A4 paper or A5 landscape paper—then it is wise to measure and mark the paper, in pencil, before inserting it into the machine and setting the margins.

2 Following the instructions given on page 79, type this table on A5 landscape paper. (a) Start the heading on the 14th single space from the top of the page. (b) Set the margin and tab stops at the points given; the figures in brackets are for 10 pitch. (c) Double spacing.

Left margin: 26(17)

Tab stops: 48(39) 64(55)

SOME POLITICAL PARTIES IN EUROPE

Socialists	Greens	Liberals
Christian Democrats	Labour	Fine Gael
Social Democrats	Conservatives	Communists
Extreme Right	Popular Party	Rainbow

Horizontal centring

Steps to determine starting point for each column—Backspacing method.

(See last section of *Handbook, Solutions, and Resource Material* for arithmetical method of horizontal centring)

(a) Backspace once for every two characters and spaces in the longest item of each column, saying them to yourself in pairs. If there is an odd letter left over in any column, carry this on to the next column.
(b) Add together the total number of spaces to be left between all the columns plus any odd character (if there is one) from the last column and divide by two—backspace this number (ignore fractions).
(c) Set left margin stop at the point thus reached.
(d) Starting from the left margin, tap space bar once for each character and space in the longest line of the first column and once for each blank space between first and second columns. Set first tab stop at this point for the start of the second column and make a note of this figure.
(e) Starting from this first tab stop, again tap space bar once for each character and space in the longest item of the second column and for each blank space between second and third columns.
(f) Set second tab stop at this point for the start of the third column and make a note of this figure.
(g) Continue in the same way for any additional columns.
(h) Return carriage/carrier/cursor and test tab stop settings.

Horizontal centring using a VDU

If you have a VDU, you can find the start of each column in the following way:
(a) Clear tab stops, and set equal left and right margins of 13 mm (half an inch).
(b) Type the longest item in the first column plus three spaces; the longest item in the second column plus three spaces, etc, and the longest item in the last column.
(c) Press the centre key, re-set left margin and set tab stops.
(d) Erase all the words and then type the heading at the left margin followed by the remainder of the exercise.

3 Carrying out the instructions given above, type the following table on A5 landscape paper. (a) Type the heading on the 14th single space from the top edge of the paper. (b) Leave three spaces between columns. (c) Double spacing.

MAJOR INDUSTRIES IN EC COUNTRIES

Industrial manufacture	Petrochemicals	Agriculture
Tourism	Textiles	Service industries
Leisure industries	Financial services	Oil
Car industry	Fishing	Shipping

3 Type the following letter from Eastways Developments (UK) Ltd on A4 letterhead paper. (a) Margins: 12 pitch 22–82, 10 pitch 12–72. (b) Take a carbon copy. (c) Insert a subject heading TRANSLATIONS. (d) Type a C6 envelope. (e) Mark the letter and envelope URGENT.

Ref RRH/OP

5 August 1993

Ms Emily Faulkner
Translations and Marketing Manager
Exact Translations
19 Pollard Street
LONDON
W1V 4AX

Dear Madam

We hv today rec'd a letter + a 20-page report from a client in Germany, written in his own language. Although we are able to make a fair translation, it is important th we do not, in any way, misunderstand the contents of the report.

We understand th you hv "mother tongue" translators, + shd be glad if you wd let us hv an accurate transcription of the enclosed document by Tues at the latest.

It wl also be nec for us to send a reply in German, + I shd also be glad if you wld send us, by return, yr charges.

Yrs ffly
EASTWAYS DEVELOPMENTS (UK) LTD

Rupert R Hambridge
Sales Manager

4 Type the following letter from Eastways Developments (UK) Ltd on A4 letterhead paper. (a) Margins: 12 pitch 22–82, 10 pitch 12–72. (b) Take a carbon copy. (c) Insert a subject heading MARKETING. (d) Type a C6 envelope. (e) Mark the letter and the envelope FOR THE ATTENTION OF MR BENJAMIN PAGET.

Ref RRH/OP 11 Aug 93

European Systems Partners 26 Mill St UCKFIELD Sussex TN22 5AA

Dr Sirs

I believe th yr co offers advice abt the marketing of products in Europe.

I shd be glad if you wld send me information on –

(Inset 5 spaces)

(1) Establishing the right distributors.
(2) Technical + market assessments for our products.
(3) Design + product manufacture for the German + French markets particularly.

Enclosed are full details of our business + its products.

Yrs ffly

(TYPIST – Please complete as in Ex 3 above.)

Enc

Vertical centring

The proper vertical arrangement of columns will add greatly to the effectiveness of your display. Use the same method for vertical centring as explained on page 45.

4 Type the following table on A5 portrait paper. (a) Centre vertically and horizontally. (b) Leave three spaces between columns. (c) Double spacing. (d) Before typing the exercise, make sure you know through which countries the rivers run.

SOME PRINCIPAL EUROPEAN RIVERS

The Seine	The Tiber	The Loire
The Rhine	The Elbe	The Meuse
The Thames	The Tejo	The Dee
The Spree	The Arno	The Shannon

The calculations for the vertical centring in the above exercise are given below:

(a) Number of vertical linespaces on A5 portrait paper = 50
(b) Number of vertical lines and spaces in table = 9
(c) Difference to be divided between top and bottom margins 50 − 9 = 41
(d) Divide by 2 = 20
(e) Begin typing heading on 21st line, so leaving 20 clear.

5 Type the following table on A5 landscape paper. (a) Centre vertically and horizontally. (b) Leave three spaces between columns. (c) Single spacing.

HYPHENATED WORDS

take-off	pre-set	pre-shrunk	part-exchange
safety-belt	ear-ring	so-called	copy-book
know-how	co-opt	sister-in-law	by-law
key-ring	press-button	re-entry	lay-by
tax-free	time-consuming	price-list	laissez-faire

6 Type the following table on A5 portrait paper. (a) Centre vertically and horizontally. (b) Leave three spaces between columns. (c) Double spacing. (d) Before you type the exercise, make sure you know the meanings of each pair of words.

HOMOPHONES

ascent/assent	site/sight
board/bored	stationery/stationary
faint/feint	to/too/two
piece/peace	residence/residents
practice/practise	check/cheque

Create a new document (filename SAME) and key in document 6 for 10-pitch printout. Embolden the main heading. When you have completed this task, proofread (screenread) carefully and correct if necessary. Print out original and store on disk under filename SAME.

See Practical Typing Exercises, Book One, page 19, for further exercises on

When using a word processor/computer, information that you key in may be stored on magnetic disks. Many organizations keep names and addresses in storage for immediate retrieval and use when writing to customers/clients.

Freepost

An organization wishing to receive a reply (or response to an advertisement) from customers, without them having to pay postage, may (by obtaining a licence from the Post Office) tell the customers to use the word FREEPOST on the envelope. The word is usually typed in capitals on a line by itself after the name of the organization.

Memo

It is sometimes necessary to type an envelope for a memo, especially if it is marked PRIVATE or CONFIDENTIAL. When addressing the envelope, do not type the word 'To', which appears on the memo form, but just the name and designation, if there is one, of the addressee. If the memo is marked PRIVATE, URGENT, CONFIDENTIAL, etc, then this special mark must also be typed, preferably before the name of the addressee. If you are given the address of the addressee, then obviously this must also be typed on the envelope.

In many organizations, courtesy titles (Mrs, Mr, Miss, Ms) are not used when typing memos, and quite often originators use initials only. Follow examiner's script in an examination and housestyle in business.

Carbon copies

All business firms keep an exact copy of letters, invoices, and other documents they send out. For this purpose the typist may use carbon film. To take a carbon copy:

(a) Place face downwards on a flat surface the sheet on which typing is to be done.

(b) On top of this, with matt/dull surface upwards, place a sheet of carbon film.

(c) Place on top of these the sheet of paper on which the carbon copy is to be made. This is usually a sheet of bank (flimsy) paper, as compared with the top sheet which is usually bond (better quality) paper. If additional copies are required, repeat steps (b) and (c).

(d) Pick up all sheets together and insert into machine with coated surface of carbon film facing cylinder.

(e) Make sure that feed rolls grip all sheets at the same time.

Erasing on carbon copies Do not handle the carbon film more than is absolutely necessary, as you may transfer marks to both top and carbon copies if your fingers are dirty.

(a) *Correction paper/Lift-off tape* Before inserting the correction paper for the top copy in front of the printing point, or using the lift-off tape, insert the special correction paper prepared for carbon copies between the matt side of your carbon film and the carbon copy. Then place the correction paper for the top copy in front of the printing point and type the incorrect letter through all sheets. *Remove the strips of paper* and type the correct letter(s).

(b) *Correction fluid* Apply the appropriate fluid to the error on the carbon copy. It is imperative that the fluid should be quite dry before any attempt is made to type in the correction.

(c) *Rubber* Before erasing, insert a strip of thickish paper between the matt side of your carbon film and the carbon copy. Then erase on the top copy. Remove the strip of paper and erase on the carbon copy. If you are taking more than one carbon copy, insert strips of paper behind the matt surface of each sheet of carbon film. Erase on the carbon copy/copies. *Remove the strips* and then return the carriage/carrier to the typing point and type the correct letter(s).

Photocopying

Most companies now use a copier and you may be asked to 'photocopy' or 'photostat' an original document, instead of taking a carbon copy. There are many different makes and models, but the machines are simple to operate, and you will soon learn how to use the particular model in your office. In many offices, the typist will type the letters pc, followed by a number, at the bottom of a document (letter, memo, etc) to indicate the number of photocopies to be taken, eg, pc 5.

NCR (no carbon required)

This stationery is popular for multiple-page forms. The paper has been chemically treated and the impression, made on the original, appears on the copies without the use of carbon film.

Typing column headings—Blocked style

In addition to the main heading of a table, each column may have a heading. The length of the column heading must be taken into account when deciding which is the longest line in each column. When there are headings above columns, proceed as follows:

(a) Find longest line in each column. It could be the heading or a column item.

(b) Backspace as usual to find left margin, remembering to take into account the spacing between columns, and set left margin and tab stops, and make a note of these figures. Column headings and column items start at left margin and at the tab stops set for the longest line of each column/heading.

(c) Turn up two single (one double) after the main headings.

(d) Turn up two single (one double) after the column headings.

7 Following the above instructions, type this exercise on A5 landscape paper. (a) Centre the whole table vertically and horizontally. (b) Leave three spaces between columns. (c) Double spacing.

EUROPEAN COUNTRIES

Turn up one double

Currencies

Turn up one double

Country	Currency	Country	Currency	Country	Currency
Belgium	Franc	Germany	Mark	Italy	Lira
Denmark	Krone	Greece	Drachma	Luxembourg	Franc
France	Franc	Ireland	Punt	Netherlands	Guilder
Spain	Peseta	UK	Pound	Portugal	Escudo

Turn up one double

8 Type the following exercise on A5 portrait paper. (a) Centre the table vertically and horizontally. (b) Leave three spaces between columns. (c) Single spacing. (d) Before you type the exercise, find the name of Denmark's Copenhagen airport and insert it in your typed copy.

INTERNATIONAL AIRPORTS

Turn up two single

Turn up two single

Country	City	Name of Airport
Netherlands	Amsterdam	Schipol
Greece	Athens	Athinai
Germany	Berlin	Tempelhof
Denmark	Copenhagen	
Spain	Madrid	Barajas
France	Paris	Charles de Gaulle
Portugal	Lisbon	Lisbonne
Italy	Rome	Leonardo da Vinci

9 Type the following exercise on A5 landscape paper. (a) Centre the table vertically and horizontally. (b) Leave three spaces between columns. (c) Single spacing.

EC COUNTRIES

Capital cities

Country	Capital city	Country	Capital city
Denmark	Copenhagen	Spain	Madrid
Belgium	Brussels	Italy	Rome
Luxembourg	Luxembourg	Greece	Athens
Netherlands	Amsterdam	France	Paris
Portugal	Lisbon	UK	London

TYPIST Retain abbreviations

(a) Must always be used with a person's name, eg, Miss P T Allsop F Garni Esq Jnr Mr B D Hayden Mrs G Jahn Ms E H Kershaw Mr and Mrs J Hewitt or Mr and Mrs John Hewitt*
(b) Use either Mr or Esq when addressing a man, never both
(c) Rev replaces Mr or Esq, eg, Rev H I Livingstone
(d) Partnerships—the word Messrs may be used before the name of a partnership, eg, Messrs Ling & Sons Messrs Naughton & Co Messrs Nynett & Shaw
(e) Courtesy titles are not used in the following cases:
  (i) before the name of a limited company, eg, K Shuker & Co Ltd Tehan & Watts PLC L Hocking & Sons Ltd
  (ii) with impersonal names, eg, The British Non-ferrous Metal Co
  (iii) when a title is included in a name, eg, Sir Brian Warrender & Co Sir Christopher Derricott-Browne
  (iv) with the names of societies, associations, clubs, etc, eg, Tile Hill Tennis Club.

* It should be noted that many married couples now prefer the use of the husband's and wife's initials, eg, Mr J and Mrs M Hewitt or Mr John and Mrs Mary Hewitt. In business, follow housestyle.

Addressing envelopes

Approximately one-third in from left edge ↓

First line half way down → Mr R Maybury MA BSc
'The Shrubbery'
Holly Road
Post town in capitals → TEWKESBURY
Glos
One space between the two halves of code → GL20 5AA

Each item on a separate line

C6 envelope — 162 × 114 mm ($6\frac{3}{8}'' \times 4\frac{1}{2}''$)

```
URGENT

Dr J Bhattay
8 Leigh Drive
Byfleet
WEYBRIDGE
Surrey
KT14 7RD
```

2 Type the following addresses on C6 envelopes. Mark the first envelope PERSONAL and the third FOR THE ATTENTION OF MR F PORTER.

C R Maunder Esq 2 North Terrace Fenit TRALEE Co Kerry Irish Republic
Monsieur Claude Derrien Place des Fleurs Pouilly 60790 VALDAMPIERRE France
G M Morris & Co Ltd 11 Main Road LLANDEILO Dyfed SA19 6EP
Herrn Erich Boll Berner Str 9a 7800 FREIBURG Germany
Mr P McCready PhD JP 32 Manley Avenue Fetterangus CUPAR Fife KY15 5AS
Pieter van Kleef PO Box 5241 2280 AK The Hague The Netherlands
Rev I L Yoxall Holly Tree House Butterton LEEK Staffs ST13 7SY
The Tyson Engineering Co FREEPOST Belgrave Road Highgate BIRMINGHAM B5 2JD
McCluskey Bros 10 Waterford Road LARNE Co Antrim BT40 1AA

See Practical Typing Exercises, Book One, page 29, for further exercises on

These simulated office tasks are preceded by a **Typist's log sheet** (copy in the *Handbook, Solutions, and Resource Material*). Refer to the **Log sheet** for instructions and relevant details before and during the typing of the documents.

Timing

Today, because of the number of automatic functions on certain electronic keyboards (as compared with, say, a manual typewriter), it is impossible to set an average timing for any one document. In some typewriting examinations you should complete all questions; therefore, we suggest that your objective is to type the **Integrated production typing projects** within the time allowed. This time includes proofreading the typed page before removing it from the machine and making corrections where necessary.

Reading the manuscript, or typescript, through to see that you understand the contents (which is of paramount importance), deciding on linespacing and margins, reading and following instructions, are all essential typing techniques that require immediate decisions and must be carried out speedily and accurately. Therefore, within the time allowed for the project, we have allocated 10 minutes for reading through the complete script, marking the special points to watch for and corrections to be made, deciding on what paper to use, what margins to set, where carbon copies are required, etc, and another five minutes for a final check to see that each task has been attempted and each instruction followed.

Any writer, when preparing a draft or editing a script, may unwittingly make a mistake—it may be a word spelt incorrectly; an apostrophe in the wrong place, or no apostrophe at all when there should be one; it may be that the verb does not agree with the subject. You have to correct these mistakes when you are typing. In practice exercises we draw your attention to the words by circling them; in all but the first **Integrated production typing project** we do not circle them: you have to watch for the errors and correct them, just as you would do in business.

Mailable documents

The contents must make sense; no omissions (you could have a serious omission and the document may still make sense); no uncorrected errors (misspellings, incorrect punctuation, typing errors, etc); no careless corrections (if part of the wrong letter(s) is showing, the correction is not acceptable); no smudges; no creases. Consistency in spelling, in format, in typing sums of money, etc, is vital. Occasionally, your tutor may return a document marked C & M (correct and mail). This means that there is an error that will not be difficult to correct, and after a neat correction, the document may be mailed. Remember to correct the carbon copy.

Folders

Keep the typed documents in a folder marked FOR SIGNATURE, and the folder (with the tasks in document number order, together with the **Log sheet**) should be handed to your tutor when you are sure that all the documents (in any one group) are MAILABLE and ready for approval and signature where appropriate. Also, keep a separate folder for the documents that have been approved/signed—file the documents under the **Log sheet** number and in document number order.

Typist's log sheet

The information in the **Typist's log sheet** will follow a pattern: name of employer will be at the top; the name of the originator and the department (where appropriate) will be handwritten; the date may or may not be given, but letters and memos must have a date unless there are instructions to the contrary. If you have access to a word processor, a text-editing electronic typewriter, or a correction only electronic typewriter, follow the general instructions given on the **Log sheet** against the symbol  and enter your name, date and starting time near the bottom of the sheet. When all the documents have been completed and are ready for approval/signature, calculate and enter the TOTAL TYPING TIME at the bottom of the last column, and also record the date and time of completion.

Urgent

Note that any input marked with an asterisk (*) is urgent and should be dealt with first. See that it is ready for approval/ signature within 40 minutes of your starting time.

Stationery requisition

Before starting the **Integrated production typing projects**, you should read them through and decide on the quantity and kind of stationery you will require for all the tasks, and then fill in **Stationery requisition form** which you should hand to your tutor for approval.

Dates

A business document is of very little use unless it is dated and has a reference as to its origin. Documents, other than letters and memos, are usually dated at the bottom of the last page with the reference either before or after the date. When you are in business, follow the housestyle. Typewriting examiners for certain boards will penalize you if you date any document (unless there are instructions to do so) apart from letters and memos.

Superfluous wording

If you add a word(s) that is not in the script, eg, a reference in a letter when it is not given, then you may be penalized by the examiner. Similarly, if you insert a line before a footnote and there is no line in the script, then you may be penalized.

Check very carefully to ascertain what the examiner does and does not accept.

Resource material

The *Handbook, Solutions, and Resource Material* is looseleaf, and record sheets, printed letterheads, forms, form letters, etc, may be copied: these will make your typing much more realistic.

Because you still need a great deal of practice on typewriting conventions, deciding on margin settings, etc, we have supplied, in this first Integrated production typing project much more detail than that given in the projects that follow later on.

Envelopes

There are numerous sizes of envelopes, but the size will be used that best fits the letter and enclosures. The Post Office Preferred sizes are:
C5—229 × 162 mm (9" × $6\frac{3}{8}$") takes A5 paper unfolded and A4 folded once
C6—162 × 114 mm ($6\frac{3}{8}$" × $4\frac{1}{2}$") takes A4 folded twice and A5 folded once
DL—220 × 110 mm ($8\frac{5}{8}$" × $4\frac{1}{4}$") takes A4 equally folded into three and A5 folded once.
The above measurements fall within the POP (Post Office Preferred) sizes. The POP envelopes are sorted automatically, whereas larger or smaller sizes are not, and there may be an extra charge for sizes outside the POP range.

1 Type the following on A4 paper. (a) Margins: 12 pitch 20–85, 10 pitch 11–76. (b) Single spacing, with double between each numbered item. (c) Inset the numbered items six spaces from the left margin.

GUIDE FOR TYPING ENVELOPES

The Post Office prefer addresses on envelopes to be displayed in accordance with the following guidelines.

1 The name and address should always be parallel to the longer side of the envelope.

2 On most envelopes the address should be started about one-third in from the left edge.

3 Do not leave less than 38 mm from the top edge of the envelope before typing the first line; preferably start halfway down so that the address is not obliterated by the postmark. Each line of the address should occupy a separate line.

4 Single spacing is preferable on smaller envelopes - double spacing on larger envelopes - and the post town should be typed in CLOSED CAPITALS.

5 The postcode is the last line in the address and should have a line to itself. The code is always typed in BLOCK CAPITALS. Do not use full stops or any punctuation marks between or after the characters in the code. Leave one clear space between the 2 halves of the code.

6 Special instructions such as PERSONAL, CONFIDENTIAL, PRIVATE or FOR THE ATTENTION OF, which appear on the document to be enclosed in the envelope, should be typed 2 spaces above the name and address.

Forms of address—Open punctuation

DEGREES AND QUALIFICATIONS—no punctuation. No spaces between the letters representing a degree or qualification, but one clear space between each group of letters, eg, Mrs (space) A (space) Sinclair (space) MA (space) PhD   Mrs A Sinclair MA PhD

POST OFFICE RECOMMENDATIONS

The Post Office now use OCR (optical character recognition) machines for reading and sorting mail at a high speed: 35 000 items an hour. However, the machines can be used only if certain sized envelopes (please see top of this page) and methods of addressing are followed:

(a) The post town (in capitals) county (where appropriate) and postcode should each form the last three lines of the address. For overseas mail, the country name should be the last item.
(b) One space must be left between the two halves of the code and NO punctuation IN or AFTER the code; NEVER underline any of the items in the address; whenever possible, use no punctuation at all in the name and address on envelopes.
(c) The OCR machines cannot read script or italic typefaces; addresses typed on envelopes which are not white, buff or cream; proportionately spaced type; or crooked application of address labels. The typeface should be 10, 11 or 12 characters to the inch.

TOWN TWINNING ASSOCIATION

OFFICE SERVICES—REQUEST FORM

This sheet contains instructions that must be complied with when typing the documents. Read the information carefully before starting, and refer back to it frequently.

Typist's log sheet

Originator JACK SIMONS Chairman   Department ——   Date 23.6.93.   Ext No –

Typists operating a word processor, or electronic typewriter with appropriate function keys, should apply the following automatic facilities: top margin; carrier/cursor return; line-end hyphenation; underline OR bold print (embolden); error correction; centring; any other relevant applications.

Remember (a) to complete the details required at the bottom of the form; (b) to enter typing time per document in the appropriate column; and (c) before submitting this **Log sheet** and your completed work, enter TOTAL TYPING TIME in the last column so that the Typist's time may be charged to the originator.

Document No	Type of document and instructions	Copies – Original plus	Input form¶	Typing time per document	Total typing time Ɏ
1	Notice of Twinning Ceremony	1 original	AT		
2	Personal letter.	1 original	AT		
3	Notice of visit by delegates from Unterhaching. Use A4 paper.	1 original	AT		
* 4	Letter to Cllr Mrs Abbotts on A4 headed paper.	1 original	AT		
5	News items – A5 landscape.	1 original	MS		
6	List of clubs + associations in Unterhaching. Use A5 landscape paper.	1 original	T		
7	Memo on A5 headed paper.	1 original	AT		
			TOTAL	TYPING TIME	

TYPIST – please complete:

Typist's name: Date received: Date completed:

Time received: Time completed:

If the typed documents cannot be returned within 24 hours, the office services supervisor should inform the originator. Any item that is urgent should be marked with an asterisk (*).

¶ T = Typescript   AT = Amended Typescript   MS = Manuscript   SD = Shorthand Dictation   AD = Audio Dictation

Ɏ To be charged to the originator's department.

Follow instructions given at top of page 42. Margins: 12 pitch 22–82, 10 pitch 12–72.

A Review alphabet keys

1 The dozens of climbers were frequently exhausted when trying
to complete the fantastic job of climbing the very high rock
mountain.

B Improve accuracy on use of shift key

2 Vale Kay Union Ruth Gwen Edna Lily Adam Nora Zena John Terry
3 York Coxon Olive Frank Henry Devon Innes Queen Wilson Barrie
4 Ask Miss Edna Trim to see Mr P St John Barrington on Monday.
5 Adam, Olive, Frank, Lily and Ruth left Devon for York today.

C Improve accuracy on word-building drill

6 tend attend attends attended attending attendance attendants
7 be belie belief believe believes believed believing believer
8 We believe their attendance has tended to be poor this term.
9 The attendants believe that the attendance will now improve.

D Improve control of both hands

10 loaf pure knife lived judge upper ounces populate minimized.
11 jive nine house begin carol dream evenly imported detection.
12 I lived in the upper regions where people were hard to find.

E Spelling skill *Correct the one misspelt word in each line. (Answer: page 181)*

13 forcible salaried arguements underrate courageous emphasized.
14 modelled steadily inhabited posseses especially vaccinated.
15 He emphasized that he did not underate all their arguments.

Skill measurement *30 wpm* *$1\frac{1}{2}$ minutes* *Not more than 2 errors*

SM30 You will be pleased to learn that we have made more machines 12
this year than we did last year, and that we are also making 24
all vital spare parts. Over the next 2 months we shall take 36
orders only for the new models we are producing. **(SI 1.22)** 45

SM31 There is nothing that annoys a business man more than clerks 12
who forget to do jobs given to them. A very good idea is to 24
have a pad on your desk, so that you can write down straight 36
away anything that you may be required to do. **(SI 1.27)** 45

1 | 2 | 3 | 4 | 5 | 6 | 7 | 8 | 9 | 10 | 11 | 12 |

Record your progress *$1\frac{1}{2}$ minutes*

R22 Dear Ms Knight, Since July 1992 we have had your name on our 12
mailing lists, and although we have, from time to time, sent 24
you details of many exclusive properties, you have not tele- 36
phoned as you said you would. We are now anxious to know if 48
you have any queries and still wish to buy a desirable resi- 60
dence at an amazingly low price. 66

1 | 2 | 3 | 4 | 5 | 6 | 7 | 8 | 9 | 10 | 11 | 12 |

Document 1 Production target—12 minutes

TYPIST – Use A4 paper please & follow the display shown below.

T W I N N I N G   C E R E M O N Y

WITNEY, Oxfordshire - UNTERHACHING, Bavaria

10 July 1993

Europa Hymn

WELCOME

by Chairman of Witney's Twinning Association

FORMAL ADDRESSES

EMP for Berkshire
Witney's Mayor
Unterhaching's Mayor

← leave 2 blank lines here

SIGNING OF THE WITNEY-UNTERHACHING CHARTER

← " " " " "

Bavarian, German and British Anthems

Document 2 Production target—12 minutes

TYPIST – Please retype on A5 portrait paper making the necessary alterations.

4 Downes Lane
WITNEY
Oxon
OX8 6AX

Insert date here

Mr and Mrs D Gowering

TYPIST – You will find Mr & Mrs Gowering's address in the Data Files (filename HOST on page 184

Dear Mr and Mrs Gowering

I am very sorry to hear that you will no longer be able to host a member of the twinning delegation from Unterhaching because of your daughters illness. I do hope she will make a complete recovery.

Yours sincerely

Insetting matter from left margin

Matter may be inset from the left margin to give a certain part of the work greater emphasis. This matter may or may not consist of numbered items. You must follow any instructions given to you as to how many spaces to indent. There is always one clear linespace before and after inset matter. When insetting matter you may either:

(a) Set a tab stop at the point where each of the lines in the inset portion will commence; or
(b) re-set the left margin. When using this method, it is most important to remember to go back to the original margin when you have finished typing the inset portion. It is wise to make a reminder mark on the copy at the point where you need to revert to the original margin again.

Some electronic machines allow for a second temporary margin to be set while retaining the original margin.

3 Type the following on A4 paper. (a) Use single spacing, with double between the paragraphs. (b) Margins: 12 pitch 22–82, 10 pitch 12–72.

THE COUNCIL OF EUROPE

The Council of Europe was set up in 1949 and consists of representatives from 25 countries.

It enables them

Inset 5 spaces

> to exchange views, discuss problems which affect them all and, most important, to get to know one another, so leading to a climate of confidence and peace throughout the continent.

In 1991 its membership consisted of 25 countries with Poland set to join as soon as it could meet the full rules for membership.

4 Type the following on A5 portrait paper. (a) Single spacing. (b) Margins: 12 pitch 13–63, 10 pitch 6–56.

USING THE CE MARK

A CE mark generally indicates th the product on wh the mark appears conforms to the standards laid down by the European Community.

Inset 5 spaces

> 1) The mark shd be a minimum of 5mm high.
> 2) The thickness of the CE letters shd be at least one-fifth of the height of the mark.
> 3) The mark shd be clear, visible & long lasting.

You may find the CE mark on items such as toys & electrical goods. It is against the law to use the mark on goods th are not covered by EC standards.

Create a new document (filename MARK) and key in document 4 for 15-pitch printout. When you have completed this task, proofread (screenread) carefully and correct if necessary. Print out original and store on disk under filename MARK. Follow the instructions for text editing on page 182.

See Practical Typing Exercises, Book One, page 28, for further exercises on Inset matter

Document 3 Production target—15 minutes

TYPIST – Double spacing please, to the following margins –
12 pitch 25 - 85
10 pitch 12 - 72

VISIT BY UNTERHACHING DELEGATES

9, 10 and 11 July 1993

The delegates will arrive at Heathrow, Terminal 2, Flight LH1676, at 1335 hours and be met by coach and 2/3 members of the twinning comitee.

9 JULY AT 1930 HOURS International evening at Langdon Hall; admission by ticket only.

10 JULY AT 1100 HOURS Twinning ceremony at Langdon Hall followed by Mayor's Reception and official luncheon.

11 JULY AT 1030 HOURS The delegates will leave by coach for a tour of Windsor and Hampton Court before going on to Heathrow, Terminal 2, for Flight LH1661 which departes at hours.

TYPIST – Please check the time the plane leaves in the Data Files (filename HOUR) on page 184, & enter here.

Document 4 Production target—15 minutes

Our ref JS/Yr initials

Insert tomorrow's date here & don't forget to mark the letter URGENT

Councillor Mrs J Abbotts
1 Church Lane
WITNEY
Oxon
OX8 4ST

Dear Mrs Abbotts

UNTERHACHING

Thank you for your letter which I received this morning asking for some information about the town of Unterhaching.

Unterhaching has a population of approximately 18 000. It is 20 minutes by S-Bahn from the centre of Munich. It has a Town Council of 24 members (to be increased to 30 when the population reaches 20 000).

It has a new Town Hall (Rathaus) where 45 staff are employed and a combined primary/secondary school (Hauptschule) which caters for 500 pupils from 6 to 15 years of age.

Please do not hesitate to contact me if you require further information.

Yours sincerely

Jack Simons
Chairman

Enumerated items

Paragraphs and items are sometimes numbered or lettered as shown below. The numbers or letters may stand on their own or be enclosed in brackets. Leave one clear linespace between enumerated items. Two or three character spaces follow the last figure, letter or bracket, and it is essential to be consistent. There is always one clear linespace before and after enumerated items, eg

1 [2] Name	(1) [2] Name	(A) [2] Name	a) [2] Name
2 Address	(2) Address	(B) Address	b) Address

NB If the items run on in a paragraph and are not listed one under the other, only leave one clear character space after the figure, letter or bracket.

1 Type the following on A4 paper. (a) Use single spacing if an item goes on to more than one line, but double spacing between each item. (b) Margins: 12 pitch 22–82, 10 pitch 12–72. (c) Leave two character spaces after the item number. (d) Top margin: 51 mm (2 inches), ie, turn up 13 single spaces from the top edge of the paper. (e) Make your own line-endings.

THE GRAND DUCHY OF

L U X E M B O U R G

NB With OPEN punctuation there is no full stop after the figure or letter that lists the items.

Luxembourg is an original member of the Community, and houses many European organizations, such as the European Court of Justice.

1 It covers an area of 3000 sq km and is by far the smallest of the EC member states.

2 It has a population of about 0.4 million, and has 5 MEPs.

3 Its economy is totally dependent on EC membership; its major industries being iron and steel, and agriculture.

2 Type the following on A5 portrait paper. (a) Use single spacing, with double between each item. (b) Margins: 12 pitch 13–63, 10 pitch 6–56. (c) Leave two character spaces after the bracketed letters. (d) Make your own line-endings.

A I R S T R E A M

The Royal Mail International's Airstream service enables you to send mail speedily and reliably to many destinations throughout the world.

(A) Sort your mail into Europe and Rest of the World and mark the bundles using the appropriate label provided by Royal Mail International.

(B) Weigh and count the no of items in ea bundle & enter the details on the posting docket provided.

(C) Calculate the cost of posting at the bottom of the docket. Then enclose 2 copies of the completed docket in the mailbag wh is provided.

(D) TYPIST – You wl find this item in the Data Files (filename AIR) on page 183. Please type it here.

Create a new document (filename AIR) and key in document 2 for 12-pitch printout. When you have completed this task, proofread (screenread) carefully and correct if necessary. Print out original and store on disk under filename AIR. Follow the instructions for text editing on page 182.

See Practical Typing Exercises, Book One, page 27, for further exercises on

Document 5 *Production target—12 minutes*

TOWN TWINNING

NEWS ITEMS

TYPIST - Please insert the Secretary's name here. You will find it in Document 7.

Pen Friends

Our twin town wd like a list of young people who wd be interested in writing to young people of a similar age in Unterhaching. Please see the Sec, ,
if you are interested.

AGM ← In full →

A reminder that the AGM + barbeque wl be held on 24 July @ 7.30 pm. All welcome. / are

Document 6 *Production target—12 minutes*

U N T E R H A C H I N G

Clubs and Associations

Fishing Association	Volleyball Club	Soccer Club
Red Cross Group	Girl Scouts	Music School
Brass Band	Social Club	Netball Club
Boy Scouts	Shooting Club	Athletics and Judo Club

Document 7 *Production target—12 minutes*

From Jack Simons Chairman

To Mona Patridge ~~Treasurer~~ Secretary

Date

GRANT AID

I am enclosing a circular I have received from the Commission of the European Communities which states that "twinned towns (or towns being twinned) can receive financial assistance for gatherings they arrange with other towns". We should qualify for aid for our twinning ceremony with Unterhaching.

Would you please send for an application form as soon as poss.

JS/ Yr initials

Enc

Follow instructions given at top of page 42. Margins: 12 pitch 22–82, 10 pitch 12–72.

A Review alphabet keys

1 The executive was next in line for the position of Editor on
the Gazette as the skills required for the job were just the
ones possessed by him.

B Build accuracy on one-hand words

2 dresses nylon extra jolly great knoll agree pylon gave on my
3 opinion trade union aware only safe upon area joy car him at
4 In our opinion, you were aware of the trade union wage rate.
5 I agree the extra trade in nylon dresses gave him great joy.

C Build accuracy on double-letter words

6 programmes possible running supply arrive proof agree added.
7 difficult football baggage accept excess rubber attend carry
8 Is it possible to supply a proof of the football programmes?
9 We agree that it was difficult to accept the excess baggage.

D Improve control of both hands

10 swim frail action stroll punter nominate fraction impressed.
11 just dwell brains pooled number populate immodest kilowatts.
12 It would seem right to take action and nominate Joan Howlet.

E Spelling skill *Correct the one misspelt word in each line. (Answer: page 181)*

13 potato ocasion exercise hardware guardian reducing familiar
14 wholly separate definite feasible expenses gaurdian pleasant
15 On this occasion I was quite familar with the charges made.

Skill measurement *30 wpm One minute Not more than one error*

SM28 The weather is likely to remain mild in the south, with some 12
light rain, but in the north there may be ground frost which 24
could cause ice on some roads. **(SI 1.10)** 30

SM29 Road conditions have been quite difficult for some time, but 12
we are sure they will improve. We share your view, and know 24
we must be patient and careful. **(SI 1.23)** 30

1 | 2 | 3 | 4 | 5 | 6 | 7 | 8 | 9 | 10 | 11 | 12 |

Record your progress *One minute*

R21 If you are asked to compile a business letter, you must: (a) 12
use short words if they express clearly what you want to say 24
and (b) also keep your sentences short. Tackle the job with 36
zeal, acquire a good style, and avoid vague statements. 47
(SI 1.25)

1 | 2 | 3 | 4 | 5 | 6 | 7 | 8 | 9 | 10 | 11 | 12 |

Follow instructions given at top of page 42. Margins: 12 pitch 22–82, 10 pitch 12–72.

A *Review alphabet keys*

1 With maximum efficiency vivacious Eliza completed the formal tests, was judged to be the best candidate, and acquired the highest marks.

B *Improve control of figure keys*

2 wee 233 our 974 try 546 ere 343 wit 285 ire 843 too 599 6789
3 330 339 338 337 336 992 993 994 995 123 456 789 101 293 2345
4 Final 7%, payable 3 November, making 12½%. Profit £455 980.
5 Flight 417 leaves at 1350, while Flight 148B leaves at 1619.

C *Build accuracy on suffix drill*

6 using ending asking making turning morning replying advising
7 comment shipment equipment settlement adjustment arrangement
8 We will not comment about the shipments of equipment to you.
9 In the morning we shall be asking him what car he is taking.

D *Practise alternate hand drill*

10 jam hale curl lake make foam roam turn forms provide profits
11 pay burn work hale worm paid kept spar usual turkeys handles
12 My visual aid showed the profits we make on the new handles.

E *Spelling skill* *Correct the one misspelt word in each line.* *(Answer: page 181)*

13 valuable marriage function paralel secretary advertisements
14 exercise envelope physical planning colleague miscelaneous.
15 My Secretary's function was to exercise complete discresion.

Skill measurement *29 wpm* *One minute* *Not more than one error*

SM25 We hear that you plan to buy new desks, chairs and files, so 12
we are sending you a copy of our price-lists which will give 24
you a wide range of choice. **(SI 1.07)** 29

SM26 Against the clear blue morning sky, the white sails of their 12
graceful yachts made an ever-changing pattern as they danced 24
and swayed in the breeze. **(SI 1.21)** 29

1 | 2 | 3 | 4 | 5 | 6 | 7 | 8 | 9 | 10 | 11 | 12 |

Record your progress *One minute*

R19 It may be next June before I can be certain of the number of 12
folk who may be present at the Market Square for this year's 24
Fair. Four years ago our efforts added up to zero, but I am 36
sure we have already sold more tickets than in 1992. 46

1 | 2 | 3 | 4 | 5 | 6 | 7 | 8 | 9 | 10 | 11 | 12 |

(a) Usually printed and typed in red.
(b) Used to cancel an incorrect invoice.
(c) Used for crediting goods or packing cases returned.
(d) A supplier who credits a customer for goods/services relating to taxable supplies, must issue a VAT credit note, which should give: VAT registration number, amount credited for each item, rate and amount of VAT credited, etc.

4 Type the following credit note on a suitable form. Please see *Handbook, Solutions, and Resource Material* for a printed form.

CREDIT NOTE NO 1368

CASA DE EUROPA PLC
269 Britannia Way
RICHMOND Surrey TW9 1JA

Telephone 081-447 9229 Telex 56980

VAT registration No 992 3872 78 Date 15 July 1993

P K Jackson & Son Ltd
47 Ludlow Road
REDDITCH
Worcs
B98 8JZ

Original tax invoice No 4561
Date of invoice 05.07.93

Reason for credit	Quantity	Description	Total	
			£	
Damaged in transit	1	Dresden Figurine	100	00
		Total Credit	100	00
		Plus VAT	17	50
		TOTAL	£117	50
E & OE				

VAT SUMMARY

Code	%	Goods	Tax
1	17½	£100.00	£17.50

See Practical Typing Exercises, Book One, page 26, for further exercises on

Typing sums of money in columns

Refer to the instructions given on page 41 with regard to the typing of decimals. Then note the following: The £ sign is typed over the first figure in the £'s column. Units, tens, hundreds, etc, fall under one another.

Example £
230.16
12.10
0.24
147.00

1 Type the following on A5 portrait paper, taking care to type the decimal points, figures denoting units, tens and hundreds under one another. (a) Centre the exercise vertically and horizontally. (b) Leave three spaces between the columns. (c) Double spacing.

£	£	£
245.46	247.14	105.89
199.95	236.01	214.78
10.44	19.64	66.99
3.45	6.78	6.38

Interliner lever

The interliner lever may be found on the right or left side of the typewriter. Locate this on your machine. The interliner lever frees the cylinder from the ratchet control, so that the cylinder may be turned freely forward or backward as required. When the lever is returned to its normal position, your machine will automatically return to the original spacing.

Double underscoring of totals

For double lines underneath the totals, use the interliner. When typing totals, proceed as follows:

(a) Type the underscore for the first lines above the totals. (Do not turn up before typing the first lines). These lines extend from the first to the last figure of the longest item in each column including total.

(b) Turn up twice and type the totals.

(c) Turn up once, and then type the lines below the totals.

(d) Turn the cylinder up slightly by using the interliner lever and type the second lines. Then return the interliner lever to its normal position.

NOTE When typing columns with more than five figures in any column, you may leave a space between the hundred and thousand figure. (See **Variations in display**, in last section of *Handbook, Solutions, and Resource Material.*)

2 Display the following exercise on A5 landscape paper. (a) Single spacing for the main part. (b) Leave three spaces between columns. (c) Follow the instructions for the total figures. (d) Decimal points must fall under one another.

£	£	£	£	
228.90	12.34	212.34	109.87	
404.75	566.78	33.44	654.57	
323.25	90.12	105.62	1 010.85	
1 234.56	35.45	1 212.05	354.25	
789.00	1 237.95	343.18	1 213.65	
654.32	220.16	331.26	434.12	← Do not turn up
______	______	______	______	← Turn up 2 spaces
3 634.78	2 162.80	2 237.89	3 777.31	← Turn up 1 space
======	======	======	======	← Use interliner

If you are using an electronic keyboard, you may wish to use the appropriate keys for the decimal tab and for the underscore and double underscore.

A trader, registered for VAT, who supplies taxable goods to another taxable person, must issue a VAT invoice giving the VAT registration number, tax point, type of supply, etc.

3 Type the following invoice on a suitable form. Please see *Handbook, Solutions, and Resource Material* for printed form. Because of the small amount of space available, notice the use of figures for the date after 'Tax point'.

INVOICE NO 4561

CASA DE EUROPA PLC
269 Britannia Way
RICHMOND Surrey TW9 1JA

Telephone 081-447 9229 Telex 56980

VAT registration No 992 3872 78 Date 5 July 1993

P K Jackson & Son Ltd
47 Ludlow Road
REDDITCH
Worcs
B98 8JZ

Tax point 05.07.93
Type of supply Sale

Your order No PUR 1996/93 Account No J/2085 Advice note No 35949

Quantity	Description	Unit cost	Total cost
		£	£
6	Edinburgh Crystal Tumblers	30.00	180.00
2	Dresden Figurines	100.00	200.00
2	Aynsley Portland Vases	60.00	120.00

VAT SUMMARY

Code	%	Goods	Tax
1	17½	£500.00	£87.50

Total goods	500.00
Discount	0.00
Total VAT	87.50
TOTAL	£587.50

Subject to our conditions of sale. Copy on request.
E & OE

3 There is a skeleton of the form below in the *Handbook, Solutions, and Resource Material* and copies may be duplicated. Insert the form into your typewriter and then type in the handwritten words, following layout as in the textbook.

PERSONNEL RECORD CARD (PRC/1/93) Reverse side

Previous employer
R P Mitchell Ltd
3 Hawthorn Way
Doncaster
South Yorkshire DN1 1AA

From 4 February 1991 To 27 March 1992

Last position held
Shorthand Typist

Last school attended
Foster Comprehensive
Castle Hill
Doncaster
South Yorkshire DN1 1AA

From August 1985 To June 1990

Further education

Course Private Secretary's Certificate Day/Full-time Day

Books £69.25 Fees £169.00

Dates August 1990 - June 1991 Result Pass

Starting position Shorthand Typist Date 1 April 1992

Changes
Assistant Secretary

From 18 December 1992 To

SURNAME NEWTON OTHER NAMES Ruth Margaret

Forms

Business organizations have a great variety of forms that have been printed, or duplicated, with guide headings, boxes, columns, etc, and the typist has to type in additional information. When the insertion is typed on the same line as the printed heading, there are two clear spaces before the start of the insertion. Where the insertion comes below a printed heading, it is typed on the next line. However, if the column is deep and the information to be inserted is short, it will look better with a clear space between the printed heading and the inserted matter.

Information typed in opposite headings should be on the same line as the base of the printed heading and, therefore, it is important to know how close your typewriter prints to its aligning scale. Type a sentence and study exactly the space between the typing and the scale so that, when you insert a form and wish to align your typing with the bottom of the printed words, you will know how much to adjust the paper with the variable linespacer. When typing over ruled or dotted lines, no character should touch the ruled or dotted line. Therefore, with the variable linespacer adjust the typing line so that, when typed, the descending characters y, p, g, etc, are very slightly above the dotted line or underline.

INVOICE 2981

MATLOCK FURNITURE SUPPLIES Telephone 0629 074485
North Bakewell Road
MATLOCK
Derbyshire DE4 3AP

10 August 1993

Mr & Mrs T Brookes
32 Buxton Road
MATLOCK
Derbyshire DE4 1AA

NOTE After the second horizontal line, turn up two spaces and type the £ sign in the appropriate columns. Then turn up another two spaces before starting the items.
Figures—units must always be typed under units, tens under tens, etc. Follow the text layout carefully when typing the total column.
Where possible, leave two clear spaces after the vertical lines before typing the items—with the exception of the money columns where decimal points must fall underneath one another.

QUANTITY	DESCRIPTION	PRICE	TOTAL
		£	£
1	Resin Patio Table	90.00	90.00
4	Resin Leisure Chairs	25.50	102.00
1	Patio Parasol	40.00	40.00
1	Rocking Deck Chair	30.75	30.75
			262.75
	Delivery charge		12.00
	Prices include VAT E & OE		£274.75

Invoices

An invoice is the document sent by the seller to the purchaser and shows full details of the goods sold. The layout of invoices varies from organization to organization according to the data to be recorded. Invoices are printed with the seller's name, address and other useful information.

1 There is a skeleton invoice form in the *Handbook, Solutions, and Resource Material* and copies may be duplicated. Insert a copy into your machine and set left margin and tab stops for the beginning of each column. Then type the information exactly as it appears above.

2 On another invoice form display the following:

Invoice No: 3001 Supplier: Same as Ex. 1. Date: 12 August 1993
Purchaser: L D Williamson + Co 48 York Road Matlock Derbyshire DE4 1AP

3	Build-in Barbecues	23.50	70.50
3	Pairs Turning Tongs	3.75	11.25
3	'Triple' Fish Holders	4.50	13.50
			95.25
	Delivery charge		4.75
	Prices include VAT E + OE		£

TYPIST - Please calculate & type in the total. You may wish to use your calculator.

4 There is a skeleton of the form below in the *Handbook, Solutions, and Resource Material* and copies may be duplicated. Insert the form into your typewriter and then type in the handwritten words.

APPLICATION FOR EMPLOYMENT WITH AP/93/MAC

Kenkott Scotia PLC Byrnes Terrace Langside GLASGOW G41 3DI

Position applied for Shorthand Typist

Surname (in capitals) NEWTON Forenames Ruth Margaret

Address 42 Forest Road Doncaster South Yorkshire DN5 0AT

Telephone number 0302 466223 Nationality British

Date of birth 3 May 1973 Place of birth Doncaster Age 19

Married/single Single Mrs/Miss/Ms/Mr Ms

Last school and further education	From	To
Foster Comprehensive	August 1985	June 1990
Doncaster College of FE	August 1990	June 1991

Qualifications (please list your highest grade only in any one subject)

Subject	Level	Result
Maths	GCSE	'A'
Geography and History	GCSE	'B'
English	'A'	'A'
Private Secretary's Certificate	-	Pass

Previous employers

(1) Name R P Mitchell Ltd

Address 3 Hawthorn Way Doncaster South Yorkshire DN1 1AA

From 4 February 1991 To 27 March 1992

Position held Shorthand Typist Salary £9380

(2) Name ....

Address ....

From .... To ....

Position held .... Salary ....

Follow instructions given at top of page 42. Margins: 12 pitch 22–82, 10 pitch 12–72.

A Review alphabet keys

1 Flexible working is generally favoured and requested by most
employees as they can just avoid the crazy traffic.

B Build speed on word family drill

2 look took hook book nook cook best pest rest jest west nest.
3 call hall fall pall wall tall will pill bill hill fill mill.
4 He took a look at the book and said that he would call soon.
5 The birds will nest in a nook of the west wall of that mill.

C Build speed on fluency drill

6 right both they land wish held firm hand sign paid when form
7 busy lane fork pays dial make rich maps with half fuel road.
8 They wish both firms to sign the forms and pay for the land.
9 It is a busy lane to the right of a fork road by the chapel.

D Practise alternate hand drill

10 she jay hale kale pale lame flame handy signal disown dispel
11 fox ape gown town worn torn quake rigid theory thrown formal
12 He was formal and rigid, and his excuses were pale and lame.

E Spelling skill *Correct the one misspelt word in each line. (Answer: page 181)*

13 courtesy received decision knowlege competent disagreeable.
14 forcible sentence transfer companies signature inaccessable.
15 She was uncompetent and disagreeable when making a decision.

Skill measurement *29 wpm 2 minutes Not more than 2 errors*

SM27 One of the great problems of today is the pressure of noise: 12
noise in the streets, in the home, by day, and sometimes far 24
into the night. Are buses and lorries the chief cause? No. 36
As we hear these all day, we get used to them. So it is the 48
infrequent sounds, such as those made by jet planes. **(SI 1.16)** 58

1 | 2 | 3 | 4 | 5 | 6 | 7 | 8 | 9 | 10 | 11 | 12 |

Record your progress *2 minutes*

R20 Many people who pay rent are entitled to a rent allowance or 12
rebate - an allowance if a private tenant or a rebate if you 24
are a council tenant. 28

You should write to your local council. Then they will need 40
to know your income, and the larger your family the more you 52
are justified in seizing the chance of getting help, and the 64
more quickly you may expect help. **(SI 1.36)** 70

1 | 2 | 3 | 4 | 5 | 6 | 7 | 8 | 9 | 10 | 11 | 12 |

Form letter

Many documents that businesses use will contain similar information and wording and, in order to save time, form or skeleton letters, containing the constant (unchanging) information, are prepared and are duplicated or printed—only the variable items (name and address, etc) are inserted by the typist in the blank spaces which have been purposely left to accommodate these items.

The electronic keyboard and the VDU have made production of repetitive text very much easier and time-saving. The skeleton letter, containing the constant information, is keyed in and stored on a disk. When required, it can be retrieved by pressing a function key, and any insertion can be made quickly and easily (there is no difficulty with alignment when you have a VDU) and the complete letter printed out, so that it looks like an original—as distinct from a duplicated or printed document with the variables added.

Filling in form letters

The following steps should be taken when you fill in a form letter:

(a) Insert the form letter into the machine so that the first line of the body of the letter is just above the alignment scale.

(b) By means of the paper release adjust the paper so that the base of an entire line is in alignment with the top of the alignment scale (this position may vary with certain makes of machines) and so that an 'i' or 'l' lines up exactly with one of the guides on the alignment scale.

(c) Set margin stops and paper guide. The margin stops should be set to correspond with the margins already used in the duplicated letter.

(d) Turn the platen back two single spaces (four notches for machines with half-spacing) and, if not already typed, insert salutation at the left margin.

(e) Turn the platen back a sufficient number of spaces and type the reference.

(f) Turn up two single spaces and type the date.

(g) Turn up two single spaces and type the name and address of addressee.

(h) Insert any details required in the body of the letter. Remember to leave one clear space after the last character before starting to type the 'fill in'.

(i) Check carefully.

5 Following the instructions given above and using a copy of the printed form from the *Handbook, Solutions, and Resource Material* type in the handwritten details.

W M ELECTRONICS

Deerpark BELFAST BT1 1AA
Telephone 0232 644223 Telex 99783

Your Ref MAR/J
Our Ref AT/BG

14 July 1993

John R Gaunt Ltd
Bridge Street
LIMERICK
Co Limerick

Dear Sirs

We thank you for your order numbered 48/242 dated 12 July for
3 LSR Microfilm Readers/Printers
3 LSR Microfilm Cameras

The first item will be despatched on 19 July but the second item will not be sent until 22 July.

We regret this delay.

Yours faithfully
W M ELECTRONICS

To be used with 10 pitch.

6 Using another copy of the printed form letter (page 92), insert the following information:

Your Ref MAP/RES **Our Ref** AT/your initials **Date** 16 July 1993
Addressee J Ellis and Co Ltd 17 Hanover Road STRANRAER Wigtonshire DG9 7SA
Order Number 513/22 **dated** 13 July **for** 4 PERFECT COLOUR Copiers 6 Word Processor Acoustic Covers.
The second **despatched on** 19 July **but the** first **until** 23 July.

Deletions

It is often necessary to delete letters or words in a form, form letter, or a circular letter. For instance, in the exercises below you are writing to EITHER a man or a woman, so that either **Sir** or **Madam** will have to be deleted. To delete previously typed characters, use an x aligned precisely with the characters previously typed.

7 Using a copy of the printed form letter from the *Handbook, Solutions, and Resource Material* type the handwritten details from the following exercise.

W M ELECTRONICS

Deerpark BELFAST BT1 1AA
Telephone 0232 644223 Telex 99783

Your Ref ML/A13
Our Ref JCH/ID
2 August 1993
Miss J Bannerman
R Bannerman Ltd
Craigneuk
Airdrie
Lanarkshire ML6 6AA

Dear S~~ir~~/Madam

Thank you for your cheque number 045612 dated 27 July for £3200.00.

You mention that you have deducted 2½% for prompt payment, but the invoices, numbered 12361 and 12418, have been outstanding for more than 30 days and, therefore, you are not entitled to the discount.

We are sorry that we cannot allow this discount, and regret that the sum of £82.05 will be included in your statement for July.

Yours faithfully

8 Using another copy of the printed form letter, insert the following details:

Your Ref EA/AS **Our Ref** JCH/ID **date** 2 August 1993 **Addressee** Mr Richard Peterson
Barclay & Co Ltd 90 Waterloo Road BALLYMENA Co Antrim BT43 6AA
Dear Sir **cheque number** 004534 **dated** 28 July **for** £4 300 **deducted** 2½%
numbered 77829 and 82245 **more than** 30 days **sum of** £110.25 **statement for** July